T0385464

THE PAPERS OF WILLIAM F. "BUFFALO BILL" CODY

JOHN M. BURKE

Buffalo Bill from Prairie to Palace

Edited and with an introduction by Chris Dixon

University of Nebraska Press
Lincoln & London

Support for this volume was provided by the State of Wyoming

Library of Congress Cataloging-in-Publication Data
Burke, John M., d. 1917.
Buffalo Bill from prairie to palace /
John M. Burke; edited and with an
introduction by Chris Dixon.
p. cm.—(The papers of William F. "Buffalo Bill" Cody)
Originally published: Chicago;
New York: Rand, McNally & Co., 1893.
Includes bibliographical references and index.
ISBN 978-0-8032-4389-7 (cloth: alk. paper)—
ISBN 978-0-8032-4072-8 (pbk.: alk. paper)
1. Buffalo Bill, 1846–1917. 2. Pioneers—
West (U.S.)—Biography. 3. Frontier and
pioneer life—West (U.S.). 4. Entertainers—
United States—Biography. 5. West (U.S.)—
Biography. I. Dixon, Chris. II. Title.
F594.B94B87 2012
978'.033092—dc23
[B]   2012009811

Set in Iowan Old Style by Bob Reitz.

CONTENTS

ILLUSTRATIONS

SERIES EDITOR'S PREFACE

The central question facing the McCracken Research Library six years ago when it launched The Papers of William F. "Buffalo Bill" Cody was basic: Why should Cody's papers be edited and published? Cody was not a great statesman; he was not an important philosopher, nor a literary genius. Though widely recognized as a show business pioneer, his contribution to cultural consciousness and advancement has too often been, and in large measure continues to be, relegated to the margins of American history. Cody is readily accepted as a pop culture icon of his day but not always seen as a subject of serious scholarly study.

As this present volume illustrates, William Cody deserves the level of attention afforded by this documentary editing project not because of his intellectual, economic, or political contribution but, rather, in part because he was the most successful cultural export in American history. No other enterprise before or since has so boldly claimed to represent the American experience. Moreover, Cody did not merely represent American culture—he defined it for generations of Europeans. In so doing, he gave it a definition that resonates today. From Cody's prescient perspective, the United States is a pluralist, multicultural, exceptional nation. For European audiences, Buffalo Bill's Wild West stood for the frontier, and the frontier stood for America. The American West was the canvas on which Cody painted his unique and uniquely American portrait. Like any other worthy work of art, it continues to be reexamined and reinterpreted.

This current volume is part of that ongoing reexamination. *Buffalo Bill from Prairie to Palace* by John M. Burke, edited by Chris Dixon, is the third volume of The Papers of William F. "Buffalo Bill" Cody and is being published simultaneously with the fourth volume, *The Wild West in England*, by Cody and edited by Frank Christianson. These two volumes underscore the global nature of Buffalo Bill's Wild West. They document firsthand how, beginning in London in 1887, Buffalo Bill's Wild West performed the drama of frontier settlement to millions of Europeans. They also point to Cody's ability to reach ordinary people and yet appeal to the most elite circles. These new editions give us a clearer picture of a man who transcended geographic, social, cultural, and national boundaries.

We live in a world that is increasingly "flat," where our global economy does not need or even allow unique national identities. Cody had the advantage of operating in a world that delighted in differences and celebrated distinctive identities. Within that context, he posited an uncommon American character and found an energetic reception wherever he went.

To contextualize and better understand that character, the Buffalo Bill Historical Center—its staff, board, and generous supporters—have made a substantial investment in recovering and reclaiming the nineteenth-century American West through its most iconic figure. The William F. "Buffalo Bill" Cody Papers open a window onto a significant national moment—America's coming of age—as documents, photographs, newspapers, and memoirs come into view and reveal a distant but dynamic time and place: the world of Buffalo Bill.

Kurt Graham

INTRODUCTION

The Mysterious Major Burke

On March 17, 1911, Maj. John M. "Arizona" Burke, general manager and chief press agent for Buffalo Bill's Wild West, walked in a place of honor in the New York Saint Patrick's Day Parade bedecked in the green regalia fitting to the occasion. Next day, the *New York Morning Telegraph* reporting the event quoted his claim to be a "descendent of the Irish kings."[1] Such an exaggerated claim was by no means untypical of the man. Neither was it untypical that he should make misleading comments about his background.

He was not a major in any meaningful military sense of the word. He had no obvious connection to Arizona. His name contained no middle initial M in any of the earliest official records. His claim to Irish descent was, however, unquestionable although he was not necessarily of a royal line.

John Burke's paternal grandfather was Irish merchant Thomas Burke who emigrated to the United States in 1833 with his wife, Ellen. Both were already in their forties.[2] Within a year they were joined by three sons, a daughter-in-law, and two grandchildren, and by 1840 all were settled in the Brandywine Hundred, New Castle, Delaware.[3] In 1838 their twenty-seven-year-old middle son, Peter, married Swiss immigrant Mary Frances Raymond and the couple had two sons: Thomas, born August 13, 1840, and John, born April 10, 1842.[4]

U.S. Federal Census records for 1850 and 1860 show eight-year-old John Burke "attending school," and eighteen-year-old John Burke—whose occupation is unfortunately an illegible scrawl in the record book—residing in the First Ward of Wilmington, Delaware, with his Irish father and Swiss mother.[5] The 1870 federal census record for the same ward shows twenty-eight-year-old Delaware-born John M. Burk—appearing for the first time with the middle initial and without the final "e"—and gives his occupation as "theatre manager." He is listed as a U.S. citizen over twenty-one years of age, both of whose parents were of foreign birth, and he was residing with his eighty-seven-year-old Irish born grandfather, Thomas Burk.[6]

Three years later, in early September 1873, John M. Burke met William F. Cody. Burke was at the time the manager of the Italian actress and dancer Giuseppina Morlacchi. She had married "Texas Jack" Omohundro, a co-star with Cody in his Buffalo Bill Combination stage production, *Scouts of the Plains*, in Saint Mary's Catholic Cathedral, in Rochester, New York, on August 31, 1873. Burke traveled with the newlyweds to join the company at Chicago one week later. The meeting began an association between Cody and Burke that lasted for the remainder of both men's lives.[7] John M. Burke was one of only four people involved with the Wild West for the entire period that it operated (1883 to 1916); the others were Cody himself, Cody's informally adopted son, Johnnie Baker; and bandmaster William Sweeney. Thus the relationship between the two men had Buffalo Bill's Wild West as its defining characteristic.

Burke, who was most often identified as "general manager" in the Wild West's own literature, served as its advance agent, location scout, talent scout, press agent, and publicity manager. He was the Wild West's "major wordsmith," having responsibility for preparing programs, handbills, and advertising booklets with the assistance of a staff that sometimes numbered as many as nine.[8] Burke organized and staged publicity events and photo opportunities, supplied interviews and copy to local newspapers, and oversaw advertising campaigns that produced as many as half a million posters in a season.[9]

This group's work was instrumental in bringing about the transformation of William F. Cody into the iconic persona of Buffalo Bill within a carefully constructed master-narrative of the western expansion of the United States that purported to authentically represent the savage life of the frontier as it retreated in the face of the advance of civilization. It is a story which, almost one hundred years later, continues to resonate in the popular imagination across the United States and the wider world. Its legacy continues to be a focus of scholarly research and debate.

Given that he invested so much of his professional energy in the creation and dissemination of Cody's biography, it is perhaps not surprising that we know so little about John M. Burke's own life. From the writings of his contemporaries, however, we can garner enough sense of his character to identify him with the archetypal, affable Irishman, although whether or not this represented a sustained, public pose is more difficult to determine.

Burke's protégé Dexter Fellows recognized him as the "tutor in the humanities" who gave him a "zestful appetite for life,"[10] and also described him as a man who, "always appeared to be the picture of sartorial perfection but to my knowledge he never wore a shirt. Fastened around his neck was a false white bosom of standard linen, and attached to the sleeves of his undershirt were white cuffs."[11]

Fellows writes of a lavish entertainer who always smoked the best cigars and whose "expense accounts kept him in hot water with Jule Keen, the show's treasurer," and "though he had an astonishing capacity for alcoholic beverages, [he] never saw him intoxicated."[12] Fellows also lays particular emphasis on Burke's generosity: "The Major was the delight of cadgers and panhandlers. Wherever he went there was a coterie of impecunious characters around him for whom he always had a drink or a meal or a dollar. In fact his hand was habitually in his pocket."[13]

Former Wild West manager Lew Parker tells a number of anecdotes that give testimony to Burke's ready wit. For example, he relates how on an 1891 train journey that stopped briefly at Monte Carlo, the great gambling capital in the south of France, without affording them time to visit the town, "He turned round to me just as the train was starting and said: 'Have you got any change in your pocket?' I said: 'Yes, what do you want?' He said: 'Give me a franc.' I gave him a franc, and he took one out of his own pocket; opened the window of the compartment and threw the two francs out of the window into the bushes, exclaiming: 'Now we can go back to America and tell them that we dropped our good money at Monte Carlo.'"[14]

Burke was in London through the winter of 1886–1887 to lay the groundwork for the Wild West's first visit to the English capital.In writing of the time, Parker tells of Burke's preference for communicating by telegraph rather than letter:

Nothing was known as to what he had done and the general condition of affairs over there, nothing but a few telegrams that did not tell enough detail to let people know what was going on; consequently Cody and Salsbury got pretty sore about it, and on Burke's return to New York, both of these gentlemen jumped on him, first Cody and then Salsbury, as they wanted to know what he had been doing, and why he had not written. "Why you received cables from me didn't you?" said Burke. "Yes," said they, but no letters. "Why, what's the use of writing letters," said Burke. "The news is a week old before you get it, whereas on the other hand, if I telegraph you to-day from London, you get it yesterday in New York, don't you?"

One can imagine the knockout of this argument, so the two chiefs decided to let it go at that.[15]

Few of Burke's many telegrams have survived the test of time. But the last, and arguably the most poignant he ever sent to William F. Cody, dated January 9, 1917, has done so. It had been widely reported that Buffalo Bill was then on his deathbed. The cable reads, "Dear friend Bill am appealing to the Celestial court to revise the medical jurys [sic] decision hoping nerve will and constitution may steer you off the trail over Great Divide and let you camp for years yet on the banks of the rippling Shoshone. Stay with them. How Koolah old pal. John M. Burke."[16]

On April 12, 1917, a little more than three months after this telegram was dispatched, John M. Burke followed his old pal over the Great Divide between life and death. He had been admitted to Providence Hospital in Washington DC the previous day, suffering from pneumonia.

An umarked grave in Mount Olivet Catholic Cemetery in that city is the final resting place of, in the words of Dexter Fellows, "the mortal remains of as fine and kindly a man as ever lived."[17]

Buffalo Bill from Prairie to Palace

In the words of Richard White, the fact that Frederick Jackson Turner and Buffalo Bill Cody both "played" Chicago in 1893 is a great historical irony.[18] Both presented narratives of America's frontier experience and, "as different as the two narratives were, they lead to remarkably similar conclusions. Both declared the frontier over."[19] Turner argued in academic discourse that the Western frontier no longer existed;[20] Buffalo Bill demonstrated in popular entertainment that civilization had triumphed over savagery.

In another telling comment on the ironic counterpoint of the two men appearing at the same time and in the same place as the Great Columbian Exhibition, White observes, "Both Turner and Buffalo Bill were storytellers, but neither was content to be a mere storyteller. Each claimed to be an educator, a historian to represent in his story an actual past. The stories they told were not so much invented (although there was some of that) as selected from the past, with the authors erasing images that did not fit. Such selectivity was necessary, for the past itself is not a story; it is the raw material from which we make coherent stories, not all of them factual."[21]

Telling the story of Buffalo Bill was an endeavor whose proportions extended well beyond the Wild West. Cody's autobiography had been published almost five years before the Wild West came into being and a "literature wagon" selling the autobiography, various dime novels, and other related publications was a regular feature of the accompanying side show.[22] It was entirely fitting that a new biography of its star should be published to coincide with the appearance of Buffalo Bill's Wild West at an event whose overarching theme was the celebration of the four-hundredth anniversary of Christopher Columbus's first voyage to the Americas in 1492. Burke was the obvious candidate to author the work. He was the man who had always "insisted on authenticity of detail in the Wild West[,] which was never called show or circus in advertising, but rather an exhibition[,] with many of John M. Burke's adjectives added to indicate that it was a highly educational exhibition."[23]

To create the new biography Burke drew on the autobiography as a key source, recasting much of its material to fit even more directly the myth of the American hero conquering the western frontier. These revisions, together with copy that he had previously penned for various programs and other material that he wrote relating to recent events such as those at Wounded Knee in 1890, were brought together with testimonials that he had garnered from prominent military figures. It was all done in Burke's own inimitable flowery and at times hyperbolic style, making for a biography that is a fascinatingly eclectic work. Joy Kasson has rightly recognized it as helping readers "appreciate Cody's own overt struggle for self-definition."[24]

Since its first publication in 1893, *Buffalo Bill from Prairie to Palace* has only officially appeared in one subsequent edition, although some of the material was reused by Burke for later Wild West programs.[25] Connor and Berger's very welcome 2005 edition brought the work to a wider audience for the first time. Connor modernized much of the archaic spelling of the first edition and Berger contextualized the biography with an introductory essay that stressed Burke's role as an innovative public relations professional who was responsible for the creation of "a seamless Integrated Marketing Communication (IMC) advertising and public relations machine."[26] The edition did not, however, include all of the photographs and line drawings which had illustrated the *princeps*.

This new edition of *Buffalo Bill from Prairie to Palace* will, therefore, make the full text and original illustrations of this crucial primary source more readily available while also providing in the notes background information on both the literary sources on which Burke has drawn and the historical events and characters mentioned in the work. The bibliography contains details of the works consulted in preparing the attending notes, other than standard reference works such as *Encyclopedia Britannica* and *Debrett's Peerage,* and it serves as a list of suggested further reading on many of the prominent figures associated with William F. Cody to whom Burke refers. Corrections have been made to aberrant spellings of proper names and obvious typographical errors have been repaired, but the text is otherwise as it appeared in the original Rand and Mc-Nally edition of 1893.

The edition has been produced as part of the print edition of The Papers of William F. "Buffalo Bill" Cody under the aegis of the project of the same name, located at the Buffalo Bill Historical Center in Cody, Wyoming.

One of the major objectives of the project is to collect materials that document the personal and professional life of a man who had thousands of employees, friends, and customers, a great many of whom wrote to him and about him. In addition to the print edition of the Papers, a key output of the project will be a digital version of this entire corpus of material, complete with authoritative transcriptions, which will be made available through the project website and continually updated as new materials are located.

The creation of this digital collection, which brings together the entire body of research materials related to William F. Cody's personal and professional life, will both enable a variety of audiences to consider not only the impact on American life by William F. Cody the cultural entrepreneur but also provide contextualizing documents from other sources and audio-visual media that exist for the final years of Cody's life. It will allow more scholars to study the man within his times, it will provide new resources to contextualize studies of other regional and national events and persons, and it will entice the casual visitor to the digital edition to explore and learn more about these vital decades of American expansion and development. The digital edition of the Papers will differ significantly from the print edition by including manuscript materials, photographs, and film and sound recordings; it will offer searching and navigational options not possible in the print edition. Both editions will include aids that gloss names, events, places, and archaic terms and will provide overview introductory essays, graphic images, and timelines.

ACKNOWLEDGMENTS

This volume would not have been possible with the support of many people. Thanks are due to Heather Lundine, formerly of the University of Nebraska Press, and Bridget Barry, her able replacement, for the support that they have shown to this project throughout; and to Ann Baker, for editorial support.

Most of the hard work "at the coalface" was conducted at Buffalo Bill Historical Center, and without the support of numerous colleagues there this book could never have had its present form, nor been ready in time. Mary Robinson and her team at the McCracken Research Library, including Karling Abernathy, Mack Frost, Samantha Harper, Karen Preis, and Karen Van Gilder, were always prompt in responding to requests for help—and tolerant of my mounting obsession with John M. Burke. Lynn Houze, of the Buffalo Bill Museum, offered invaluable support in tracking down details of Burke's early life. The team at the Papers of William F. Cody were fundamental to the entire project, and without the encouragement of managing editor Jeremy Johnston and the editorial support of Linda Clark, Deb Adams, and Gary Boyce, I would never have made the submission deadlines for the manuscript.

The financial support that allowed me to be based in Cody, Wyoming, in the summers of 2010 and 2011 was provided by the Cody Institute of Western American Studies, the Buffalo

Bill Historical Center Fellowship Program, and the Carnegie Trust for the Universities of Scotland. The trustees of each have my gratitude.

My home institution, the University of Strathclyde, in Glasgow, Scotland, has been extremely tolerant of the mounting interest that a linguist has shown in the American West and the amount of time that it has consumed. Colleagues there have been supportive of me playing Cowboys and Indians well beyond the age when such a thing is common. To Joe Farrell and Gerry McIntyre, both mentors and friends, I will be eternally indebted.

Last, but by no means least, without the genius that is Kurt Graham, series editor of the Papers of William F. "Buffalo Bill" Cody, a scholar, and a gentleman, my games of Cowboys and Indians would never have made it into print. *Ne oublie!*

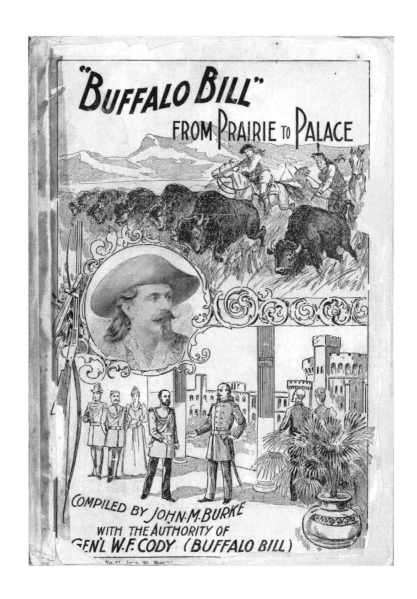

1. Buffalo Bill from Prairie to Palace.

2. W. F. Cody "Buffalo Bill."

Buffalo Bill from Prairie to Palace

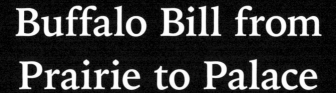

An Authentic History of the Wild West,
with Sketches, Stories of Adventure,
and Anecdotes of "Buffalo Bill,"
the Hero of the Plains

Compiled by
JOHN M. "ARIZONA JOHN" BURKE
with the Authority of
GENERAL W. F. "BUFFALO BILL" CODY

The compiler of this book desires to
give credit to General Dodge's "Thirty
Years Among the Indians," and to the
Historical Publishing Company, for a
few of the facts and incidents given in
these pages.

3. John M. Burke.

To
Those Pioneers of Progress
Who Have Led the Advance of Civilization into Savage
Lands, Defying Danger, Suffering Every Hardship,
Overcoming All Obstacles, Offering Life
As a Sacrifice When Called Upon,
The Army of the United States
I Dedicate This Book.

John M. Burke

4. Buffalo Bill.

CONTENTS

COMPILER'S PREFACE

An association of some thirty years[1] with the subject of
these pages, a familiarity with his history gained by op-
portune meetings and conversations with comrades now
living, and those since dead—who were witnesses of the
events that assisted to make the individual prominent—
makes me feel it a public duty to accede to the publisher's
request to compile a short, sharp, and veracious account of
the unique history of this picturesque character.

Born at a time, and reared in an atmosphere, the most romantic and adventurous known in the history of our American frontier, when the tidal wave of human progress, sweeping westward, was making history faster than the historians
could record it—it was his fate to be in the field, and his fortune to grasp the opportunities to meet the situation's requirements, and, in the beaten path of what seemed ordinary daily duty, to rise, by reason of his sterling qualities,
his daring, and his courage, to the distinction of a leader.

So quickly was the history of the central West recorded, as to make the Great American Desert of our childhood
seem almost a geographical mirage, a tale of the romancer. It would seem to be a fairy story were it not for the fact
of its settlement, and the evidences of its now almost ancient civilization.

The busy, hustling citizen of to-day scarcely has time to think, and does not realize that the youths of the time of Benton,[2] Beale,[3] Fremont,[4] Bridger,[5] and Carson[6] are the relics of the perfected history and work that they inaugurated.

One of the most picturesque characters that evoluted from the peculiar circumstances of the times is "Buffalo Bill," Gen.[7] W. F. Cody, N. G. S. N. The romance, the fiction, woven around his personality is dispelled in the white light of stern and veritable facts, just as the golden rays of the morning sun drive the mist from the mountain-tops.

The compiler of the accompanying pages has attempted to present to the reader, in a terse, compact compendium of facts, the story of a career that, if given in a detailed biography, would absorb volumes, believing that owing to his prominence at home and abroad the public desires some authentic knowledge of the notable events of his career. In fact, here are presented a few plain truths, unadorned, for the benefit of those too occupied to have heretofore learned the story and triumphs of the frontier lad of nine years, from the wild Western scenes of Kansas and Nebraska, from the prairies of the Platte to the parlors of the East and the palaces of Europe.

CHAPTER I

Introductory

Half a century or less ago, the people then active in the world were unable to move from place to place more rapidly than in the days before the Christian era. The fickle winds drove ships out of their course and baffled their efforts to hold on their way to their destination. On land the rapidity of progress from place to place was measured by the fleetness of a horse. The steam-engine was in its infancy; the telegraph and other electrical devices were only known through the fable of the singing tree and the talking fountain in the tales of the Arabian Nights;[1] glittering gold still lay unheeded and unseen in the beds of California streams.

The great peaks of the Rockies towered into the clouds, their grandeur and beauty unknown to a world which had not then heard the sound of the waters thundering down the cliffs of the Yosemite, a rival of Niagara. Amid the beauties of the Garden of the Gods reigned a stillness as profound as that which pervaded the Garden of Eden before the creation of man.

But already the fearless and restless white man was on discovery bent, and, with his face turned always toward the setting sun, one by one the glories of the continent were seen and heralded.

Brev.-Capt. John C. Fremont of the United States Topographical Engineers, with the famous Kit Carson as his guide, was exploring and opening up the great trail which was to connect the two oceans.

The fur traders were settling in the Northwest, and Astoria was coming into notice, while the echoes of Bonneville's adventures were heard in the Eastern world.

Among the men who found the East growing crowded was Isaac Cody,[2] who was then living in Iowa. He was a fine type of the Western frontiersman, well educated, enterprising, and fearless. Leaving his home, with his family he started across the plains. His journey continued until he reached a point in Kansas near Fort Leavenworth, and here he made camp and proceeded to build a new home.

"Little Billy" was then a boy, living the life and learning the lessons of the plains, while Humboldt[3] was wondering what secrets were hidden in the center of the continent, and the geographical societies of the world were speculating upon the mysteries that lay far beyond the banks of the "Father of Waters."

At that time this region was a little known and as dark a continent as Africa before the courage of Stanley[4] laid bare its conformation and geography. The Indians had not then been confined to reservations, but were fiercely resisting the encroachments of the white men upon their territory. They disputed, step by step, the advancement to the westward of the borders of civilization with a fiercer, because more ignorant, determination to resist subjugation than is known in the history of the world.

In this atmosphere, and amid such surroundings, this boy grew up, and his rapid development was a natural result of such conditions. Physical exercise in the open air developed his frame, and provided the steady hand and quick eye.

Surrounded by enemies, he lived amid dangers so constant and ever-present that they became part of his daily life, and fear was unknown. Self-preservation taught him to oppose strategy with strategy, and to learn the wiles of the red man in order that he might exist in his country, and study the habits of the animals infesting the country, for the dual purpose of avoiding danger and providing himself with food and raiment. At the same time this wild life broadened his moral nature, expanded his mind, and prepared it to receive great truths. Broad men are the product of broad countries; narrowness and prejudice are insular.

Sir Charles Dilke[5] has recorded the history of "Greater Britain," but during the lifetime of this frontier boy he has seen with his own eyes the growth of "Greater America." In the short span of a life still in its prime, he has seen the slow wagon-train crawling over the weary miles of wind-swept prairie harassed by Indians and other foes, and he has seen the long parallel iron rails push their way across the map of the continent until they span it from gulf to gulf and from ocean to ocean. The "prairie schooner" and the pony express have in his time given way to the Pullman coach and the electric wire.

In his boyhood the strife and struggles, the perils and privations, which had beset the Puritans in New England a century before, were being reenacted on the Western plains; and of this period in the development of our country this boy can truthfully say, "All of which I saw, and part of which I was."

In later life, when great military commanders entrusted their lives, and those of their men, to his keeping, they did it with an unhesitating confidence, begotten of the knowledge that he was born and trained upon the spot; a veritable product of the soil. His father having died while he was still young, he matured early. His widowed mother taught the boy at her knee the elements of reading and writing, and thus laid the foundation of an education which has been completed in the school of the world.

Living for years in cabins or tents, and oftener under the canopy of heaven, pursuing a career of independent activity which carried him through the various stages of cattle-herder, teamster, bronco "buster," wagon-master, stage-driver, pony-express rider, hunter, guide, scout, and soldier, he still found time to acquire an education which, added to his native refinement and gentleness of bearing, enables him to appear to advantage in any society or place. While perfection exists only in the other world, and is not claimed for him, the herder and scout has borne inspection, and passed muster, in the accepted centers of refinement and cultivation of the world.

From the Rocky Mountains to the Colosseum at Rome is a "far cry," and yet that is the history of the settler's son now known around the world as Col. William F. Cody, or "Buffalo Bill."

The pages of this book are not devoted to the recording of a legend wherein the untutored, wild, and reckless roamer of the plains has by chance, or the magic of phenomenal powers, won the open sesame to the grandeur of patriarchal palaces, but rather to the telling of how native courage and brilliant daring, combined with sincerity of purpose and purity of motive, have made savage warriors of the prairies to welcome and appreciate the joys of peace, have opened in the heart of apparently desert places storehouses of wealth, and shown princely powers that manhood, prowess, and honor are found as truly on the prairies of the great West as in the centers of art and civilization. The sturdy hero of the plains has been met by gracious hands at the portals of the palace.

The discovery that a new world existed on the western shores of the Atlantic was scarcely more a surprise to the grandees of the Old World, than the realization that far beyond the great Father of Waters there existed a country whose inhabitants were hunting buffaloes and living in rude tents on prairies and amid rugged mountains, which needed but the plow and the miner's pick for keys to unlock treasuries filled with richer products and rarer gems than the bright gleam of the mythical Aladdin's lamp e'er shone upon.[6]

Now the world recognizes and gives tardy but sincere applause to the venturesome spirits that first directed the attention of the world to the grandeur and latent power of the great West. Occasionally a noble of the East, in search of sport and adventure, visited this new country and, returning, told of its vastness and magnificence. Romancers, upon a few facts, accepted with hesitation, built stories which, though thoroughly entertaining, were regarded as novels, never as histories.

Taking up the thread of the beautiful story so graphically told by the facile pen of Washington Irving[7] in his narration of the fur traders' trials, adventures, and discoveries, and weaving all into a contemporaneous history, our

5. The Result of Bad Guiding.

Cody and his fellows have gathered together the living actual facts of the prairies, and held them up to the wondering, admiring gaze of the world in the court-yards of the palaces of Europe. The barefooted urchin, that, astride of his fleet-footed bronco, rode with a smile through every danger, carrying news and cheer from old homes in the East to the strugglers of the prairies, has since been accorded courtly welcome by crowned monarchs, to whom he has exhibited in triumph trophies of American valor and American enterprise. Kingly warriors have dragged captives chained to their chariot-wheels as proofs of their victories; subjects have shouted loud pæans of praise and glory of their lords and princes returning as victors; but when, save in the history of William F. Cody, have the conquered walked hand in hand with the conqueror, willing witnesses to his glorious achievements; or when, before, have kings and queens and emperors joined in according glad applause to a victor whose only royal heritage was his native manhood, and whose only spoils of victory were willing captives to peace and civilization.

From this man's life, deeds, and successes others may glean lessons of endurance and courage in days of trial, of hope in moments of despair, and of gentleness and generosity in the hour of triumph.

With the earnest wish that such results may accrue from a perusal of these pages, let us first recall Buffalo Bill's record as a gallant and trusty scout.

CHAPTER II

The Scout

Gen. Richard Irving Dodge,[1] General Sherman's chief of staff, correctly states, in his "Thirty Years Among Our Wild Indians": "The success of every expedition against Indians depends, to a degree, on the skill, fidelity, and intelligence of the men employed as scouts and guides, for not only is the command habitually dependent on them for good routes and comfortable camps, but the officer in command must rely on their knowledge of the position and movements of the enemy."

Our best Indian officers are quick to recognize these traits in those claiming frontier lore, and to no one in the military history of the West has such deference been shown by them as to W. F. Cody, as is witnessed by the continuous years of service he has passed, the different commands he has served, the expeditions and campaigns he has been identified with, his repeated holding, when he desired, the position of Chief of Scouts of the United States Army, and the intimate association, and contact resulting from it, with Gen. W. T. Sherman[2] (with whom he was at the making of the Comanche and Kiowa Treaty) in 1866, Gen. Phil. Sheridan[3] (who has often given him special recognition and chosen him to organize ex peditions, notably that of the Duke Alexis),[4] old General

Harney,[5] Generals Forsyth,[6] Merritt,[7] Brisbin,[8] Emory,[9] Gibbon,[10] Terry,[11] Mackenzie,[12] Carr,[13] W. S. Hancock,[14] Crook,[15] Pope,[16] Miles,[17] Ord,[18] Auger,[19] Royall,[20] Hazen,[21] Duncan,[22] Palmer,[23] Penrose,[24] and the late lamented General Custer.[25] His history, in fact, would be almost a history of the middle West; and, though younger, equaling in term of service and in personal adventure, Kit Carson, old Jim Bridger, California Joe,[26] Wild Bill,[27] and the rest of his dead associates.

As another evidence of the confidence placed in his frontiersmanship, it may suffice to mention the celebrities whose money and position most naturally sought the best protection the Western market could afford, and who chose to place their lives in his keeping: Sir George Gore,[28] the Earl of Dunraven,[29] James Gordon Bennett,[30] Duke Alexis, General Custer, Lawrence Jerome,[31] Remington,[32] Professor Ward of Rochester,[33] Professor Marsh of Yale College,[34] Maj. J. G. Heckscher,[35] Doctor Kingsley (Canon Kingsley's brother),[36] and others of equal rank and distinction. In all books of the plains his exploits with Carr, Miles, and Crook, in the summer of 1876, when he killed Yellow Hand in front of the military command in an open hand- to-hand fight, are recorded.

The following letter of his old commander, the celebrated Indian fighter, Gen. E. A. Carr, written years ago relative to him, is a tribute as generous as any brave man has ever made to another:

"From his services in my command, steadily in the field, I am qualified to bear testimony as to his qualities and character.

"He was very modest and unassuming. He is a natural

gentleman in his manners as well as in character, and has none of the roughness of the typical frontiersman. He can take his own part when required, but I have never heard of his using a knife or a pistol, or engaging in a quarrel where it could be avoided. His personal strength and activity are very great, and his temper and disposition are so good that no one has reason to quarrel with him.

"His eyesight is better than a good field-glass; he is the best trailer I ever heard of, and also the best judge of the 'lay of country'—that is, he is able to tell what kind of country is ahead, so as to know how to act. He is a perfect judge of distance, and always ready to tell correctly how many miles it is to water, or to any place, or how many miles have been marched. . . .

"Mr. Cody seemed never to tire, and was always ready to go in the darkest night or the worst weather, and usually volunteered, knowing what the emergency required. His trailing, when following Indians, or looking for stray animals, or for game, is simply wonderful. He is a most extraordinary hunter.

"In a fight, Mr. Cody is never noisy, obstreperous, or excited. In fact, I hardly ever noticed him in a fight unless I happened to want him, or he had something to report, when he was always in the right place, and his information was always valuable and reliable.

"During the winter of 1868 we encountered hardships and exposure in terrific snow-storms and sleet. On one occasion that winter Mr. Cody showed his quality by quietly offering to go with some dispatches to General Sheridan across a dangerous region of 300 miles where other principal scouts were reluctant to risk themselves.

6. Danger Ahead.

"Mr. Cody has since served with me as post guide and scout at Fort McPherson,[37] where he frequently distinguished himself.

"In the summer of 1876 Cody went with me to the Black Hills region, where he killed Yellow Hand. Afterward he was with the Big Horn and Yellowstone expedition. I consider that his services to the country and the army by trailing, finding, and fighting Indians, and thus protecting the frontier settlers, and by guiding commands over the best and most practicable routes, have been invaluable."

Thus it will be seen that notwithstanding it will sometimes be thought his fame rests upon the pen of the romancer, had they never been attracted to him—and they were solely by his sterling worth—W. F. Cody would none the less have been a remarkable character in American history.

The history of such a man, attractive as it has already been to the most distinguished officers and fighters in the United States Army, must prove doubly so to men, women, and children who have heretofore found only in novels the hero of rare exploits, on which imagination so loves to dwell.

As proof that our great military leaders and the officers of the United States Army recognize the value of Buffalo Bill as a scout, guide, and Indian fighter, and that though I am writing of one of whom more stories of romance have been written than of any other individual living or dead, it will be well to turn to the letters of commendation from prominent personages in another part of this book, and the quotations which are given in this chapter from such authorities as General Sheridan's "Autobiography," Captain Price's[38] "Across the Continent with the Fifth Cavalry," Colonel Dodge's "Thirty Years Among the Indians," etc.

These endorsements stamp Buffalo Bill as one whose deeds speak for themselves, and show conclusively that he is not a pen-made man, but worthy of all said and written of him.

Across The Continent with the Fifth Cavalry

(CAPT. GEORGE F. PRICE.)

"After Cody was appointed chief scout and guide for the Republican River expedition, he was conspicuous during the pursuit of the Dog Soldiers, under the celebrated Cheyenne chief, Tall Bull, whom he killed at Summit Springs, Colo. He also guided the Fifth Cavalry to a position whence the regiment was enabled to charge upon the enemy and win a brilliant victory. He afterward participated in the Niobrara pursuit, and later narrowly escaped death at the hands of hostile Sioux on Prairie Dog Creek, Kan., September 26, 1869. He was assigned to Fort McPherson when he expedition was disbanded, and served at that station (was a justice of the peace in 1871) until the Fifth Cavalry was transferred to Arizona. He served during this period with several expeditions, and was conspicuous for gallant conduct in the Indian combat at Red Willow and Birdwood creeks, and also for successful services as chief scout and guide of the buffalo-hunt which was arranged by General Sheridan for the Grand Duke Alexis of Russia.

"Cody was then assigned to duty with the Third Cavalry, and served with that regiment until the fall of 1872, when he was elected a member of the Nebraska Legislature, and thus acquired the title of 'Honorable.'

"At the beginning of the Sioux War in 1876 he hastened to Cheyenne, Wyo., joined the Fifth Cavalry, which had recently returned from Arizona, and was engaged in the affair at War Bonnet (Indian Creek), Wyo.[39] He then accompanied the Fifth Cavalry to Goose Creek, Mont.,[40] and served with the Big Horn and Yellowstone expedition until September. Cody abundantly proved during this campaign that he had lost none of his old-time skill and daring in Indian warfare. He enjoys a brilliant reputation as a scout and guide, which has been fairly earned by faithful and conspicuous service.

"William F. Cody is one of the best scouts and guides that ever rode at the head of a column of cavalry on the prairies of the Far West. His army friends, from general to private, hope that he may live long and prosper abundantly.

"Should the wild Sioux again go on the war-path, Cody, if living, will be[41] found with the cavalry advance, riding another 'Buckskin Joe,' and carrying his Springfield rifle, 'Lucretia,'[42] across the pommel of his saddle."

This merited note of applause will find an echo in every patriotic American heart which recognizes and remembers that it was in the Fifth Cavalry that Gens. Robert E. Lee, Albert Sidney Johnston, Hardee, Emory, Van Dorn, Custer,[43] and other noted generals served, and which was formerly known as the Second Dragoons.

From Gen. Phil Sheridan's "Autobiography." After relating his conception of the *first winter campaign* against Indians on the then uninhabited and bleak plains, in the winter of 1868, he says:

"The difficulties and hardships to be encountered had led several experienced officers of the army and some frontiersmen, like old Jim Bridger, the famous scout and guide of earlier days, to discourage the project. I decided to go in person, bent on showing the Indians that they were not secure from punishment because of inclement weather—an ally on which they had hitherto relied with much

7. Guiding in a Blizzard.

assurance. We started, and the very first night a blizzard struck us and carried away our tents. The gale was so violent that they could not be put up again; the rain and snow drenched us to the skin.

Shivering from *wet and cold, I took refuge under a wagon,* and there spent such a miserable night that when morning came the gloomy predictions of old man Bridger and others rose up before me with greatly increased force. The difficulties were now fully realized; the blinding snow, mixed with sleet; the piercing wind, thermometer below zero—with green bushes only for fuel—occasioning intense suffering. Our numbers and companionship alone prevented us from being lost or perishing, a fate that stared in the face the frontiersmen, guides, and scouts on their solitary missions.

"An important matter had been to secure competent guides for the different columns of troops, for, as I have

said, the section of *country to be operated in was comparative-*
ly unknown.

"In those days the railroad town of Hays City[44] was
filled with so-called 'Indian scouts,' whose common boast
was of having slain scores of redskins; but the real scout—
that is, a guide and trailer knowing the habits of the Indians—was very scarce, and it was hard to find anybody familiar with the country south of the Arkansas, where the
campaign was to be made. Still, about the various military
posts there was some good material to select from, and
we managed to employ several men, who, from their experience on the plains in various capacities, or from natural instinct and aptitude, soon became excellent guides
and courageous and valuable scouts, some of them, indeed, gaining much distinction. Mr. William F. Cody ('Buffalo Bill'), whose renown has since become world-wide,
was one of the men thus selected. He received his sobriquet from his marked success in killing buffaloes to supply fresh meat to the construction parties on the Kansas
Pacific Railway. He had lived from boyhood on the plains
and passed every experience—herder, hunter, pony-express
rider, stage-driver, wagon-master in the quartermaster's
department, and scout of the army, and was first brought
to my notice by distinguishing himself in bringing me an
important dispatch from Fort Larned[45] to Fort Hays,[46] a
distance of sixty-five miles, through a section infested
with Indians. The dispatch informed me that the Indians
near Larned were preparing to decamp, and this intelligence required that certain orders should be carried to Fort
Dodge,[47] ninety-five miles south of Hays. This too being
a particularly dangerous route—several couriers having

8. Buffalo Bill as Buffalo Hunter.

been killed on it—it was impossible to get one of the various Petes, Jacks, or Jims hanging around Hays City to take my communication. Cody, learning of the strait I was in, manfully came to the rescue, and proposed to make the trip to Dodge, though he had just finished his long and perilous ride from Larned. I gratefully accepted his offer, and after a short rest he mounted a fresh horse and hastened on his journey, halting but once to rest on the way, and then only for an hour, the stop being made at Coon Creek,[48] where he got another mount from a troop of cavalry. At Dodge he took some sleep, and then continued on to his own post—Fort Larned—with more dispatches. After resting at Larned he was again in the saddle with tidings for me at Fort Hays, General Hazen sending him this time with word that the villages had fled to the south of the Arkansas. Thus, in all, Cody rode about three hundred and fifty miles in less than sixty hours, and such an exhibition of endurance and courage at that time of the year and in such weather was more than enough to convince me that his services would be extremely valuable in the campaign, so I retained him at Fort Hays till the battalion of the Fifth Cavalry arrived, and then made him chief of scouts."

Read through the fascinating book, "Campaigning with Crook (Maj.-Gen. George Crook, U. S. A.) and Stories of Army Life," due to the graphic and soldierly pen of Capt. Charles King[49] of the United States Army, published in 1890.

Incidentally the author refers in various pages to Colonel Cody as scout, etc., and testifies to the general esteem and affection in which Buffalo Bill is held by the army.

The subjoined extracts from the book will give our readers an excellent idea of the military scout's calling and its dangers:

"'By Jove! General,' says Buffalo Bill, sliding backward down the hill, 'now's our chance. Let our party mount here out of sight and we'll cut those fellows off. Come down, every other man of you.'

"Glancing behind me, I see Cody, Tait, and 'Chips,' with five cavalrymen, eagerly bending forward in their saddles, grasping carbine and rifle, every eye bent upon me, watching for the signal. Not a man but myself knows how near they are. 'That's right, close in, you beggars! Ten seconds more and you are on them! A hundred and twenty-five yards—a hundred—ninety—now, lads, in with you.' . . .

"There's a rush, a wild ringing cheer; then bang, bang, bang! and in a cloud of dust, Cody and his men tumble in among them, Buffalo Bill closing on a superbly accoutered warrior. It is the work of a minute; the Indian has

9. Buffalo Bill's Duel with Chief Yellow Hand.

fired and missed. Cody's bullet tears through the rider's leg into the pony's heart, and they tumble in a confused heap on the prairie. The Cheyenne struggles to his feet for another shot, but Cody's second bullet hits the mark. It is now close quarters, knife to knife. After a hand-to-hand struggle, Cody wins, and the young chief Yellow Hand drops lifeless in his tracks after a hot fight. Baffled and astounded, for once in a lifetime beaten at their own game, their project of joining Sitting Bull nipped in the bud, they take hurried flight. But our chief is satisfied; Buffalo Bill is radiant; his are the honors of the day."—*From p. 35.*

General Cody holds his commission in the National Guard of the United States (State of Nebraska), an honorable position, and as high as he can possibly attain. *His connection with the Regular United States Army* has covered a continuous period of *fifteen years,* and desultory connection of thirty years—in the most troublous era of that superb corps' Western history—as guide, scout and chief of scouts—a position unknown in any other service, and the confidential nature of which is told in the extract from General Dodge's work, quoted below. This privileged position, and the nature of its services in the past, may be more fully appreciated when it is understood that it commanded, besides horses, subsistence, and quarters, $10 per day ($3,650 per year), all expenses, and for special service, or "life and death" volunteer missions, special rewards of from $100 to $500 for carrying a single dispatch, and brought its holder the confidence of commanding generals, the fraternal friendship of the commissioned officers, the idolization of the ranks, and the universal respect and consideration of the hardy pioneers and settlers of the West.

10. Cowboys Lassoing Wild Horses.

In addition to the distinguished officers previously named in this chapter, General Cody may also well be proud of his service under Generals Bankhead, Fry, Crittenden, Sweitzer, Rucker, Smith, King, Van Vliet, Anson Mills, Reynolds, Greely, Penrose, Sandy Forsyth, Dudley, Canby, Blunt, Hayes, Guy Henry,[50] and others.

As a fitting close to this chapter of Cody's record as a scout, and as epitomizing the character of his services, the writer quotes from page 628 of Colonel Dodge's "Thirty Years Among the Indians":

"Of ten men employed as scouts, nine will prove to be worthless; of fifty so employed, one my prove to be really valuable; but though hundreds, even thousands of men have been so employed by the Government since the war, the number of really remarkable men among them can be counted on fingers. The services which these men are called on to perform are so important and valuable that the officer who benefits by them is sure to give the fullest credit, and men honored in official reports come to be great men on the frontier. Fremont's reports made Kit Carson a renowned man. Custer immortalized California Joe. Custer, Merritt, Carr, and Miles made William F. Cody ("Buffalo Bill") a plains celebrity *'until time shall be no more.'"*

CHAPTER III

What Is a Cowboy?

Around the name of cowboy hangs a romance that will never die.

It is a romance interwoven with deeds of daring, nerve, and big-heartedness that will survive long after civilization has stamped out every need for the brave men who have been known by the name of cowboy.

Our country is one that has sprung surprises upon the world from its very beginning, and it has produced men possible in no other land.

Without the services of the cowboy the vast grazing-lands of America would have been worthless.

As the buffalo, like the Indian, perished before the march of emigration westward, there came to take their place vast herds of beef-cattle, feeding on the plains where the once wild monarchs of the prairies had roamed.

With these immense herds it was necessary to have herders, and they became known by the somewhat picturesque cognomen of cowboy.

They are known from the flower-bespangled prairies of the Lone Star State to the land of the Frozen North, and their worth is recognized by those who know them as they are, for to their care is given the vast wealth of the cattlemen of the country, which is not alone in the beef furnished for the markets but to be found also in the tan-yards and factories of the East.

By many, who do not know him as he is, the cowboy is despised and generally feared.

He is looked upon as a wild, reckless fellow, armed to the teeth, keeping half-full of bad whisky, and always ready for a fight or some deed of deviltry.

How little is he known, and thus abused, for no braver hearts, no more generous motives, are to be found among men than are those that beat beneath the hunting-shirt of the cowboy, whether he comes from the country bordering on the Rio Grande, the great plains of the Southwest, the level prairies of the West, or the grazing-lands of Wyoming.

During night and day, storm and sunshine, danger and death, they are at their post of duty, always ready to be called upon, shrinking from no hardship, driven off by no peril, suffering untold privations, but ever ready to protect and care for the valuable herds that they control.

At times, when a temporary relief from duty comes to them, is it a wonder that they break forth into reck-less hilarity?

They mean no harm to any one, and if, as in all com-munities, one goes beyond all bounds and the death of a comrade follows, the many must suffer for the deeds of the few.

The cowboy is composed of that stern stuff of which heroes are made, and the poet and the novelist have al-ways found in this rover of the plains the richest materi-al for song and story.

In olden times it was that the boys of every land turned toward the sea as the Mecca of their hopes and ambitions.

They saw upon its broad bosom a field of adventure, a life of romance; and they sought to emulate great captains, good and bad.

But with the coming of steam-vessels the romance of the seas faded into oblivion; foreign lands were brought near; the mystery of the blue waters was solved in a most matter-of-fact way, and the growing youths of the country turned to new fields of adventure.

Columbus had won the admiration of would-be young heroes, and the heroic deeds of the grand old sailor were read with avidity, the boy longing some day to emulate them.

Even Kidd, Lafitte, Morgan,[1] and other pirate captains became heroes in the minds of the average boy, who longed to run away to sea and make his name known in the world.

But steam dispelled these ambitions, and the American boy was forced to turn his hopes upon the land of the setting sun.

Daniel Boone[2] was a hero to admire; David Crockett,[3] Kit Carson, and other became the beau ideal of border heroes, and the heart of the youth thrilled in reading of these men in buckskin.

And these men of the Wild West, of whom Buffalo Bill is the most conspicuous figure, made it possible for other border heroes to appear.

They sprung from the ranks of the army, from the emigrant's cabin, and from among those rangers of the plains, the cowboys.

These brave fellows have produced many a hero in their ranks, and they have been ever ready to battle for the weak against the strong.

11. A Bucking Bronco.

The ranch and the cattle interests are being encroached upon by the advance of civilization, the mask of mystery is being torn from the wild borderland by the westward march of the iron horse, and in a few more years like the scout, the guide, the trapper, and the hunter, the cowboy will be a thing of the past.

To be acknowledged as a true cowboy, and to the prairie born, one must possess accomplishments for the perilous and arduous work they have to undergo.

He must be a perfect horseman, handle a rope, catch a calf, throw and tie a steer, stop a crazy cow in a stampede, lasso a mustang, and be a good shot, guide, scout, and Indian fighter as well.

Let me here refer to a few incidents of a trip over the plains of a herd of cattle to the markets of the North, through the wild and unsettled portions of the Territories, varying in distance from fifteen hundred to two thousand miles, time three to six months, extending through the Indian Territory and Kansas to Nebraska, Colorado, Dakota, Montana, Idaho, Nevada, and sometimes as far as California. Immense herds, as high as thirty thousand or more, are moved by single owners, but are driven in bands of from one to three thousand, which, when under way, are designated "herds." Each of these have from ten to fifteen men, with a wagon-driver and cook, and the "king-pin of the outfit," the boss, with a supply of two or three ponies to a man, an ox-team, and blankets; also jerked-beef and corn-meal—the staple food. They are also furnished with mavericks, or "doubtless-owned" yearlings, for the fresh-meat supply. After getting fully under way, and the cattle broke in, from ten to fifteen miles a day is the average, and everything is plain sailing in fair weather. As night comes on the cattle are rounded up in a small compass, and held until they lie down, when two men are left on watch, riding round and round them in opposite directions, singing or whistling all the time, for two hours, that being the length of each watch. The singing is absolutely necessary, as it seems to soothe the fears of the cattle, scares away the wolves or other varmints that may be prowling around, and prevents them from hearing any other accidental sounds, or dreaming of their old homes; and if stopped would in all probability be the signal for a general stampede. "Music hath charms to soothe the savage breast," if a cowboy's compulsory scrawling out lines of his own composition:

> Lie nicely now, cattle, don't heed any rattle;
> But quietly rest until morn;
> For if you skedaddle, we'll jump in the saddle,
> And head you as sure as you're born,
> can be considered such.

Ordinarily so clumsy and stupid-looking, a thousand beef-steers can rise like a flock of quail on the roof of an exploding powder-mill, and will scud away like a tumble-weed before a high wind, with a noise like a receding earthquake. Then comes fun and frolic for the boys. Many a cowboy has lost his life in one of these wild stampedes of cattle, which would put an army of men to flight in a mad charge down upon them.

The next great trouble is in crossing streams, which are invariably high in the driving season. When cattle strike swimming-water, they generally try to turn back, which eventuates in their "milling"—that is, swimming in a circle—and if allowed to continue would result in the drowning of many. Then the daring herder must leave his pony, doff his togs, scramble over their backs and horns to scatter them, and with whoops and yells, splashing, dashing, and didos in the water, scare them to the opposite bank. This is not always done in a moment, for a steer is no fool of a swimmer. One has been seen to hold his own for six hours in the gulf after having jumped overboard.

12. A Cattle Stampede.

As some of the streams are very rapid, and a quarter to a half mile wide, considerable drifting is done. Then the naked herder has plenty of amusement in the hot sun, fighting green-head flies and mosquitoes, and peeping around for Indians, until the rest of the lay-out is put over—not an easy job. A temporary boat has to be made of the wagon-box by taking the canvas cover over the bottom, with which the ammunition and grub is ferried across, and the running gear and ponies are swum over afterward. Indian fights and horse-thief troubles are part of the regular rations. Mixing with other herds and cutting them out, again avoiding too much water at times and hunting for a drop at others, belongs to the regular routine.

Such is the cowboy of the wild West, who, if not without faults, has virtues to compensate for the little eccentricities that cling to men of the frontier.

13. A Group of Hostiles.

CHAPTER IV

The Riders of the World

Many customs and habits, by reason of their peculiar surrounding and requirements, have become necessities, and, indeed, second nature to some people; while to others, whose observation has shown the graces and beauties of these same customs and habits, they are studied with great diligence and application, and acquired, as far as such things can be acquired, as accomplishments.

To the Bedouin of the Arabian Desert, the Cossack, the Vaquero, the Gaucho, and last, but the peers of any of these, our native Indian and our own cowboy, the horse is a necessity; and woe be unto that man who by fraud, stealth, or force attempts to despoil the owner of his animal, his pet. Pleasures, comforts, necessities, aye, living itself, would be impossible to either of these is his horse was not part of his worldly possessions. The desert, the pampas, the llanos, and the prairie without horses would, for the uses of man, be as an ocean without ships or boats. But to the fashionables of the world the art of horsemanship is a beautiful and admirable accomplishment, a means of healthful exercise. The rider's grace of carriage, his easy seat, his courageous bearing, like the fit of his handsome tailor-made riding-suit, are objects of pride to himself, and causes of congratulation from his

14. Nip and Tuck.

associates. Gentlemen riders occasionally replace their jockeys on the race-course for the display of their grace and ability. But, after all, how poor their best efforts seem, how awkward their most graceful carriage, and how uncertain and timid their most heroic riding appears when put in actual contrast to the native ease, grace, daring, and picturesque riding of those "to the manor born." The one is, to quote from familiar slang, "born in the saddle," "looks as if part of his horse," while the other easily betrays his hours of study and of practice.

As children we have all read of the Arab, but we remember him principally by recollecting his love for his horse. From our school-boy days the Arab and his horse have been as one to us. His somewhat fantastic costume and the complicated trappings of his steed were beautiful pictures to us, and we recall them yet. These Bedouins of the Arabian Desert are not only recognized as among the best horsemen of the world, but are the beau ideal of Eastern pathfinders. The Cossack of the Caucasian lines is by inheritance and inclination among the most fearless and graceful horsemen of the world. His system of warfare, which bears a striking similarity to that which prevailed on the American frontier a few years ago, is the finest school for the development of military horsemanship since the days of Saladin[1] and *Cœur de Lion*.[2] The Cossacks of the Caucasian line are entitled to be called the flower of that great horde of irregular cavalry, the Cossack Military Colonies, that dwell along the southern frontier of the Russian Empire. They spring from the same branch of the great Cossack family, the Zaporogians, which Byron immortalized in his great poem "Mazeppa."[3] On their light steppe horses, which are as fierce and active as themselves, they have proven themselves worthy of their fierce and warlike sires. Experts as swordsmen, as well as horsemen, they met their old enemies, the Russians, on equal terms.

As picturesque, and more gaudy in appearance and trapping than either the Bedouin or the Cossack, is the wily Vaquero of our neighboring Mexico. Agile, hardy, and dashing, adepts in the work of lasso-throwing, as well as with arms, they are alike interesting in exhibition and dangerous as foes.

But of all these native-born and wonderful horsemen of land other than our own, perhaps the most complete, the most daring and dangerous in war, the most phenomenal trailer, the greatest pathfinder, is the wonderful Gaucho from the llanos of the Argentine Republic. From his earliest infancy the half-wild horses have been his intimates and familiars. When the American or English boy is just learning to stand on his feet alone, the infant Gaucho is being taught by his fond mother to steady himself on the back of one of the ponies of the herd. At the age of four years he can ride the wildest colt that roams the pampas, and from that time he and his horse are practically one; and to unseat him would be almost to tear from the horse a portion of his own anatomy. He is by virtue of his home life and occupations completely dependent on his horse. He spends most of his life on horseback, and is associated with the wild equine to a greater degree than any member of the other equestrian races of the world. Armed with the deadly bolas he is a terrible foe to either bird, beast, or man. The bolas consists of a number of rawhide thongs fastened to a central thong and with an iron ball at each of the ends. He is possibly the most expert lassoer in the world; and when in pursuit of animal or bird he hurls the deadly bolas with unerring skill. From a distance of sixty feet he causes it to inextricably entangle about the legs, bringing the victim helpless to the ground. When tracking his foe across the pathless continent, his fearful skill and persistence make the work of the Cuban bloodhound and the Bedouin of the desert appear like child's play. It is interesting to note that the Gaucho himself makes nearly everything connected with his outfit, from the saddle in which he rides to the boots which cover his feet.

15. Wild Riders of the Plains.

Though these horsemen of the Orient and of South America are picturesque types of riders of the world, the list would indeed be incomplete if we omitted our own Indian and cowboy. To the former no price is too high, no danger too threatening to risk, no undertaking too hazardous to attempt, that will win for him a horse. His wealth is told in the number of his horses, and while he may keep his promise of peace to the settler, he can rarely resist "borrowing" one of his horses if occasion seems to him to demand the need of it. Whether in pursuit of game, indulging in his peculiarly interesting sports, or on the war-path, his pony is his friend and companion. It would at times appear as though the wish, the thought, of the rider was in some mysterious way communicated to the horse without word of mouth or touch of bridle-rein, so quick are their changes of movement or direction and so seldom is a correction made.

Indian warfare was made far more dangerous to the

pioneer of comparatively later days by reason of the red man's introduction to the horse. In the earliest conflicts between the hereditary owners of this continent and the white aggressor, the horse and his uses were unknown to the former. His fighting, like his hunting, had to be done on foot. An Indian attack in those days could not be made with the suddenness or the rush, nor could his retreat be so quickly accomplished, as in after years. And it was not until Cortez[4] brought over his horses that the "long-felt want" was satisfied. Now, like a veritable Centaur, he strides his animal, his command so complete that it appears his arms and hands are not needed for use in his horsemanship, but left free to handle his bow and arrow or his rifle.

Just here it may be well to say a few words relative to the noble animal whose duties and services have commanded the admiration of mankind.

It seems to be a settled fact that the horse is of Moorish origin, as also is his accompaniment, the saddle.

To follow the theory of other able writers, the horse is thought to be a native of the plains of Central Asia, but the wild species from which it is derived is not certainly known. The Asiatic horse with its one digit was in turn evolved from ancestors with polydactyl feet. Some instances have been known in modern times, and ancient records give stories, of horses presenting more than one toe. Julius Cæsar's[5] horse is said to have had this peculiarity. Suetonius,[6] the writer, describes this horse as being almost human, with the hoofs cleft like toes. This author says: "It was born in Cæsar's own stables, and as the soothsayers declared that it showed that its owner would be lord of the world, he reared it with great care, and was the first to mount it. It would allow no other rider."

Most of the polydactyl horses found in the present day have been raised in the southwest of America, or from that ancestry bred. In this way their connection with the mustang, or semi-wild stock of that region, becomes at least probable.

This same raw-boned, small, or medium-sized horse, called the mustang, possesses a well-authenticated claim to noble origin. Horses of good Berber blood were brought over by the Spanish conquerors under Cortez and De Soto,[7] and it is a most reasonable supposition that these invaders selected the very best and strongest specimens of the breed for use in their daring ventures. It is not surprising that the native of Mexico, when for the first time they saw approaching them men on horses, both clad in glittering armor, were filled with terror. To them it seemed that man and horse were one, a veritable four-legged warrior, and they fled precipitately to the fastnesses of their own mountains to escape contact with this monstrosity.

In good time the climate and surroundings wrought many changes in the horse that first landed on the shores of Mexico, and the breed eventually became what is now known as the "American mustang," perhaps the hardiest specimen of the genus horse now known. From this origin evolved the finest breeds of horses now claimed to be American bred.

During the visit of the Wild West to Paris, General Cody, by invitation, called on Rosa Bonheur,[8] the famous painter of horses. Three years prior to this time Miss Bonheur had received from America three fine mustang ponies, two of which had, despite all effort, remained uncontrollable and therefore, of course, useless to her. These latter she generously tendered to General Cody as a present. Her surprise when Cody calmly accepted the offer, and assured her that "his boys" would have but little trouble in catching and controlling these animals, can hardly be described. True to his assurance, Cody soon had two of his "boys" on hand, and in a short times the apparently uncontrollable "Appach" and "Clair de Lune" were lassoed by the "boys," saddled and mounted. This scene was witnessed not only by the great artist herself but by numbers of marveling neighbors, who, by peeping through their window-shutters, saw for the first time a lasso hunt. The quick, accurate, and successful work of the American cowboy astonished and interested all these witnesses to a wonderful degree.

To the cowboy's dexterous horsemanship, added to his courage and endurance, has been largely due the protection of the lives and property of the early emigrants to the great West. For years the dissemination of news was entirely dependent upon these heroic riders. Now the success and preservation of the vast cattle interests are made possible only by the watchful care of the cowboy and his pony—the one practically helpless without the other.

The "view halloo" of the English hunting gentleman may be inspiriting to those accustomed to it, but how it lacks in vigor, in earnestness, in actual music, the famous cowboy yell as he and his pony dash upon game or hostile Indians. This latter carries with its sound the conviction of heartiness, determination, and enthusiasm with which he begins a sport, faces a danger, or encounters a foe. To those who have seen Gen. W. F. Cody ("Buffalo Bill") give exhibitions of this method of riding, it will readily be understood how difficult it is in words to illustrate the strange peculiarity of its singular attractiveness.

To this man of ideas is due the thought of gathering together in one congress the representatives of all these types of horses and riders. And, as with Cody to resolve is to act, this interesting assemblage is ready for public contemplation at the World's Fair.

It may not be inappropriate in this chapter to quote the words of the famous king of poets in eulogy of that noble animal, the horse.

Shakespeare on the Horse.[9]

Imperiously he leaps, he neighs, he bounds,
And now his woven girths he breaks asunder;
The bearing earth with his hard hoof he wounds,
Whose hollow womb resounds like heaven's thunder;
The iron bit he crushes 'tween his teeth,
Controlling what he was controlléd with.

His ears up-pricked, his braided hanging mane
Upon his compassed crest now stands on end;
His nostrils drink the air, and forth again,
As from a furnace, vapors doth he send;
His eye, which scornfully glisters like fire,
Shows his hot courage and his high desire.

Sometimes he trots, as if he told the steps
With gentle majesty and modest pride;
Anon he rears upright, curvets, and leaps,
As who should say, "Lo! thus my strength is tried;

And this I do to captivate the eye
Of the fair breeder that is standing by."

What recketh he his rider's angry stir,
His flattering "Holla," or his "*Stand, I say*"?
What cares he now for curb or pricking spur,
For rich caparisons or trapping gay?
He sees his love, and nothing else he sees,
Nor nothing else with his proud sight agrees.

Look! When a painter would surpass the life
In limning out a well-proportioned steed,
His art with nature's workmanship at strife,
As if the dead the living should exceed,
So did this horse excel a common one,
In shape, in color, courage, pace, and bone.

Round-hoof'd, short-jointed, fetlocks shag and long,
Broad breast, full eye, small head, and nostrils wide,
High crest, short ears, straight legs, and passing strong,
Thin mane, thick tail, broad buttock, tender hide.
Look! What a horse should have he did not lack,
Save a proud rider on so proud a back.

Buffalo Bill's Equine Heroes

Mr. Cody is a great lover of man's best friend among the animal kingdom—the horse. The peculiar career he has followed has made his equine friend such a sterling necessity as a companion, an assistant, a confidant, that he admits, as every frontiersman and scout does, a great deal depends, even life itself in innumerable emergencies, on the general sagacity of this noble brute. For the purposes

16. Comrades.

of the trail, the hunt, the battle, the pursuit, or the stampede it was essentially necessary to select, for chargers with which to gain success, animals excelling in the qualities of strength, speed, docility, courage, stamina, keen scent, delicacy of ear, quick of sight, sure-footed, shrewd in perception, nobleness of character, and general intelligence. History records, and a grateful memory still holds dear, numberless famous quadruped allies that Buffalo Bill has during his long career possessed, and many are the stories told on the frontier and in the army of Old Buckskin Joe, Brigham, Tall Bull, Powder-Face, Stranger, and Old Charlie.

Old Buckskin Joe was one of his early favorites, who by long service in army-scouting became quite an adept, and seemed to have a perfect knowledge of the duties required of him. For this reason, when ordered to find and report the location of the savages in their strongholds, at times hundreds of miles away over a lonely country, infested by scouting parties of hostiles liable at any instant to pounce upon one, Old Buckskin was always selected by Cody to accompany him on the trail when the work was dangerous. Mounted on another horse, he would let Buckskin follow untrammeled, even by a halter, so as to reserve him fresh in case of discovery and the terrible necessity of "a ride for life." Quick to scent danger, he instinctively gave evidence of his fears, and would almost assist his saddling or quickly insert his head in the bridle, and once on his back Joe was always able to bid defiance to the swiftest horses the Indians possessed, and the longer the chase the farther they were left in his rear. On one occasion his master descried a band of 100 warriors, who gave them chase from the headwaters of the Republican River to Fort McPherson, a distance of 195 miles. It was at a season when the ponies were in good condition, and the savage band, though thirsting for the scalp of their well-known foe, Pa-he-has-ka (the long-haired scout),[10] dropped behind until on the last fifty miles but fifteen of the fleetest were in pursuit, Buckskin leaving them out of sight twenty miles from the fort.

This ride, famed in army annals, caused Old Buckskin to go blind, but the gratitude of his master was such that Joe was kept and carefully attended to until his death, which occurred a few years ago at Cody's home, North Platte. Buckskin was accorded a decent funeral, and a tombstone erected over his remains inscribed "Old Buckskin Joe, the horse that on several occasions saved the life of Buffalo Bill by carrying him safely out of the range of Indian bullets. Died of old age, 1882."

Brigham was another celebrity of his race, and it was on his back Mr. Cody clinched his undisputed title of "King Buffalo-killer," and added permanency to the name of Buffalo Bill by killing *sixty-nine buffalo in one run;* and such was this steed's knowledge of hunting that game that he discarded saddle and bridle while following the herd, killing the last half while riding this renowned pet of the chase *bareback.*

Many other tried and true ones have enhanced his love for their race, the last of the famous old-timers being owned and ridden by him in his daily exhibitions with the Wild West, traversing the continent five times, traveling thousands of miles, and never missing a performance. Old Charlie possessed all the virtues that go to form a "noble horse." Charlie was broken in by Mr. Cody, and has never been ridden by any one else (except Miss Arta Cody,[11] an accomplished horse-woman), and for many years has been the participant of all his master's skirmishes, expeditions, long rides, and hunts; has been ridden over all kinds of rough country, prairie-dog towns, mountain and plain; has never stumbled or fallen, being beyond a doubt one of the surest-footed animals man ever rode; and for endurance is a second Buckskin Joe, if not better, on one occasion, in an emergency, having carried his master over a prairie road *one hundred miles in nine hours and forty-five minutes,* rider and trappings weighing 243 pounds. Old Charlie's great point was his wonderful intelligence, which caused him to act in a manner as to almost lay claim in his conduct to judiciousness. In the most lonely or unattractive place, or in one of the most seductive to equine rambles, when his master removed saddle and bridle, he

17. Kicking Bear, Oglala Sioux War Chief.

could trust Charlie to stay where he was left, wrap himself in a blanket, take the saddle for a pillow, go to sleep contented, knowing his faithful steed would be close at hand, or, after browsing fully, would come and lie close beside him, sink into slumber, with ear at tension, one eye open, and at the slightest disturbance arouse him to meet the threatened danger. All the Indians in the country, keen as he was to scent them, intuitively as he dreaded them, could not make him leave, or stampede him, until his owner was mounted, challenging in this respect the instincts of the highest class of watch-dog.

He cared not how much load you put on his back, having carried 500 pounds of buffalo-meat; would pull as much by tying a lariat to the pommel as an ordinary horse with a collar; would hold the strongest buffalo or steer, but when a harness was placed on his back and a collar round his neck he would not pull an ounce, and if not soon relieved would viciously resent the (to him) seeming degradation.

Alas! poor Charlie died while crossing the ocean on the homeward-bound voyage, and was buried at sea with all the honors that would have been shown to a human being.

In his death Buffalo Bill lost a friend he will never forget.

18. A Redskin Scout.

CHAPTER V

Indian Home Life

To Indians at peace, and with food in plenty, the winter camp is their home. After the varying excitements, the successes and vicissitudes, the constant labors of many months, the prospect of the winter's peace and rest, with its home life and home pleasures, comes like a soothing balm to all.

To those of the warriors who have passed the age of passionate excitements, this season brings the full enjoyment of those pleasures and excitements yet left to them in life. Their days are spent in gambling, their long winter evenings in endless repetitions of stories of their wonderful performances in days gone by, and their nights in the sound, sweet sleep vouchsafed only to easy consciences.

The women also have a good time. No more taking down and putting up the tepee; no more packing and unpacking the ponies. To bring the wood and water, do the little cooking, to attend to the ponies, and possibly to dress a few skins is all the labor devolved upon them.

To the young of both sexes, whether married or single, this season brings unending excitement and pleasure. Now is the time for dances and feasts, for visits and frolics and merry-making of all kinds, and for this time the "story-teller" has prepared and rehearsed his most marvelous recitals. Above all, it is the season for love-making; "love rules the camp," and now is woman's opportunity.

Without literature, without music or painting as arts, without further study of nature than is necessary for the safety of the needs of their daily life, with no knowledge or care for politics or finance or the thousand questions of social or other science that disturb and perplex the minds of civilized people, and with reasoning faculties little superior to instinct, there is among Indians no such thing as conversation as we understand it. There is plenty of talk, but no interchange of ideas; no expression and comparison of views and beliefs, except on the most commonplace topics. Half a dozen old sages will be sitting around, quietly and gravely passing the pipe, and apparently engaged in important discussion. Nine times out of ten their talk is the merest camp tattle, or about a stray horse or sick colt, or where one killed a deer or another saw a buffalo-track. All serious questions of war and chase are reserved for discussion in the council lodge.

During the pleasant months he has constantly the healthy stimulus of active life; during the winter he is either in a state of lethargy or of undue excitement. During the day, in the winter season, the men gamble or sleep, the women work or idle, as suits each; but the moment it gets dark everybody is on the qui vive, ready for any fun that presents itself. A few beats on a tom- tom bring all the inmates of the neighboring lodges; a dance or gambling bout is soon inaugurated, and oftentimes kept up until nearly morning.

The insufficiency and uncertainty of human happiness has been the theme of eloquent writers of all ages. Every man's happiness is lodged in his own nature, and is, to a certain extent at least, independent of his external circumstances and surroundings. These primitive people demonstrate the general correctness of this theory, for they are habitually and universally happy people. They thoroughly enjoy the present, make no worry over the possibilities of the future, and "never cry over spilled milk." It may be argued that their apparent happiness is only insensibility, the happiness of the mere animal, whose animal desires are satisfied. It may be so. I simply state facts, others may draw conclusions. The Indian is proud, sensitive, quick-tempered, easily wounded, easily excited; but though utterly unforgiving, he never broods. This is the whole secret of his happiness.

In spite of the fact that the wives are mere property, the domestic life of the Indian will bear comparison with that of average civilized communities. The husband, as a rule, is kind; ruling, but with no harshness. The wives are generally faithful, obedient, and industrious. The children are spoiled, and a nuisance to all red visitors. Fortunately the white man, the "bugaboo" of their baby days, is yet such an object of terror as to keep them at a respectful distance. Among themselves the members of the family are perfectly easy and unrestrained. It is extremely rare that there is any quarreling among the women.

There is no such thing as nervousness in either sex. Living in but the one room, they are from babyhood accustomed to what would be unbearable annoyances to whites. The head of the lodge comes back tired from a hunt, throws himself down on a bed, and goes fast to sleep, though his two or three wives chatter around and his children tumble all over him. Everybody seems to do just as he or she pleases, and this seems no annoyance to anybody else.

Unlike her civilized sister, the Indian woman, "in her hour of greatest need," does not need any one. She would be shocked at the idea of having a man doctor. In pleasant weather the expectant mother betakes herself to the seclusion of some thicket; in winter she goes to a tepee provided in each band for the women. In a few hours she returns with a baby in its cradle on her back, and goes about her usual duties as if nothing had happened.

Preparations for war or the chase occupy such hours of the winter encampment as the noble red man can spare from gambling, love-making, and personal adornment.

Each Indian must make for himself everything which he can not procure by barter, and the opportunities for barter of the more common necessities are very few, the Indians not having even yet conceived the idea of making any articles for sale among themselves.

The saddle requires much time and care in its construction; some Indians can never learn to make one; consequently this is more an article of barter than anything commonly made by Indians.

No single article varies so much in make and value as the bridle. The bit is always purchased, and is of every pattern, from the plain snaffle to the complicated contrivance of the Mexicans. The bridle of one Indian may be a mere headstall of rawhide attached to the bit, but without frontlet or throat-latch, and with reins of the same material, the whole not worth a dollar; that of another may be so elaborated by patient labor, and so garnished with silver, as to be worth a hundred dollars.

The Southern Indians have learned from the Mexicans the art of plaiting horse-hair, and much of their work is very artistic and beautiful, besides being wonderfully serviceable. A small smooth stick, one-fourth of an inch in diameter, is the mold over which the hair is plaited. When finished, the stick is withdrawn. The hair used is previously dyed of different colors, and it is so woven as to present pretty patterns. The hair, not being very strong, is used for the head-stall; the reins, which require strength, are plaited solid, but in the same pattern, showing skill, taste, and fitness.

The name "lariat" (Spanish, *riata*) is applied by all frontiersmen and Indians to the rope or cord used for picketing or fastening their horses while grazing, and also to the thong used for catching wild animals—the lasso. They are the same, with a very great difference. The lasso may be used for picketing a horse, but the rope with which a horse is ordinarily picketed would never be of use as a lasso.

A good riata (lasso) requires a great deal of labor and patient care. It is sometimes made of plaited hair from the manes and tails of horses, but these are not common except where wild horses are plentiful, one such riata requiring the hair of not less than twenty animals. It is generally made of rawhide of buffalo or domestic cattle, freed from hair, cut into narrow strips, and plaited with infinite patience and care, so as to be perfectly round and smooth. Such a riata, though costing less money than that of hair, is infinitely superior. It is smooth, round, heavy, runs easily and quickly to noose, and is as strong as a cable. Those tribes, as the Ute, who are unable to procure beef or buffalo skins, make beautiful lariats of thin strips of buckskin plaited together; but as these are used only for securing their horses they are usually plaited flat.

To make these articles is all that the male Indian finds to do in his ordinary winter life. Without occupation, without literature, without thought, how man can persuade himself to continue to exist can be explained only on the hypothesis that he is a natural "club man," or a mere animal.

"From rosy morn to dewy eve" there is always work for the Indian woman. Fortunately for her the aboriginal inhabitants have as yet discovered no means of making a light sufficient to work by at night. It is true they beg or buy a few candles from military posts or traders, but these are sacredly preserved for dances and grand occasions.

But, slave as she is, I doubt if she could be forced to work after dark even if she had light. Custom, which holds her in so many inexorable bonds, comes to her aid in this case. In every tribe night is the woman's right, and no matter how urgent the work which occupies her during the daylight, the moment the dark comes she bedecks herself in her best finery and stands at the door of the lodge, her ear strained for the first beat of the tom- tom which summons her to where she is the, for once, queen and ruler.

There was formerly one exception to this immunity from night work, but it has gone with the buffalo. At the time of the "great fall hunt" there was no rest nor excuse for her. She must work at any and all hours. If the herds were moving, the success of the hunt might depend on the rapidity with which the women performed their work on a batch of dead buffalo. These animals spoil very quickly if not disemboweled, and though the hunters tried to regulate the daily kill by the ability of the s***ws[1] to "clean up" after them, they could, not in the nature of things, always do so.

When the buffalo was dead the man's work was done; it was woman's work to skin and cut up the dead animal; and oftentimes, when the men were exceptionally fortunate, the women were obliged to work hard and fast all night long before the task was finished.

The meat, cut as closely as possible from the bones, is tied up in the skin, and packed to camp on the ponies.

The skin is spread, flesh side upward, on a level piece of ground, small slits are cut in the edges, and it is tightly stretched and fastened down by wooden pegs driven through the slits into the ground. The meat is cut into thin flakes and placed upon poles or scaffolds to dry in the sun.

All this work must be done, as it were, instantly, for if the skin is allowed to dry unstretched it can never be made use of as a robe, and the meat spoils if not "jerked" within a few hours.

This lively work lasts but a few weeks, and is looked upon by the workers themselves pretty much in the same way as notable housewives look upon the early house-cleaning—very disagreeable, but very enjoyable. The real work begins when, the hunt being over, the band has gone into winter quarters, for then must the women begin to utilize "the crop."

Some of the thickest bulls' hides are placed to soak in water in which is mixed wood ashes, or some natural alkali. This takes the hair off. The skin is then cut into the required shape and stretched on a form, on which it is allowed to dry, when it not only retains its shape but becomes almost as hard as iron. These boxes are of various shapes and sizes—some made like huge pocket-books, others like trunks. All are called "parfleche."

As soon as these parfleches, or trunks, are ready for use, the now thoroughly dried meat is pounded to powder between the stones. About two inches of this powdered meat is placed in the bottom of a parfleche and melted fat is lightly poured over it. Then another layer of meat is served in the same way, and so on until the trunk is full. It is kept hot until the entire mass is thoroughly saturated. When cold, the parfleches are closed and tightly tied up. The contents so prepared will keep in good condition for several years. Probably the best feature of the process is that nothing is lost, the flesh of old and tough animals being, after this treatment, so nearly as good as that of the young that few persons can tell the difference. This is the true Indian bread, and is used as bread when they have fresh meat. Boiled, it makes a soup very nutritious. So long as the Indian has this dried meat and pemmican he is entirely independent of all other food. Of late years all the beef issued to the Indians on the reservations, and not needed for immediate consumption, is treated in this way.

The dressing of skins is the next work. The thickest hides are put in soak of alkali for materials for making shields, saddles, riatas, etc. Hides for making or repairing lodges are treated in the same way, but after the hair has been removed they are reduced in thickness, made pliable, and most frequently soaked.

Deer, antelope, and other skins are beautifully prepared for clothing, the hair being always removed. Some of these skins are so worked down that they are almost as thin and white as cotton cloth.

But all this is the mere commencement of the long and patient labor which the loving wife bestows on the robe which the husband is to use on dress occasions. The whole inner surface is frequently covered with designs beautifully worked with porcupine-quills, or grasses dyed in various colors. Sometimes the embellishments are paintings. Many elegant robes have taken a year to finish.

Every animal brought into the camp brings work for the s***w. The buck comes in with a deer and drops it at the door. The s***w skins it, cuts up and preserves the meat, dresses the skin and fashions it into garments for some member of the family. Until within a very few years the needle was a piece of sharpened bone; the thread a fiber of sinew. These are yet used in the ornamentation of robes, but almost all the ordinary sewing is done with civilized appliances.

All Indians are excessively fond of bead-work, and not only the clothing, moccasins, gun-covers, quivers, knife-sheaths, and tobacco-pouches, but every little bag or ornament, is covered with this work. Many of the designs are pretty and artistic. In stringing the beads for this work an ordinary needle is used; but in every case, except for articles made for sale, the thread is sinew.

The life in the winter encampment has scarcely been changed in any particular, but with the earliest spring come evidences of activity, a desire to get away; not attributable, as in the "good old time," to plans of forays for scalps and plunder, but to the desire of each head of a lodge or band to reach, before any one else does, the particular spot on which he has fixed for his location for the summer. No sooner has he reached it than all hands, men, women, and children, fall to work as if the whole thing were a delightful frolic.

The last five years, more than any twenty preceding them, have convinced the wild Indians of the utter futility of their warfare against the United States Government. One and all, they are thoroughly whipped; and their contests, in the future, will be the acts of predatory parties (for which the Indians at large are no more responsible than is the Government of the United States for the acts of highwaymen in the Black Hills, or train-robbers in Missouri), or a deliberate determination of the bands and tribes to die fighting rather than by the slow torture of starvation to which the Government condemns them.

But the buffalo is gone; so also nearly all the other large game on which the Indians depended for food. They are confined to comparatively restricted reservations, and completely surrounded by whites. They are more perfectly aware of the stringency of their situation than any white man can possibly be, for they daily feel its pressure.

With no chance of success in war, with no possibility of providing food for themselves, they thoroughly comprehend that their only hope for the future is in Government aid, grazing cattle, and tilling the soil.

They do not like it, of course; it would be unnatural if they did. They accept it as the dire alternative against starvation.

Basing arguments on the Indian contempt for work, many men in and out of Congress talk eloquent nonsense of the impossibility of ever bringing them to agricultural

19. Oglala Chiefs.

20. Breaking Glass Balls at Full Speed.

pursuits. The average Indian has no more hatred of labor, as such, than the average white man. Neither will labor unless an object is to be attained. Both will labor rather than starve. Heretofore the Indian could comfortably support himself in his usual and preferred life without labor; and there being no other incentive he would have only proved himself an idiot had he worked without an object.

But now, with the abundant acres of land that his white conquerors, with simple justice, have allotted to him in the shape of reservations, with no opportunity to think of the excitement, honor, and glory of battle, his life is changed. He now finds that fences are to be made, ground broken up, seed planted; and the peerless warrior, with "an eye like an eagle," whose name a few short years ago was a terror and whose swoop was destruction, must learn to handle the plow, and follow, in fact, what he has often claimed in desire and spirit to follow, "the white man's road."

CHAPTER VI

Expert Shooting

Every custom, vocation, or study that has for its object the protection of home, self, or one's just rights, the defense of the weak or the protection of the innocent, is justly denominated "manly," and commands universal respect and admiration. If such attributes or qualifications as a steady nerve, a clear, penetrating gaze, and intensity and earnestness of purpose, are combined with quickness of action and courageous bearing, the admiration grows stronger and the respect deeper.

Years ago scarcely anybody save the professional duelist would ever have thought of making an accomplishment of rifle or pistol shooting, unless, like the enlisted soldier or the dweller on the prairies, a practical knowledge of fire-arms and their uses became an absolute necessity for self-protection or the performance of duty. Yet now so-called "fancy shooting" is considered rather a "fad," and its aptest exponents are objects of laudation and applause. The huntsman is no longer a slayer of game and wild beasts as a means of subsistence for himself and family, or for sale to neighbors or in the public market. The elephant is now rarely killed for his tusks, the tiger for his skin, or the buffalo (what few there are left of this species) for his flesh. Now the "chase" is a mere sport, like "hunting the covers" in Merrie England, and men boast of their prowess as hunters much as they do of their skill at billiards. Yet an expert with the rifle or the pistol is an object of applause and admiration, and even the more courageous of the fair sex love to try their skill at a target. For a time the old pastime of archery was revived, but, whether its difficulties or its present-day impracticability was the cause, it has been abandoned by the fashionable world, and shooting-galleries are now the "thing" rather than archery clubs.

In the march of progress the club, the lance, the javelin, and the long-bow have been thrown aside, and modern invention has given us the cannon, the shotgun, the musket, the rifle, and the pistol. Some writers have even argued, and ably too, that the invention of gunpowder had a most powerful and active effect upon the civilization of the world.

However, the acts of aiming and discharging the projectile, and successfully striking the target, be it animate or inanimate, possess a rare fascination for the world at large. What boy has not enjoyed raptures of delight at the story of William Tell,[1] and the fact of his having shot the apple from his son's head has made a more lingering and lasting impression upon the readers of the story than his struggle to liberate his countrymen from the tyranny personified in Gessler; and you iconoclasts give mortal offense to the youth of the world when you dare assert that their hero of Switzerland is a myth. There is no story more interesting, told to the good little boy who regularly attends his Sunday-school, than that of David's wonderful marksmanship when, by throwing a pebble from a sling, he struck the mighty Goliath and slew him.[2] David's after-history, his glories and his sacerdotal power, though ofttimes told the youthful Biblical scholar and repeated to him in sermons when he grows older, may have an effect, but still it is the incident of David's meeting with the giant and his victory over him that most surely impresses him.

To learn the science of accurate shooting by constant practice in a gallery especially prepared for that purpose, the target being inanimate and incapable of retaliation, may, and often does, result in aptitude with the revolver and the rifle. To preserve this cleverness, however, the conditions must always be the same. The proper light must fall correctly upon the target; nothing to disturb the serenity of the surroundings or to distract the attention of the shooter must be permitted.

A grade higher comes the hunter. His targets are living, breathing objects. Sometimes he may stealthily approach, unobserved, and secure of aim while the object is at rest; again, the bird flies, the beast runs, and then his scientific calculation must be quick and accurate. But in both of these the disturbing element of probable, almost certain, retaliation is lacking. The excitement of rivalry or the enthusiasm, added to the uncertainty, of the chase may somewhat agitate the nerves of the shooter. His own safety is assured, however. How often do we read of a meeting on the miscalled "field of honor" of two men, both famous as pistol-gallery shots; men with whom to hit the "bull's-eye" nine times out of ten shots is a common occurrence, yet who exchange leaden compliments that are as barren of results as would be the feeding of a hungry man on "angel food." What is the cause of this? It is the actual, assured knowledge that in this instance the targets are equally animate, equally prepared thoroughly for retaliatory action, both equally anxious, and as capable of hitting the target the one as the other, and a sure consequence is that the nerves of both shooters are "like sweet bells, jangled, out of tune."

The soldier whose lessons in the handling of fire-arms have been learned on many a hard-fought field has acquired a steadiness of nerve, a sort of reckless fearlessness, and, at times, even a contempt for danger which its constant presence has taught him. All honor to the soldiers who in steady column, shoulder to shoulder, or in dashing charge to the shrill cry of the bugle, have fearlessly breasted the scathing fire of the enemy's guns. But in this case the inspiriting association of comrades, the encouraging sense of companionship, cheers them on, and they at least momentarily fail to really appreciate the thorough seriousness of their situation.

How different from all these pictures is that of the daring scout, the intrepid cowboy, the faithful guide, of the unsettled West. To either of these danger is so constant, so frequent in its visitations, that it has become an expected presence. An ear quick to detect a rustle of the leaves, a footfall on the turf, the click of the hammer of a rifle; an eye to instantaneously penetrate into the thickness of the brush; to detect, locate, and photograph a shifting speck on the horizon; to measure distance at a glance, and to fix the threatening target's vulnerable point in an instant are absolute necessities. Added to these, as an absolute essential, must be nerves as tense as steel. A tremor of the arm, nay, the slightest quiver of muscle, that sends the bullet a hair's-breadth from the point aimed at, may cost not only the death of the shooter, but the lives of those depending on him for safety. No fancy shooting this; for more than life—honor and reputation, the preservation of sacred trusts and cherished lives committed to his care, depend upon his coolness, his courage, and his accuracy. In a moment all will be over for good or ill, and upon his single personality all depends. The stake is fearful.

These indubitable facts considered, is it surprising that these danger-baptized heroes of the West stand to-day as the most marvelous marksmen of the world?

The amateur sportsman, the society expert rifle-shot, the ambitious youth, and even woman, to whom all real manly exploits and true heroism are admirable, all take sincere pleasure in witnessing the feats of marksmanship of the cowboy, scout, or guide expert, and wonder at his marvelous accuracy. It is because actual necessity was the foundation upon which their expertness was built that these surpass all others in the science. What appears wonderful to others is in them but the perfection of art.

Looking at expert shooting as a pastime, a science, or a means of protection or self-preservation, the awakening of the manhood of the country and the up-growing youth to its possibilities is surely to be commended and encouraged. No man is more to be credited with the accomplishment of this than Gen. W. F. Cody. His romantic and picturesque history and his wonderful accomplishments have attracted to him the attention of America and Europe, and no one man is more capable of exemplifying the science of shooting than he. A graduate, with high honors, of the school where expert shooting is taught by

21. A Noonday Halt on the Prairie.

the best practice and actual experience, he is master of his art. The object-lessons he gives are of incalculable benefit to the ambitious student of marksmanship, and sources of delight to all. His trusty rifle is now a social friend, whose intimacy is founded on dangers averted, heroic deeds accomplished, and honors nobly won.

CHAPTER VII

A Most Famous Ride

In the spring of 1868, at the outbreak of the violent Indian war, General Sheridan, from his headquarters at Hays City, dispatched Cody as guide and scout to Captain Parker[1] at Fort Larned. Several bands of Comanches and Kiowas were in the vicinity, and Buffalo Bill, after guiding General Hazen and an escort of twenty men to Fort Zarah,[2] thirty miles distant, started to return to Larned alone. At Pawnee Rock,[3] about half-way, he found himself suddenly surrounded by about forty warriors. By professions of friendship and warm greeting of "How, how!" Bill saw he could alone depend on cunning and strategy to escape. Being taken before Satanta,[4] who Bill knew was expecting, a short time before, a large herd of cattle which had been promised by General Hazen, he boldly complained to the wily chief of his treatment, and informed him that he had been ordered to find him and deliver "a big heap lot whohaws." The cupidity of old Satanta enabled Bill to regain his arms. Although declining an escort, he was followed, much to his alarm, by a dozen well-mounted redskins. Keeping up "a heap of thinking," Cody at last reached a depression that hid him from view, and succeeded, by putting the mule at his highest speed, in getting fully a mile in advance before the trailers discovered his object.

Upon seeing the fleeing scout, there were no further grounds for suspecting his motives; so the Indians, who were mounted on excellent ponies, dashed after him as though they were impelled by a promise of all the whisky and bacon in the big father's commissary for his scalp. Bill was trying to save his hair, and the Indians were equally anxious to save it, so that the ride, prompted by these diametrically opposed motives, was a furious as Tam o' Shanter's.[5] After running over about three miles of ground, Bill turned his head, only to be horrified by the sight of his pursuers gaining rapidly on him. He now sank the spurs a little deeper into his mule, let out another inch of the reins, and succeeded in increasing the speed of his animal, which appeared to be sailing under a second wind.

It was thus the chase continued to Ash Grove,[6] four miles from Fort Larned, at which point Bill was less than half a mile ahead of the Indians, who were trying to make line shots with him and his mule as a target. Reaching Pawnee Fork, he dashed into that stream, and as he gained the opposite shore, and was rounding a thick clump of trees, he was rejoiced to meet Denver Jim,[7] a prominent scout, in company with a private soldier, driving a wagon toward the post.

A moment spent in explanation determined the three men upon an ambush. Accordingly the wagon was hastily driven into the woods, and posting themselves at an advantageous point they awaited the appearance of the redskinned pursuers. "Look out!" said Bill; "here they come, right over my trail." True enough, the twelve painted warriors rode swiftly around the clump of brush, and the next instant there was a discharge of shots from the ambush which sent two Indians sprawling on the ground, where they kicked out their miserable existence. The others saw the danger of their position, and making a big circle rode rapidly back toward their war-party.

When the three men reached Larned, Buffalo Bill and Denver Jim each displayed an Indian scalp as trophies of a successful ambush, and at the same time apprised Captain Parker of the hostile character of Satanta and his tribe.

On the following day about eight hundred warriors appeared before the fort, and threatened to storm it; but being met with a determined front they circled the post several times, keeping the soldiers inside until their village could move off. Considerable fear was entertained at the fort, owing to the great number of hostile Indians who practically invested it, and it was determined by Captain Parker as of the utmost importance to send dispatches to General Sheridan, informing him of the situation. Fort Hays was sixty-five miles distant from Fort Larned, and, as the country was fairly swarming with the worst kind of "bad" Indians, Captain Parker tried in vain to find some one who would carry the dispatches, until the request was made to Buffalo Bill. This expedition was not within Bill's line of duty, and presented dangers that would have caused the boldest man to hesitate; but finding all the couriers absolutely refusing to perform the necessary service, he agreed to deliver the message, provided that he could select the horse that he wanted to ride. Of course this requirement was readily assented to, and at 10 o'clock at night, during a terrible storm, the brave scout set out, knowing that he had to run a very gauntlet of hostiles, who would make many sacrifices if by so do-ing they could lift his coveted scalp.

The profound darkness of the night afforded him some security from surprise, but his fears of riding into an Indi-an camp were realized when he reached Walnut Creek.[8] A barking dog was the first intimation of his position, but this was speedily followed by several Indians pursuing him, being directed by the sounds of his horse's feet. By hard riding and good dodging, however, he eluded these, and meeting with no further mishap than being thrown over his horse's head by reason of the animal suddenly stepping into a gopher-hole, he reached Fort Hays short-ly after daylight, and delivered the dispatches he carried before General Sheridan had arisen from bed.

After delivering the message Bill went over to Hays City, where he was well acquainted, and after taking some refreshments lay down and slept for two hours. Thinking then that General Sheridan might want to ask him some questions regarding the condition of affairs at Larned, he returned to the fort and reported to him. He was some-what astonished to find that General Sheridan was as anx-ious to send a messenger to Fort Dodge, ninety-five miles distant, as Captain Parker had been to communicate with his superior officer at Fort Hays; and more surprised was he to fine that of the numerous couriers and scouts at the fort not one could be induced to carry the general's dis-patch, though the sum of $500 was offered for the ser-vice. Seeing the quandary in which General Sheridan was placed, Bill addressed that official, and said, "Well, Gen-eral, I'll go over to the hotel and take a little more rest, and if by 4 o'clock you have not secured some one to car-ry your dispatches, I will undertake to do it."

The general replied: "I don't like to ask so much of you, for I know you are tired; but the matter is of great importance and some one must perform the trip. I'll give you a fresh horse, and the best at the fort, if you'll undertake it."

"All right, General; I'll be ready at 4 o'clock," replied Bill, and then he went over to the hotel; but meeting with many friends, and the "irrigating" being good, he obtained only the rest that gay companionship affords. At the appointed time Bill was ready, and receiving the dispatches at the hands of General Sheridan he mounted his horse and rode away to Fort Dodge. After his departure there was much debate among the scouts who bade him goodby respecting the probability of his getting through, for the Indians were thick along the whole route, and only a few days before had killed three couriers and several settlers. Bill continued his ride all night, meeting with no interruption, and by daylight next morning he had reached Saw-Log Crossing,[9] on Pawnee Fork which was seventy-five miles from Fort Hays. A company of colored cavalry, under Major Cox,[10] was stationed here, and it being on the direct route to Fort Dodge, Bill carried a letter with him from General Sheridan requesting Major Cox to furnish him with a fresh horse upon his arrival there; this the major did; so after partaking of a good breakfast Bill took his remount and continued on to Dodge, which point he gained at 10 o'clock in the morning, making the ninety-five miles in just eighteen hours from the time of starting.

The commanding officer at Fort Dodge after receiving the dispatches remarked: "I am very glad to see you, Cody, and I'll tell you that the trip just made is one of the most fortunate I know of. It is almost a miracle how you got through without having your body filled as full of holes as a pepper-box. The Indians are swarming all around within fifty miles of here, and to leave camp voluntarily is almost equal to committing suicide. I have been wanting to send a message to Fort Larned for several days, but the trip is so dangerous that I can't find any one who will risk it, and I wouldn't blame the bravest man for refusing."

"Well, Major, I think I might get through to Larned; in fact I want to go back there, and if you will furnish me with a good horse I'll try to carry your message."

"I don't think it would be policy for you to make the trip now, especially since you have done so much hard riding already. Besides, the best mount I could give you would be a government mule."

"All right, Major, I don't want the best; second-best is good enough for me; so trot out your mule. I'll take a little nap, and in the meantime have your hostler slick up the mule so that he can slide through with me like a greased thunder-bolt should the reds jump on us."

Bill then went off, and, after "liquidating" in true Western style, lay down in the major's quarters, where he slept soundly until nearly 5 o'clock in the evening, when, having replenished his canteen, he mounted the patient mule and set out for Fort Larned, which was sixty-five miles east of Fort Dodge.

After proceeding as far as Coon Creek, which was nearly half-way, Bill dismounted for the purpose of getting a drink of water. While stooping down the mule got frightened at something and jerked loose; nor did the stupid animal stop, but followed the trail, keeping ahead of the weary and chagrined scout for *thirty-five miles*. Half a mile from the fort Bill got within rifle range of his exasperating steed and gave him a furlough to the eternal grazing-grounds.

After reaching Larned—carrying the bridle and saddle himself—Buffalo Bill spent several hours in refreshing sleep, and when he awakened he found General Hazen trying to induce some of the couriers to take his dispatches to General Sheridan in Fort Hays. Having been warmly and very justly praised for the long and perilous rides he had just completed, Bill again proffered his service to perform the trip. At first General Hazen refused to dispatch him on the mission, saying, "This is like riding a free horse to death; you have already ridden enough to kill an ordinary man, and I don't think it would be treating you properly to permit you to make this additional journey."

But when evening came and no other volunteer could be engaged, as a matter of last resort Bill was given a good horse and the dispatches entrusted to him for transmission. It was after nightfall when he started on this last trip, and by daylight the next morning he was in Fort Hays, where he delivered the dispatches. General Sheridan was profoundly astonished to see Bill before him again in so short a time, and after being informed of his wonderful riding during the three days the general pronounced it a feat that was never equaled; and even now General Sheridan maintains that no other man could accomplish the same distance under similar circumstances. To this day the rides here described stand on record as the most remarkable ever made. They aggregated *three hundred and fifty-five miles in fifty-eight riding hours,* or an average of more than *six miles an hour,* including an enforced *walk of thirty-five miles.*

22. Plenty Horses, Oglala Sioux Brave.

When it is considered that all this distance was made in the night-time, and through a country of hostile Indians, without a road to follow or a bridge to cross the streams, the feat appears too incredible for belief were it not for the most indisputable evidence, easily attainable, which makes disbelief impossible.

General Sheridan was so favorably impressed with the self-sacrificing spirit and marvelous endurance of Buffalo

Bill, and being already acquainted with his reputation as a brave man, that he called the scout to his headquarters directly after receiving Major Hazen's dispatches, and said, "Cody, I have ordered the Fifth Cavalry to proceed against the Dog Soldier Indians, who are now terrorizing the Republican River district; and as the campaign will be a very important one, I want a first-class man to guide the expedition. I have therefore decided to appoint you guide, *and also chief of scouts of the command.*"

CHAPTER VIII

Letters of Commendation from Prominent Military Men

The following letter was received with a photograph of the hero of "The March to the Sea," Gen. W. T. Sherman:

23. General W. T. Sherman.

New York, December 25, 1886

To Col. William Cody:

With the best compliments of one who in 1886 was guided by him up the Republican, then occupied by the Cheyennes and Arapahoes as their ancestral hunting-grounds; now transformed into farms and cattle ranches, in better harmony with civilization, and with his best wishes that he succeed in his honorable efforts to represent the scenes of that day to a generation then unborn.

W. T. Sherman, General.

24. Lieutenant-General P. H. Sheridan.

Headquarters Army of the United States,

Washington, D.C., January 7, 1887

Col. William F. Cody was a scout and served in my
command on the Western frontier for many years.
He was always ready for duty, and was a cool, brave
man, with unimpeachable character. I take pleasure in
commending him for the many services he has rendered
to the army, whose respect he enjoys for his manly
qualities.

P. H. Sheridan, Lieutenant-General.

25. Brevet-Major-General James B. Fry.

New York, December 28, 1886.

Col. William F. Cody

Dear Sir: Recalling the many facts that came to me while I was adjutant-general of the Division of the Missouri under General Sheridan, bearing upon your efficiency, fidelity, and daring as a guide and scout over the country west of the Missouri River and east of the Rocky Mountains, I take pleasure in observing your success in depicting in the East the early life of the West.

Very truly yours,
James B. Fry,
Assistant Adjutant-General,
Brevet-Major-General U.S.A.

26. Major-General Nelson A. Miles.

Los Angeles, Cal., January 7, 1878.

Col. William F. Cody

Dear Sir: Having visited your great exhibition in St. Louis and in New York City, I desire to congratulate you on the success of your enterprise. I was much interested in the various lifelike representations of Western scenery, as well as the fine exhibition of skilled marksmanship and magnificent horsemanship. You not only represent the many interesting features of frontier life, but also the difficulties and dangers that have been encountered by the adventurous and fearless pioneers of civilization. The wild Indian life as it was a few years ago will soon be a thing of the past, but you appear to have selected a good class of Indians to represent that race of people. I regard your exhibition as not only very interesting, but practically instructive. Your services on the frontier were exceedingly valuable. With best wishes for you success, believe me,

　Very truly yours,
　Nelson A. Miles,
　Brigadier-General U.S.A.

27. Brigadier-General George Crook.

Omaha, Neb., January 7, 1887.

Hon. William F. Cody

Dear Sir: I take great pleasure in testifying to the very efficient service rendered by you "as a scout" in the campaign against the Sioux Indians during the year 1876. Also that I have witnessed your Wild West exhibition. I consider it the most realistic performance of the kind I have ever seen.

Very sincerely, your obedient servant,
George Crook, Brigadier-General U.S.A.

28. Brevet-Major-General Eugene A. Carr.

"He Is King of Them All."

Headquarters Mounted Recruiting Service,

St. Louis, Mo., May 7, 1885.

Maj. John M. Burke

Dear Sir: I take pleasure in saying that in an experience of about thirty years on the plains and in the mountains I have seen a great many guides, scouts, trailers, and hunters, and Buffalo Bill (W. F. Cody) is "king of them all." He has been with me in seven Indian fights, and his services have been invaluable.

Very respectfully yours,

Eugene A. Carr, Brevet-Major-General U.S.A.

29. Major-General W. Merritt.

United States Military Academy,

West Point, N.Y., January 11, 1887

. . . I have known W. F. Cody ("Buffalo Bill") for many years. He is a Western man of the best type, combining those qualities of enterprise, daring, good sense, and physical endurance which made him the superior of any scout I ever knew. He was cool and capable when surrounded by dangers, and his reports were always free from exaggeration. He is a gentleman in a better sense of the word which implies character, and he may be depended on under all circumstances. I wish him success.

> *W. Merritt,*
> Brevet-Major-General U.S.A.
> Late Major-General Volunteers.
> War Department, Adjutant-General's Office
> Washington, August 10, 1886.

To whom it may concern:
Mr. William F. Cody was employed as chief of scouts under Generals Sheridan, Custer, Crook, Miles, Carr, and others in their campaigns against hostile Indians

on our frontier, and as such rendered very valuable and distinguished service.

R. C. Drum,[1] Adjutant General.

30. Major-General W. H. Emory.

Washington, D.C., February 8, 1887

Mr. Cody was chief guide and hunter to my command when I commanded the district of North Platte, and he performed all his duties with marked excellence.

W. H. Emory, Major-General U.S.A.

31. Colonel James W. Forsyth.

Headquarters Seventh Cavalry,

Fort Mead, D. T., February 14, 1887

My Dear Sir: Your army career on the frontier, and your present enterprise of depicting scenes in the far West, are so enthusiastically approved and commended by the American people and the most prominent men of the United States Army, that there is nothing left for me to say. I feel sure your new departure will be a success.

    With best wishes, I remain, yours truly,

    James W. Forsyth, Colonel Seventh Cavalry

32. Brigadier-General H. C. Bankhead.

Jersey City, 405 Bergen Avenue, February 7, 1887

Hon. Wm. F. Cody

My Dear Sir: I fully, and with pleasure, indorse you as the veritable Buffalo Bill, United States scout, serving with the troops operating against hostile Indians, with whom you secured renown by your services as a scout and successful hunter. Your sojourn on the frontier at a time when it was a wild and sparsely settled section of the continent fully enables you to portray that in which you have personally participated--the pioneer, Indian fighter, and frontiersman. Wishing you every success, I remain,

Very respectfully yours,

H. C. Bankhead, Brigadier-General U.S.A.

33. Colonel W. B. Royall.

Hotel Richmond,

Washington, D.C., January 9, 1887

W. F. Cody ("Buffalo Bill") was with me in the early days when I commanded a battalion of the Fifth Cavalry, operating against the hostile Sioux. He filled every position and met every emergency with so much bravery, competence, and intelligence as to command the general admiration and respect of the officers, and became chief of scouts of the department. All his successes have been conducted on the most honorable principles.

W. B. Royall, Colonel Fourth Cavalry U.S.A.

34. Brevet-Brigadier-General N. A. M. Dudley.

Headquarters First Cavalry,

Fort Custer, M.T.

I often recall your valuable services to the Government, as well as to myself, in years long gone by, especially during the Sioux difficulties, when you were attached to my command as chief of scouts. Your indomitable perseverance, incomprehensible instinct in discovering the trails of the Indians—particularly at night, no matter how dark or stormy—your physical powers of endurance in following the enemy until overtaken, and your unflinching courage, as exhibited on all occasions, won not only my own esteem and admiration, but that of the whole command.

With my best wishes for your success,
I remain, your old friend,
N. A. M. Dudley, Colonel First Cavalry,
Brevet-Brigadier-General U.S.A.

35. Brevet-Major-General Jno. H. King.

Tallahasse, Fla., January 12, 1887

Hon. William F. Cody: I take great pleasure in recommending you to the public as a man who has a high reputation in the army as a scout. No one has ever shown more bravery on the Western plains than yourself. I wish you success in your proposed visit to Great Britain.

Your obedient servant,
Jno. H. King, Brevet-Major-General U.S.A.
State of Nebraska

To all whom these presents shall come, greeting:

Know ye, that I, John M. Thayer,[2] governor of the State of Nebraska, reposing special trust and confidence in the integrity, patriotism, and ability of the Hon. William F. Cody, on behalf and in the name of the State do hereby appoint and commission him as aide-de-camp of my staff, with the rank of colonel, and do authorize and empower him to discharge the duties of said office according to law.

In testimony I have hereunto subscribed my name and caused to be affixed the great seal of the State.

["Grand Seal of the State of Nebraska,
March 1, 1887."]
Done at Lincoln this 8th day of March, ⬜ ⬜ 1887.
John M. Thayer.
By the Governor: G. L. Laws, Secretary of State[3]

CHAPTER IX

Buffalo Bill's Boyhood

Having in the preceding pages given the scenes, conditions, surroundings, and types of characters that made up the theater of action in which Buffalo Bill bore so prominent a part, with the letters from gallant commanders stamping his career with the brand of truth, it is fitting to start my hero from the threshold of boyhood, and follow him through his most adventurous and phenomenal life up to the present day, where he stands unchallenged as the Chevalier Bayard[1] of American bordermen.

Buffalo Bill made his debut upon the stage of life in a little log cabin situated in the backwoods of Scott County, Iowa. His father and mother were good honest people, poor in this world's goods, but rich in hope, faith in each other and the result of their efforts, and confidence in the future.

While struggling for success as a farmer Isaac Cody became seriously affected by the California gold fever that raged at that times; a party was organized, an outfit provided, and a start was made. A failure resulted, and all comprising the party returned to their respective homes at Le Claire.

Bill was sent to school, where he familiarized himself with the alphabet; but further progress was arrested by a suddenly developed love for boating on the Mississippi, which occupied so much of his time that he found no convenient opportunity for attendance at school, his parents, however, not having the slightest idea of his self-imposed employment as a boatman.

Shortly after his removal to Le Claire Mr. Cody was chosen justice of the peace, then was elected to the Legislature, positions which he held with honor but without profit.

A natural pioneer, he hunted for new field of adventure and following his inclination he disposed of a small ranch he owned, packed his possessions in one carriage and three wagons, and started for the plains of Kansas. Mr. Cody had a brother living at Weston[2], near the Kansas line, a well-to-do merchant of that place, with whom he stopped until he could decide upon a more desirable location for his family. It was on this trip that Buffalo Bill had his first sight of a negro, of whom he stood in great awe. It was also while on this expedition he ate his first wheat bread, something he had never heard of before, corndodgers being the chief staff of life at that time.

Mr. Cody remained but a short while at Weston, when he went to the Kickapoo Agency in Leavenworth, Kan.[3] He established a trading-post at Salt Creek Valley,[4] while he settled his family upon a ranch near by. At that time Kickapoo was occupied by numerous tribes of Indians, who were settled upon the reservations, and through the territory ran the great highway of California and Salt Lake City. In addition to the thousands of gold-seekers who were passing through by way of Fort Leavenworth, there were many Mormons going westward, and this extensive travel made trade profitable. With these caravans were those fractious elements of adventurous pioneering, the typical Westerner, with white sombrero, buckskin clothes, long hair, moccasined feet, and a belt full of murderous bowies and long pistols. Instead of impressing him, however, with trepidation, they inspired in him an ambition to become likewise. Their skillful feats of horsemanship, which he witnessed, bred in him a desire to become an expert rider, and when, at seven years of age, his father gave him a pony the measure of his happiness was filled to overflowing. Thenceforth his occupation was horse-back-riding, and he made himself useful to his father in many ways.

During his early life at this post Buffalo Bill spent much of his time with the Indians, who taught him how to shoot with bow and arrow, and he joined in their other sports, soon learning the Kickapoo language more readily than he had his alphabet. Being friendly with the Indians Mr. Cody at times gave them barbecues, at which they indulged in their fantastic war-dances, the sight of which excited admiration in the youthful William. It was at this time that Buffalo Bill first met his friend Alexander Majors[5] of the freighting firm of Russell & Majors, and he has since then been his lifelong friend.

Writers of American history are familiar with the disorders which followed upon the heels of the Enabling Act.[6] The western boundary of Missouri was ablaze with the camp-fires of intending settlers. Thousands of families were sheltered under the canvas of the ox-wagons, awaiting the announcement of the opening of the Territory; and when the news was heralded they poured over the boundary-line and deluged the new domain. Those who came from Missouri were intent upon extending slavery into the Territory, while those who came from Illinois, Iowa, and Indiana were opposed to bringing slaves into the new Territory. It was over this question that the border warfare began; men were shot down in their homes, by the fireside, in the furrows behind the plow; widows and orphans multiplied; the arm of industry was paralyzed. The incendiary torch lit up the prairie, burning homes and destroying their storehouses and granaries. Anguish sat on every threshold, pity had no abiding-place, and for several years the besom of destruction rendered every heart on the borderland sad and despondent. In this war of vengeance the Cody family did not escape. One night a body of armed men surrounded the Cody home. Knowing what they had come for, Mr. Cody disguised himself and walked out of the house and managed to escape. Discovering this, the band carried off all the valuables in the house and about the premises, drove off the horses, and Bill's pony among them; but the pony escaped and came back to his young master. Learning that another attempt was to be made to capture Mr. Cody, having learned of his hiding-place, Mrs. Cody started Bill off on his pony to give warning to his father of his danger. The boy had ridden only a few miles when he came upon a party of men camped at the crossing of Stranger Creek. Hearing one of them call out, "That is Cody's son, catch him," the brave lad instantly started to dash through them, knowing that it was a matter of life and death to his father. He was instantly pursued, but eluded capture, joined his father, and warned him of his danger. From that time on

Mr. Cody's visits to his home were made secretly, and soon after it was that he lost his life, dying from the effects of a wound he received.

After the death of his father, though a mere boy, Buffalo Bill applied for employment to Mr. Alexander Majors of the firm of Majors & Russell, overland freighters. Mr. Majors said to him, "Billy, my boy, I will give you $25 a month as messenger, and this sum is what I pay a man for the same work."

Bill gladly accepted the offer, and at ten years of age began work. For two months, mounted on a little gray mule, Bill's duties were to herd cattle. At the end of that time he was paid his $50 in one-half dollar pieces, and, putting the bright silver coins into a sack, he started for home, feeling himself a millionaire. Every dollar of that money he gave to his mother. Thus began his services for the firm of Majors & Russell, afterward Russell, Majors & Waddell, in whose employ he spent seven years in different capacities, such as messenger, wagon master, pony-express rider, and stage-driver.

36. Little Emma, Daughter of Long Wolf.

CHAPTER X

Bill Kills His First Indian

Like all boys Bill had a sweetheart with whom he was "dead in love," in a juvenile way, of course. He had a rival of whom he was terribly jealous. One day, attacked by his rival, who was an older and larger boy, Buffalo Bill defended himself with his pocket-knife, wounding the youth slightly. The cry at once arose, "Bill Cody has killed Steve Gobel!" and, terribly frightened at what he had done, Bill immediately took refuge in flight, the teacher in hot pursuit. Fortunately for Bill one of Russell & Majors's freight trains was passing beyond the hills on its way to the West. Reaching it he recognized the wagon-master with whom he had before served. He was concealed in one of the wagons until night, when he went to his home, bade his mother and sisters good-by, and continued on with the train to the far West. The trip proved one of delightful experience to the boy, and on his return he was paid off with the rest of the employees, when he went to herding cattle for the same firm.

After a few months spent at this work, he started with a herd of beef-cattle for Gen. Albert Sidney Johnston's army, which was then marching across the plains to fight the Mormons. Reaching South Platte River they were camped for dinner, and had no idea of danger near, when, with shouts and yells, a band of Indians dashed in upon them. A hot fight followed, and three of the party were killed. Buffalo Bill, with the rest of the band, was driven to seek safety under the river-bank, keeping the Indians at a safe distance with their guns. It was on this occasion that Buffalo Bill killed his first Indian, being at that time but eleven years old. As the cattle had been stampeded by the Indians, and the horses also, the little party was forced to return to Fort Kearny.[1] After many hardships and passing through many dangers, the fort was reached, though several of the party were wounded and had to be carried by their comrades. A company of cavalry and force of infantry, with one gun, were sent out to endeavor to capture the cattle, Buffalo Bill and his comrades accompanying the expedition. Upon reaching the place where the fight occurred, the bodies of their comrades were found literally cut to pieces, and but few of the stampeded cattle were captured.

Upon his return to Fort Leavenworth the young Indian fighter found that he was published far and wide as the youngest Indian killer on record; in fact a juvenile celebrity. What bearing this taste of laudation had on his future career may easily be inferred.

The following summer Buffalo Bill engaged $40 per month, in gold, to go with the wagon-trains carrying supplies to Gen. Albert S. Johnston's army. The trail of the train was through Kansas into Nebraska, near the Big Sandy,[2] then running sixty miles along the Little Blue,[3] striking the Platte River near old Fort Kearny;[4] then up the South Platte, then across to the North Platte, near the mouth of the Blue Water,[5] where General Harney fought his great battle in 1855[6] with the Sioux and Cheyenne Indians. From this point the train continued on to the Great Salt Lake Valley. At that time Russell, Majors & Waddell had upon the overland trails nearly seven thousand wagons; 75,000 oxen, 2,000 mules, and 8,000 men were employed, while the capital invested amounted to $2,000,000. The expedition was without adventure of importance until the South Platte River was reached. The country was alive with buffalo roaming in all directions, and among them were found some of the herd of cattle stampeded by the Indians long before. Discovering the herd of buffaloes ahead, they at the same time sighted a party of returning Californians, and, being between two fires, the buffalo herd stampeded at once, and broke down the hills, some thousands of them rushing through the wagon-train. Wagons were turned over, poles were broken, buffaloes were mixed up among the terrified oxen and shouting men, who were unable to manage their teams. Many of the oxen broke their yokes and stampeded, and the frantic buffaloes played havoc with the train. This caused several days' delay to repair damages and gather up the scattered teams. When the train reached within eighteen miles of the Green River,[7] in the Rocky Mountains, a party of twenty horsemen came up. They were covered at once with guns, and the wagon-train men found that they were in the hands of the Mormons, who were at that time engaged in hostilities against the Army of the United States.[8] It was impossible to resist, and Simpson was forced to submit, first, however, soundly abusing the apostles.

The Mormons took from the wagons all the provisions they could carry, then set fire to the train and drove off the oxen. The trainmen, however, were allowed to retain their arms, one wagon, six yoke of oxen, and provisions enough to last the party until Fort Bridger could be reached.

It was late in November when the party reached the fort, and they decided to spend the winter there, in company with about four hundred other employees of Russell, Majors & Waddell, rather than attempt to return, which would have exposed them to many dangers and the severity of the coming winter. During this period of rest the commissary became so depleted that the men were placed on one-quarter rations; and at last, as a final resort, the poor, dreadfully emaciated mules and oxen were killed for food for the famishing men.

Fort Bridger being located in a prairie, fuel had to be carried nearly two miles, and after the mules and oxen were butchered the men were compelled to carry the wood on their backs or haul it on sleds.

But for the timely arrival of a train-load of provisions for Johnston's army many of the party would certainly have died of hunger.

Arrangements having been made for a return to Fort Leavenworth, all the employees at Fort Bridger[9] concluded to accompany the returning cavalcade. Simpson was chosen brigade wagon-master of the new outfit, consisting of two trains and 400 men.

When the train approached Ash Hollow[10] Simpson decided to leave the main road and follow the North Platte to its junction with the South Platte. The two trains had become separated, some fifteen or twenty miles between them, the latter train in charge of Assistant Wagon-master George Woods, under whom Billy was acting as "extra."

Simpson, accompanied by Woods, desiring to reach

the head train, ordered Billy to "cinch" (saddle) up and follow him. When the three reached Cedar Bluffs[11] they suddenly discovered a score of Indians emerging from the head of a ravine less than half a mile distant and coming toward them with great speed.

"Dismount and shoot your mules," was the quick order issued by Simpson, who was at once alive to the situation. As the stricken animals dropped in their tracks the two men and little boy crouched down behind their bodies, which lay together in a triangle, and using their dead bodies as breast-works opened fire on the Indians with Mississippi jaegers[12] and revolvers, killing three and wounding two ponies. The redskins, surprised at the hot-bed they had struck, circled around and sped away again, halting several hundred yards distant, evidently for consultation. This gave the trio time to load their weapons and prepare for a second charge, which they felt sure would be made.

The Indians were armed with bows and arrows, which of course required close range to be effective, and this gave the little party an advantage which partly compensated for the superior number of their enemy.

Little Billy showed so much pluck in the dangerous position he occupied that Simpson could not help praising him, and by way of further encouragement he said, "My brave little man, do you see that Indian on the right, riding out from the party to reconnoiter?"

"Yes, I'm watching him," was the reply.

"Well, suppose you give him a shot, just by way of experiment."

Billy at once extended himself, and resting his gun on the body of the mule before him took steady aim and fired.

"Bully boy! A splendid shot!" shouted Simpson, as he saw the Indian topple from his horse, struck in the side. The distance was fully three hundred yards.

After a long parley the Indians scattered, and came charging back again, whooping in a delirium of excitement. When they had approached within less than one hundred yards the besieged party turned loose on them, shooting two more out of the saddle; but the Indians rushed on, discharging a shower of arrows, one of which pierced George Woods's right shoulder, producing a most painful wound. For a second time the red warriors were repulsed, and they drew off again, evidently for the purpose of resorting to other tactics. Getting beyond the range of the jaegers the Indians formed in a large circle, tethered their ponies, and disposed themselves for a siege, with the evident intention of starving out the brave trio. About three hours afterward, however, the cracking of bull-whacker's whips was heard, and soon the advancing train was seen coming over the hill. The Indians, appreciating what this meant, and gaining their ponies, rode down on the little party again, discharging another flight of arrows and receiving a volley of bullets in return. No damage was inflicted on either side in the last charge, and the three were saved.

After bandaging Woods's wound the train started again and met with no further detention or accident, reaching Leavenworth in July, 1858. Wild Bill had been a special companion of Billy's during the entire trip, and so warm had become the attachment between them that the latter gave him a pressing invitation to go with him to his home for a short visit; an invitation that was accepted by Wild Bill.

CHAPTER XI

The Boy Miner

Billy had been at home scarcely one month before he engaged himself as assistant wagon-master to another train
which was made up at Fort Laramie to carry supplies to
a new post just established at Cheyenne Pass.[1] He got
through this adventure without losing a team or a man.

Returning to Laramie he engaged with a Mr. Ward,
the post trader, to trap for beaver, mink, and otter on the
Chug Water,[2] and poison wolves for their peltries. This
enterprise was not profitable, and two months after Billy
returned to Laramie, and in a few days, in company with
two others, he started back to Leavenworth.

When they reached the Little Blue the three were
jumped by a party of Indians. The darkness saved them,
after a chase of several hours. After "losing" the Indians
the trio discovered a cave in which they resolved to spend
the night. Lighting a match they were horrified to find the
place tenanted by the bones and desiccated flesh of murdered emigrants. Without further investigation the three,
badly frightened, regardless of cold and snow, pushed rapidly onward. An all-night journey brought them to Oak
Grove,[3] and there taking in a fresh supply of necessaries
they resumed their homeward march, reaching Leavenworth in February, 1859.

Billy was now fourteen years old, and unusually large for one of that age. His education having been neglected he, yielding to his mother's entreaties, resolved to attend a school just opened in the neighborhood of Grasshopper Falls,[4] and for a period of ten weeks applied himself with diligence and made most gratifying progress. This was the longest term of schooling he ever attended, and it is doubtful if all the schooling he ever received would aggregate six months; though he is now comparatively well educated, his knowledge has been acquired almost wholly by extensive travel and association with polished people.

On the return of spring the old impulse seized on Billy again to seek the far West, where adventure and danger incite the restless spirit of brave men. The recent discovery of gold at Pike's Peak[5] was a further motive for this move.

Billy, despite his years, was now a man in size, and in common with thousands of others he seized a pick and set out for the wonderful diggings. After digging around Aurora[6] for a few days the *ignis fatuus*[7] led him farther up the mountains to Black Hawk,[8] where he settled, and worked most assiduously for a period of two months without finding as much as a handful of pay dirt. In the meantime provisions were so high that it took a Jacob's ladder[9] to reach the smell of cold beans.

Billy became not only tired but disgusted with the result of his mining labors and resolved to get out of the country. He had no difficulty in finding others in camp of the same turn of mind as himself, and such as he desired as companions he induced to accompany him back. Of the numerous caravans and individuals who adopted as their motto "Pike's Peak or bust," Billy and his party fell back on the latter end of the bold legend. They were so badly "busted" (?), in fact, that the only conveyance left them was their legs. Setting out on these the party proceeded to the Platte River, where the idea possessed Billy that they might make the remainder of their journey to Leavenworth on an improvised raft.

By various means, but chiefly by killing game along the way, the party subsisted comfortably while they floated down the stream on a rickety collection of logs. Matters were satisfactory enough until they reached Jule's ranch, or Julesburg,[10] where having met a swifter current the raft struck a snag and went to pieces with a suddenness no less astonishing than the bath which instantly followed. Fortunately, though the North Platte is a broad stream it is generally shallow, and the party had to swim but a short distance before they found a footing, and then waded ashore.

Everything having been lost with the raft, including their arms and such provisions as they had, the party stopped at Julesburg to wait for something to turn up.

It so happened that the great Pony Express had just been established between Omaha and Pike's Peak, and other far Western points, including San Francisco. This route ran by Julesburg, where the company had an agent in the person of George Chrisman, who was well acquainted with Billy, the two having freighted together for Russell, Majors & Waddell.

Finding Billy out of employment, and express riders being scarce, Chrisman offered him a position as rider, which was gladly accepted.

The requirements for this occupation were such that

very few were qualified for the performance of the duties. The distance and time required to be made were fifteen miles per hour. Only courageous men could be employed on account of the dangers to be encountered, and such laborious riding could be endured by very few. Nevertheless Billy was an expert horseman, and having the constitution and endurance of a bronco he braved the perils and duties of the position and was assigned to a route of forty-five miles.

CHAPTER XII

Story of the Pony Express

The glamour and pageantry of the crusaders in the eleventh and twelfth centuries were revived in the fifteenth and sixteenth by Columbus, Cortez, and Pizarro,[1] and repeated in the nineteenth by Taylor,[2] Scott,[3] Doniphan,[4] and Fremont. As a resultant were the wonderful gold discoveries of 1849, in California, and a State born full-fledged and armed in a day, as Minerva from the brain of Jove.[5] Among the wonderful and prolific accomplishments of Western thought and genius was the conceptions and successful fruition of the Pony Express, a scheme that could only have been conceived and launched amid the mountain grandeur of the Western plains. It could have birth in no other place, and can be duplicated nowhere else. The world presents no theater for its reenactment. It was formulated by Senator Gwin of California,[6] and fashioned and matured to success by Russell, Majors & Waddell of the overland mail coach system of 1859, as established by Congress.

The telegraph extended from the Atlantic seaboard to St. Joseph and from San Francisco to Sacramento. Two thousand miles of desert intervened. The ocean communications, via Central America, occupied twenty-two days, with propitious sea voyages.

Could this be reduced? The stages took from twenty-one to twenty-five days, according to the weather. Duke Gwin, as he was afterward called, suggested to W. H. Russell of the stage line that if the time could be shortened for communication on a central line, and kept open all the year, a great increase of travel and emigration, and the location of a railroad by the Government on a central route, would be the result. The conference resulted in the habiliment of the Pony Express, which eventuated in carrying a telegraph mail upon ponies from St. Joseph to Sacramento, 1,982 miles, regularly, from April, 1860, to September, 1861, in ten days, schedule time, and the special express in December, 1860, with a message of President Buchanan[7] to Congress, on secession, in seven days and seventeen hours, a feat never before and never again accomplished. This was done through a desert country occupied by prowling savages and swept by violent storms, furious blizzards, and blinding snows. Crossing immense mountain ranges and trackless wastes of sand and sage-brush, grappling with mountain torrents and with nature's wildest orgies, the hardy riders, whose watchword was "excelsior," always made (Deo volente)[8] the schedule time to the objective point. At St. Joseph and Sacramento, until the completion of the telegraph across the continent, the expectant crowd was never held in wait over an hour before the messenger waved his red flag of safety, and in the next instant slid from his panting steed and hastened to the office of the company with his bag of dispatches, worth its weight in gold.

During the Mexican War Congress added two new regiments of mounted volunteers to the regular army under orders to lay out a military road on the route taken

37. Riding Pony Express.

by Fremont in 1843 to Oregon. They were to locate posts, and changed old Fort Kearny, then at the mouth of Tabor Creek, where Nebraska City is now located, to the crossing of the Platte River, where Kearney is now situated, and called it New Fort Kearny, one at Laramie on the Platte River, fifty miles north of Laramie City, now a station situated on the Union Pacific Railroad, and one at old Fort Hall, a Hudson Bay trading-post near the present site of Pocatello.[9] This was called the military route, and was the road traveled by most of the emigrants to California in 1849. Passing by Soda Springs[10] and south of Snake River to the headwaters of the Humboldt, or St. Mary's River,[11] through Nevada, it passed through the South Pass and struck Bear River, now in Idaho and Utah. The emigration

38. Shooting over Horse's Back.

of 1850 diverged southward from Laramie and past Green River at its junction with Hams Fork,[12] through Echo Cañon and Salt Lake Valley westwardly via Reese River, striking the Humboldt lower down, and crossing the Sierra Nevada at the Truckee Pass and by Donner Lake. This was a much more direct trail to California and was used mostly thereafter by emigrants in 1850–51. In 1854 two stage routes were established, one by Texas and El Paso, on the Gila River, to Southern California, and one via Salt Lake, the latter much the shorter, but mountainous. McGraw & Co. had the route on the military road from Independence by Fort Leavenworth under a government subsidy, and in 1859 Russell, Majors & Waddell became the owners of this mail line and operated it successfully for years.

In 1859 Senator Gwin, then United States Senator from California, and a devoted Union man, appealed to the stage company to expedite travel and communications on the military road, so as to have a central line available to the North and South alike, and to demonstrate the possibilities of operating it in midwinter. Strange to say, this grand

Union man and able statesman went into the Rebellion and lost his wonderful prestige and influence in California, as well as a fortune, in his fealty to his native State of Mississippi, and in 1866 was made the Duke of Sonora by Maximilian,[13] in the furtherance of some visionary scheme of Western empire, but soon died. His propositions were duly considered and responded to by that famous firm, representatives of thrift, enterprise, energy, and courage, who well deserve the commendation of history and the gratitude of their countrymen.

Russell was a Green Mountain[14] boy, who before his majority had gone West to grow up with the country; and after teaching a three-months' school on the frontier of Missouri had hired to old John Aull of Lexington, Mo., at $30 per month, to keep books, and was impressed in lessons of economy by the anecdotes of Aull that a London company engaged in the India trade had saved £80 per annum in ink by omitting to dot the "i's" and cross the "t's," when he was emptying his pen by splashing the office wall with ink. Alexander Majors is still living, venerable with years and honors, a mountain son of Kentucky frontier ancestry, the colleague and friend of Daniel Boone; and William Waddell, an ancestral Virginian of the blue-grass region of Kentucky, bold enough for any enterprise, and able to fill any missing niche in Western wants.

The Pony Express was born from this conference, and the first move was to compass the necessary auxiliaries to assure success. Sixty young, agile, athletic riders were engaged and 420 strong and wiry ponies procured, and on the 9th of April, 1860, the venture was simultaneously commenced from St. Joseph and Sacramento City. The

39. Runaway Horse.

result was a success in cutting down the time more than one half, and it rarely missed making the schedule time in ten days, and in December, 1860, making it in seven days and seventeen hours. The stations were from twelve to fifteen miles apart, and one pony was ridden from one station to another, and one rider made three stations, and a few dare-devil fellows made double duty and rode eighty or eighty-five miles. One of them was Charles Cliff, now a citizen of St. Joseph, who rode from St. Joseph to Seneca and back on alternate days. He was attacked by Indians at Scotts Bluff, and received three balls in his body and twenty-seven in his clothes. Cliff made Seneca and back in eight hours each way.

Another of these daring riders of this flying express was Pony Bob.

But the one of these pony riders who has won greatest fame was William F. Cody ("Buffalo Bill"), who passed through many a gauntlet of death while in his flight from station to station bearing express matter that was of the greatest value.

The express was closed on the completion of a telegraph line by Ed Creighton[15] of Omaha from that point to Sacramento City. The mail-bags were two pouches of leather, impervious to rain and weather, sealed, and strapped to the rider's saddle before and behind, carrying two ounces letters or dispatches at $5 each.

The keepers of the stations had the ponies already saddled, and the riders merely jumped from the back of one to another; and where the riders were changed the pouches were unbuckled and handed to the already mounted postman, who started at a lope as soon as his hand clutched them. As these express stations were the same as the stage stations, the employees of the stage company were required to take care of the ponies and have them in readiness at the proper moment. The bridles and saddles were light weight, as were the riders, and the pouches were not to contain over twenty pounds of weight. There were two pouches of two pockets each, and secured by oil-silk, then sealed, and the pockets locked and never opened between St. Joseph and Sacramento.

This channel of communication was largely used by the Government and by traders and merchants, and was a paying venture, first semi-weekly and then daily, and but for the building of the telegraph would have become a wonderful success.

Every two or three hundred miles there were located at the stations division agents to provide for emergencies in case the Indian raids or stampedes of ponies, and at the crossing of the Platte at Fort Kearny there was then employed the notorious Jack Slade, a Vermont Yankee, lost to the teachings of his early and pious environments, turned into a frontier fiend. He shot a Frenchman named Jules Bevi, whose patronymic is preserved in the present station of Julesburg on the Union Pacific Railroad. Slade nailed one of his ears to the station door and wore the other several weeks as a watch-charm. He drifted to Montana, and in 1865 was hanged by the vigilantes on suspicion of heading the road agents who killed Parker of Atchison and robbed a train of $65,000. His tragic end, as related by Doctor McCurdy, formerly of St. Joseph, contains an element of the pathetic. He lived on a ranch near Virginia City, Mont., and every few days came into town and filled up on "benzine," and took the place by shooting along the streets and riding into saloons and proclaiming himself to be the veritable "bad man from Bitter Creek." The belief that he was connected with matters worse than bad whisky had overstrained the long-suffering citizens. The suggestive and mysterious triangular pieces of paper dropped upon the streets, surmounted with the skull and arrows, called the vigilantes to a meeting at which the death of Slade and two companions was determined. On the fated morning following the meeting he came to town duly sober and went to a drug-store for a prescription, and while awaiting its preparation he was suddenly covered with twelve shotguns and ordered to throw up his hands. He complied smilingly, but proposed to reason with them as to the absurdity of taking him for a bad man. The only concession was permission to send a note to his wife at the ranch, and an hour was allotted him to make peace with the Unknown; ropes were placed around the necks of the three, and at the end of the time they were given short shrift, and were soon hanging between heaven and

40. Saddle.

earth. While the bodies were swaying the wife appeared on the scene, mounted, with a pistol in each hand, determined to make a rescue; but seeing that it was too late she quailed before the determined visages of vigilantes, and soon left the vicinity, carrying away, as it was believed, a large amount of the proceeds of Slade's robberies.

Most of the famous actors in that memorable enterprise known as the Pony Express have passed beyond the confines of time and gone to join the great majority. In the summer of 1861 the Pony Express passed, with the overland stage line, into the ownership of Ben Holladay,[16] one of those wonderful characters developed from adventure and danger, and nurtured amid the startling incidents of frontier life. Born near the old Blue Licks battlefield,[17] he was at seventeen Colonel Doniphan's courier to demand from Joe Smith and Brigham Young[18] the surrender of Farwest.[19] At twenty-eight he entered Salt Lake Valley with fifty wagon-loads of merchandise and was indorsed by Brigham as being worthy of the confidence of the faithful. This secured him a fortune. At thirty-eight, at the head of the overland mail route, and at forty-five, the owner of sixteen steamers on the Pacific, carrying trade and passengers to Panama, Oregon, China, and Japan. The stage route was sold to Butterfield,[20] and ran until the completion of the Union Pacific Railroad.

One the streets of Denver daily can be seen the grand figure of Alexander Majors, carrying his four-score years with a vigor that would shame half of the youth of the city. Six feet, lithe and straight as the red man he so often dominated, he is noted as the last of the Mohicans,[21] and only waits, without fear and without reproach, for the final summons to that better land where the expresses are all faithfully gathered and the faithful rewarded by commendations for duty well performed.

And more wonderful than the express itself is the history of the six lustrums since it ceased to exist. Two thousand miles of desert waste have been largely developed in a rich and valuable agricultural and pastoral region. The iron horse has supplanted the fiery bronco, and thought flashes with lightning rapidity from ocean to ocean. Civilization has crowned that terra incognita with seven States and built large and beautiful cities. Peace has spread her halo of beauty over the savage haunts and churches have supplanted the horrible orgies of Indian massacre. The mountains have yielded their treasures to the steady hand of industry—richer by far than the fabled Ophir[22]—and the Pactolian streams[23] have gladdened the hearts of toiling thousands. All honor to the pioneers who blazed the way for this civilization.

With this page of frontier history—the days of the Pony Express—will forever be associated the name of Billy Cody.

CHAPTER XIII

A Ride for Life

"There's Injun signs about, Billy, so keep your eyes open." So said the station boss of the Pony Express trail, addressing Buffalo Bill, who had dashed up to the cabin, his horse panting like a hound, and the rider ready for the fifteen-mile flight to the next relay. "I'll be on the watch, Boss, you bet," said Billy Cody, the pony rider, and with a yell to his fresh pony he was off like an arrow from a bow.

Down the trail ran the fleet pony like the wind, leaving the station quickly out of sight, and dashing at once into the solitude and dangers of the vast wilderness.

Mountains were upon either side, towering cliffs here and there overhung the trail, and the wind sighed through the forest of pines like the mourning of departed spirits.

Gazing ahead, the piercing eyes of the young pony rider saw every tree, bush, and rock, for he knew but too well that a deadly foe, lurking in ambush, might send an arrow or a bullet to his heart at any moment.

Gradually, far ahead down the valley, his quick glance fell upon a dark object above the boulder directly in his trail.

He saw the object move and disappear from sight down behind the rock.

Without appearing to notice it or checking his speed in the slightest he held steadily upon his way.

41. Bill Cody.

But he took in the situation at a glance, and saw that upon each side of the boulder the valley inclined.

Upon one side was a fringe of heavy timber, upon the other a precipice, at the base of which were massive rocks.

"There is an Indian behind that rock, for I saw his head," muttered the young rider, as his horse flew on.

Did he intend to take his chances and dash along the trail directly by his ambushed foe?

It would seem so, for he still stuck to the trail.

A moment more and he would be within range of a bullet, when, suddenly dashing his spurs into the flanks of his pony, Billy Cody wheeled to the right, and in an oblique course headed for the cliff.

This proved to the foe in ambush that his presence there was suspected, if not known, and at once there came the crack of a rifle, the puff of smoke rising above the rock where he was concealed.

At the same time a yell went up from a score of throats, and out of the timber on the other side of the valley darted a number of mounted Indians, and these rode to head off the rider.

Did he turn back and seek safety in a retreat to the station?

No; he was made of sterner stuff, and would run the gauntlet.

Out from behind the boulder, where they had been lying in ambush, sprang two painted braves, in all the glory of their war-paint.

Their horses were in the timber with their comrades, but they were armed with rifles, and having failed to get a close shot at the pony rider they sought to bring him down at long range.

The bullets pattered under the hoofs of the flying pony, but he was unhurt, and his rider pressed him to his full speed.

With set teeth, flashing eyes, and determined to do or die, Will Cody rode on in the race for life, the Indians on foot running swiftly toward him and the mounted braves sweeping down the valley at full speed.

The shots of the two dismounted Indians failing to bring down the flying pony, or their human game, the mounted redskins saw that their only chance was to overtake their prey by their speed.

One of the number, whose war-bonnet showed that he was a chief, rode a horse that was much faster than the others, and he drew quickly ahead.

Below, the valley narrowed to a pass not a hundred yards in width, and if the pony rider could get to this well ahead of his pursuers he would be able to hold his own along the trail in the 10-mile run to the next relay station.

But though he saw that there was no more to fear from the two dismounted redskins, and that he would come out well in advance of the band on horseback, there was one who was most dangerous.

That one was the chief, whose fleet horse was bringing him on at a terrible pace, and threatening to reach there almost at the same time with the pony rider.

Nearer and nearer the two drew toward the path, the horse of Will Cody slightly ahead, and the young rider knew that a death struggle was at hand.

He did not check his horse, but kept his eyes alternately upon the pass and the chief.

The other Indians he did not then take into consideration.

At length that happened which he had been looking for.

When the chief saw that he would come out of the race some thirty yards behind his foe, he seized his bow and quick as a flash had fitted an arrow for its deadly flight.

But in that instant Will Cody had also acted, and a revolver had sprung from his belt and a report followed the touching of the trigger.

A wild yell burst from the lips of the chief and he clutched madly at the air, reeled, and fell from his saddle, rolling over like a ball as he struck the ground.

The death cry of the chief was echoed by the braves coming on down the valley, and a shower of arrows was sent after the fugitive pony rider.

An arrow slightly wounded his horse, but the others did no damage, and in another second Will Cody had dashed into the pass well ahead of his foes.

It was a hot chase from then on until the pony rider came within sight of the next station, when the Indians drew off, and William Cody dashed in on time, and in another minute was away on his next run.

CHAPTER XIV

Held Up by Road Agents

While riding Pony Express another adventure happened to Buffalo Bill which illustrates his nerve under most trying circumstances and great cleverness in getting out of scrapes.

It was when Buffalo Bill was in the Pony Express service between Red Buttes[1] and Three Crossings,[2] which included the perilous crossing of the Platte River, half a mile in width.

He rode into the station at the end of his run to find that the man who was to go on from there had been killed by road agents the night before.

There was nothing else for him to do but take the ride himself, so Bill started promptly to do so. He darted away upon his double duty, and yet as he rode away he considered that as his fellow-rider had been killed by road agents, he stood a very fair chance of sharing the same fate.

It had become known in some mysterious manner, past finding out, that there was to be a large sum of money sent through by Pony Express, and this was what the road agents were after.

Missing it after killing the other rider, Will Cody very naturally supposed that they would make another effort to secure the treasure.

So when he reached the next relay station he walked about a while longer than was his wont.

This was to perfect a little plan he had decided upon, which was to take a second pair of saddle-pouches and put something in them and leave them in sight, while those that held the valuable express packages he folded up in his saddle-blanket in such a way that they would not be seen unless a search was made for them.

The truth was Buffalo Bill knew he carried the valuable package and it was his duty to protect it with his life.

So with this clever scheme to outwit the road agents, if held up, he started once more upon his flying ride.

He carried his revolver ready for instant use and flew along the trail with every nerve strung to meet any danger he might have to confront.

He had an idea where he would be halted, if halted at all, and it was a lonesome spot in a valley, the very place for a deed of crime to be committed.

As he drew near the spot Buffalo Bill was on the alert, and yet when two men suddenly stepped out from among the shrubs and confronted him it gave him a start in spite of his nerve.

They had him covered with their rifles, and they brought him to a halt with the words, "Hold! Hands up, Pony Express Bill, for we knows yer, and what yer carries."

"I carry the express; and it's hanging for two if you interfere with me," was the plucky response.

"Ah, we don't want you, Billy, unless you force us to call in your checks; but it's what you carry we want."

"It won't do you any good to get the pouch for there isn't anything valuable in it."

42. Bull Dallied to Horse's Saddle.

"We are to be the judges of that, so throw us the valuables or catch a bullet. Which will it be, Billy?"

The two men stood directly in front of the pony rider, each one covering him with a rifle, and to resist was certain death.

So Buffalo Bill began to unfasten the pouches slowly, while he said, "Mark my words, men, you'll hang for this."

"We'll take chances on that, Bill."

The pouches being unfastened now, Buffalo Bill raised them in one hand, while he said in an angry tone, "If you will have them, take them."

With this he hurled the pouches at the head of one of the men, who quickly dodged and turned to pick them up, just as Buffalo Bill fired upon the other man with his revolver in his left hand.

The bullet shattered the man's arm while, driving the spurs into the flanks of his mare, Buffalo Bill rode directly over the man who was stooping to pick up the pouches, his back to the pony rider.

The horse struck him a hard blow that knocked him down, while he half fell on top of him, but was recovered by a touch of the spurs and bounded on, while the daring pony rider gave a wild triumphant yell as he sped on like the wind.

The fallen man, though hurt, scrambled to his feet as quickly as he could, picked up his rifle, and fired after the retreating youth, but without effect; and Will Cody rode on, arriving at the station on time and reporting what had happened.

He had however no time to rest, for he was compelled to start back with his express pouches. He thus made the remarkable ride of 324 miles without sleep, and stopping only to eat his meals, and resting but a few minutes then. For saving the express pouches he was highly complimented by all, and years afterward he the satisfaction of seeing his prophecy regarding the two road agents verified, for they were both captured and hanged by vigilantes for their many crimes.

43. An American.

CHAPTER XV

A Year of Adventures

Receiving an invitation from an old friend named Dave Harrington to accompany him on a trapping expedition up the Republican River, Buffalo Bill gladly accepted it, and prepared for the perilous trip.

The two started out from Salt Creek Valley with an outfit consisting of a wagon filled with traps and provisions, drawn by a yoke of oxen.

It was near the middle of November when the two started on the expedition, Mrs. Cody standing in the door when the team moved off, wiping the tears from her eyes and giving bounteous blessings to her beloved boy, watching with painful emotions until the white cover of the wagon which sheltered her dearest treasure became hidden by the prairie undulations in the distance.

The two made excellent progress, and met with no detention, arriving at the mouth of Prairie Dog Creek[1] early in December. Here they found an abundance of beaver, and trapped with such success that they secured 300 beaver and 100 otter skins before the severe weather interfered with their occupation.

Having obtained a full load of pelts it was decided to remain in the dug-out which they had constructed until the beginning of spring, when the return trip could be made without dangerous exposure.

During the period of waiting the two occupied much of their time shooting elk, large numbers of which were roaming constantly within convenient proximity. On one occasion while out hunting and in pursuit of a large herd of elk, while passing around a large rock projecting over a small ravine, Billy made a false step and was precipitated onto the rocks below, the fall breaking his leg between the knee and ankle. This accident, always serious, was doubly so under the circumstances, when no surgical aid could be had, nor any but a miserably insufficient attention could be given to mitigate the injury. To add still further to the misfortunes of the suffering boy, only a few days before this accident one of the oxen had broken a leg and Harrington had been compelled to shoot the animal. Here the two trappers were, in the midst of winter storms, without a team, and Billy rolling in an agony which his partner was unable to relieve.

After discussing the situation for some time, Harrington said, "Well, Billy, this is a bad box, and the only way to get out is for me to reach the nearest settlement and get a team to haul you home."

The poor boy, though he well knew that the nearest place from which succor could be obtained was fully 125 miles distant, and appreciated all the terrors of a long and painful waiting alone among the hungry wolves and bands of equally ferocious Indians, told Harrington to do as he thought best about making the trip.

It is no less pathetic than astonishing the devotion which is so often found among the Western pioneers, whose uncouth language and grizzly garb, if taken as an index to their true character, would lead to the inference that they are destitute of that human kindness which redeems mankind and compensates our vices.

Brave Dave Harrington, just like Cody himself, bighearted, noble, generous, self-sacrificing, immediately prepared for the tedious winter journey. Collecting about and within convenient reach of Billy plenty of dried beef, water, and other provisions needful for the sufferer's subsistence, Dave set out on the long trip, bidding his companion to be cheerful and expect his return in twenty-one days.

Finding himself utterly alone, poor Billy—I say "poor" because the facts can not fail to arouse the deepest pity and make us sympathize with him even now in remembrance, because sensibly affected by the realization of his terrible situation, Billy lay on his rude bed, nursing the inflamed and painful fracture, nothing to relieve his lonesomeness save the howl of prowling wolves peering through the mud and sticks and under the door. Ten days passed, when one evening Billy was aroused by a singular noise outside the door. He heard voices, and his experienced ear told him they were Indians. Suddenly a dozen Sioux, led by Chief Rain-In-The-Face,[2] broke into the dugout. Billy rose up from his pallet and faced them as well as he could, expecting instant death; but fortune favored him, as the chief recognized Billy, having met him often at Laramie. The chief at once told Billy that his life was safe; but the Indians remained all night, feasting on the provisions found there, and when they left in the morning carried away his weapons.

To add to his suffering a terrible snow-storm began, and Billy knew that it would retard the coming of Harrington. Starvation now threatened, and his leg became

44. Roped Bull in Bush.

more painful each day. At last the twenty-first day dawned; the fuel had burned out; the suffering boy was forced to gnaw chunks of frozen venison.

On the twenty-ninth day Dave Harrington arrived at the hut with two oxen which he had driven through the snow. The meeting between the two can not be described, and Billy heard how Harrington had braved every danger and hardship to come back to his rescue. A bed was made of furs and blankets in the wagon, and making Billy as comfortable as possible Harrington set out for Junction City.[3] The sun now came out and melted the snow, and they experienced no further difficulty.

Arriving at Junction City they sold their furs at a good price, and also the team, and went to Leavenworth with a government mule train. Harrington would not desert Billy, and accompanied him home, where every kindness was shown to the brave man who had saved Billy's life. Soon after their arrival at the Cody home Harrington was taken ill, and after an illness of one week died. Even to this day to speak of Dave Harrington to Buffalo Bill, he will have something kind to say in memory of his dearest friend.

It was months before Buffalo Bill recovered the use of his leg so that he could go again to work; then he applied for work on the Pony Express, and was engaged on a long and dangerous run.

The condition of the country along the North Platte had become so dangerous that it was almost impossible for the Overland Stage Company to find drivers, although the highest wages were offered. Billy at once decided to turn stage-driver, and his services were gladly accepted.

While driving a stage between Split Rock[4] and Three

45. The Attack on the Overland Coach.

Crossings he was set upon by a band of several hundred Sioux. Lieutenant Flowers, assistant division agent, sat on the box beside Billy, and there were half a dozen well-armed passengers inside. Billy gave the horses the reins, Lieutenant Flowers applied the whip, and the passengers defended the stage in a running fight. Arrows fell around and struck the stage like hail, wounding the horses and dealing destruction generally, for two of the passengers were killed and Lieutenant Flowers badly wounded. Billy seized the whip from the wounded officer, applied it savagely, shouted defiance, and drove on to Three Crossings, thus saving the stage.

This last trip proved so disastrous that it was decided to use a band of mounted men to patrol the trail. This force was placed under the command of Wild Bill, and Billy Cody accompanied the expedition they made into the Indian country. It proved to be a complete success, and the hostiles were severely punished, many being killed and hundreds of horses captured.

While connected with the stage line Billy started out alone on a bear-hunt. He had camped for the night and was picking a sage-hen which he had shot, when he heard the whinny of a horse up the mountain. He at once proceeded to investigate, and came upon a dug-out with several horses staked out near. Hearing voices within, and concluding they were trappers or hunters, he at once rapped on the door. The door was opened, and by the firelight he saw eight men, who he at once knew were outlaws. Two of these men Billy recognized as having been discharged by the Overland Stage Company. Billy told them how he came to find their cabin, and he was asked where his horse was.

"I left him tied at my camp down the mountain. I'll leave my gun here and go and bring him up," replied Billy, anxious to get out of the hornet's-nest in which he found himself.

Two of the villains at once offered their services to accompany him, to his great regret; but he could do nothing else than go with them, fully realizing the danger of his situation. He knew if he returned to the cabin he would be killed, and so he decided to act to save himself. Quick as lightning he struck one of the outlaws a stunning blow over the head with his pistol, and as the other turned shot him dead; then running to his horse he leaped into the saddle and fled down the mountains. The trail was so rugged, however, that his progress was slow, and the shot having been heard in the cabin the outlaws were soon in full pursuit; but fortunately Billy managed to make his escape, eluding his pursuers in the darkness, but having to desert his horse to do so.

It was twelve hours before he reached Horseshoe,

exhausted and half-famished. Reporting his adventure to Alf Slade, a party of ten started at once under Billy's guidance to the outlaws' cabin. They reached there after a ride of six hours and found a new-made grave, but the place was abandoned and there was nothing left to indicate their intention to return. Billy was complimented in the most deserving way for his bravery, and was put on the road again as express rider, Wild Bill being his alternate; and the two made better time than any other riders on the road.

CHAPTER XVI

A Soldier of the Civil War

Cody learning of the serious illness of his loved mother instantly saddled his horse and made all possible speed homeward. He arrived at home to find his mother dying, and he remained by her side, a devoted nurse, until she died.

Under the prairie sod, beneath the branches of a tree planted by the hands of the loving son, sleeps the pioneer's wife and a true hero's mother. Weeks after this most melancholy incident in Billy's life he went to Leavenworth and joined the Seventh Kansas Jayhawkers,[1] who were ordered to service in Tennessee and Mississippi. After several battles in Mississippi and Tennessee and hard service there the regiment was ordered to Missouri. The courage, cunning, and woodcraft displayed by Billy had not escaped the eye of his commander, and he was made a scout with the rank of sergeant. Serving in the capacity of scout, soldier, and spy he rendered most valuable service to the North and was considered the pride of General Smith's[2] corps.

As a soldier-scout Buffalo Bill won a great name and passed through numberless adventures. While with the army in Missouri Buffalo Bill again met his old "pard" of the plains, Wild Bill, who had also won fame as a scout and spy.

46. Bringing Buffalo-meat into Camp.

Until 1865, Buffalo Bill remained in the army, and was then detailed for special service at headquarters in St. Louis. It was while there that he met Miss Louisa Frederici, a young lady with whom he at once fell in love.

Buffalo Bill's phenomenal luck did not desert him as a lover, for the lady is to-day his wife. Having fixed the date for his marriage Buffalo Bill returned to the far frontier and accepted the position of stage-driver over the same route where he had killed his first Indian. He worked as a stage-driver until he saved up a sufficient sum of money to return to St. Louis and claim his bride.

He was married in 1866, the 6th of March, and the happy couple took passage on a Missouri River steamer for Kansas, where their home was to be. Arriving in

Kansas Cody went to Salt Creek Valley, where he established a hotel known as the Golden Rule House, which he conducted with profit until the old desire for life of stirring adventures induced him to sell out and seek employment as a scout.

Going to Junction City he met Wild Bill, who was then scouting for the Government, and by his advice he proceeded to the military post at Ellsworth and at once went on duty. While scouting and guiding parties he first met General Custer, who with ten men was at Ellsworth, looking for a guide to conduct him to Fort Larned. Cody was selected for the duty, and to the day of his death Custer was a sincere friend of Buffalo Bill's.

Upon his return Cody was ordered to report to the Tenth Cavalry as scout to guide an expedition against a large band of Indians who had attacked the force working on the Kansas Pacific Railroad.

The Indians were followed rapidly and overtaken, and turning upon the regiment of colored troops they for awhile stampeded them, capturing the howitzer. Major Armes,[3] however, rallied his men, and though badly wounded recaptured the gun; but Cody discovering that another large force of Indians was near at hand a retreat was begun, in which the colored troops made remarkably good time. Night approaching, the remnant of the command succeeded in reaching Hays, and Cody declared that he would "never go Indian hunting again with colored warriors," but has since paid generous tribute to their more experienced records.

While at Ellsworth Buffalo Bill met William Rose,[4] a man of many schemes and a railroad contractor. He disclosed to Buffalo Bill a scheme to build a city and become a millionaire out of its rise in value. Cody entered into the undertaking with zest, selected a site on Big Creek one mile from Fort Hays, and the town was duly laid out and the first house built. The town was then christened Rome, and a lot was donated to every one who would erect a building thereon. In one month's time there were 200 residences, 41 stores, and 20 saloons in Rome, and lots were selling at $50 each. Rome had begun to howl. But just as the dream of wealth was about to be realized a stranger arrived in town. He was the agent for the Kansas Pacific road, and not being able to make terms with the two owners of the town, Cody and Rose, he went west of Rome and laid out a town which he named Hays City. As he placed there a machine-shop, round-house, and depot, Rome was left out in the cold, and Cody saw his anticipated fortune fade from his grasp.

47. Scouting for Buffaloes.

CHAPTER XVII

A Champion Buffalo-Hunter

Having given up the real-estate business, Buffalo Bill received a proposition from the Goddard Brothers, who had contracted to furnish subsistence for thousands of construction employees of the Kansas Pacific Railroad. The amount required was very large, to procure which involved hard riding; but the labor was small compared with the danger to be incurred from the Indians, who were killing every white man they could find in that section. Nevertheless, an offer of $500 per month for the service made Billy unmindful of the exertion or peril, and he went to work under contract to supply all the meat required. During this engagement he had no end of wonderful escapes from bands of Indians, not a few of whom he sacrificed to secure his own safety. By actual count he also killed, under his contract with the Goddard Brothers, *four thousand two hundred and eighty buffaloes.* To appreciate the extent of this slaughter, by approximate measurement these buffaloes, if laid on the ground end to end, would make a line more than five miles long; and if placed on top of each other, they would make a pile two miles high.

By special arrangements all the heads of the largest buffaloes killed by Bill were preserved and delivered to the Kansas Pacific Railroad Company, by which they were turned into excellent advertisements for the road. Many of these heads may still be seen in prominent places, marking the center of an oval board containing the advertisement of the road.

So well had Cody performed his part of the contract that the men connected with the Kansas Pacific road gave him the appellation by which he is still known throughout the world, "Buffalo Bill."

A record of all his battles with the Indians during this period of professional hunting would be so long that few could read it without tiring, for there is a sameness connected with attacks and escapes which it is difficult to recite in language always sparkling with interest. But Buffalo Bill, being a brave man under all circumstances when bravery is essential and cautious when that element subserved the purpose better, was almost daily in a position of danger, and many times escaped almost like the Hebrew children from the furnace.

So justly celebrated had Buffalo Bill now become that Kit Carson, on his return from Washington City in the fall of 1867, stopped at Hays City to make his acquaintance. Carson was so well pleased with Bill's appearance and excellent social qualifications that he remained for several days the guest of the celebrated buffalo-killer and scout. Upon parting, the renowned Kit expressed the warmest admiration for his host, and conveyed his consideration by inviting Bill to visit him at Fort Lyon, Colo.,[1] where he intended making his home. But the death of Carson the following May prevented the visit.

Like every other man who achieves distinction by superior excellence in some particular calling, Buffalo Bill (who had now shed the familiar title of Billy) had his would-be rivals as buffalo-killers. Among this number was a well-known scout named Billy Comstock,[2] who sought to dispute the claim of champion. Comstock was quite famous among the Western army, being one of the oldest scout and most skillful hunters. He was murdered by Indians seven years after the event about to be recorded, while scouting for Custer.

Buffalo Bill was somewhat startled one day upon receipt of a letter from a well-known army officer, offering to wager the sum of $500 that Comstock could kill a greater number of buffaloes in a certain given time, under stipulated conditions, than any other man living. This was, of course, a challenge to Buffalo Bill, who, upon mentioning the facts, found hundreds of friends anxious to accept the wager, or who would put up any amount that Bill's claim to the championship could not be successfully disputed by any person living.

The bet was promptly accepted, and the following conditions agreed to: A large herd of buffaloes being found, the two men were to enter the drove at 8 o'clock a.m., and employ their own tactics for killing until 4 o'clock p.m., at the end of which time the one having killed the largest number was to be declared winner of the wager and also the "champion buffalo-killer of America." To determine the result of the hunt, a referee was to accompany each of the hunters on horseback and keep the score.

The place selected for the trial was twenty miles east of Sheridan, Kan., where the buffaloes were plentiful, and the country being a level prairie rendered the hunt easy and afforded an excellent view for those who wished to witness the exciting content.

Comstock was well mounted on a strong, spirited horse, and carried a 44-caliber[3] Henry rifle. Buffalo appeared on his famous horse Old Brigham; and in this he certainly had great advantage, for this sagacious animal knew all about his rider's style of hunting buffaloes, and therefore needed no reining.

The party rode out on the prairie at an early hour in the morning, and soon discovered a herd of about one hundred buffaloes grazing on a beautiful stretch of ground just suited for the work in hand. The two hunters rode rapidly forward, accompanied by their referees, while the spectators followed 100 yards in the rear. At a given signal the two contestants dashed into the center of the herd, dividing it so that Bill took the right half while Comstock took those on the left.

Now the sport began in magnificent style, amid the cheers of excited spectators, who rode as near the contestants as safety and non-interference permitted. Buffalo Bill, after killing the first half-dozen stragglers in the herd, began an exhibition of his wonderful skill and strategy; by riding at the head of the herd and pressing the leaders hard toward the left, he soon got he drove to circling, killing those that were disposed to break off on a direct line. In a short time witnesses of this novel contest saw Buffalo Bill driving his portion of the herd in a beautiful circle, and in less than half an hour he had all those in his bunch, numbering thirty-eight, lying around within a very small compass.

Comstock, in the meantime, had done some fine work, but by attacking the rear of his herd he had to ride directly away from the crowd of anxious spectators. He succeeded in killing twenty-three, which, however, lay irregularly over a space three miles in extent, and therefore while he killed fewer than his rival, he at the same time manifested less skill, which by contrast showed most advantageously for Buffalo Bill.

All the party having returned to the apex of a beautiful knoll, a large number of champagne bottles were produced, and amid volleys of flying corks toasts were drunk to the buffalo heroes, Buffalo Bill being especially lauded, and now a decided favorite.

But these ceremonies were suddenly interrupted by the appearance of another small herd of buffalo cows and calves, into which the two contestants charged precipitately. In this "round" Bill scored eighteen, while Comstock succeeded in killing only fourteen.

The superiority of Buffalo Bill was now so plainly shown that his backers, as well as himself, saw that he could afford to give an exhibition of his wonderful horsemanship, while continuing the contest, without fear of losing the stakes. Accordingly, after again regaling themselves with champagne and other appetizing accessories, the cavalcade of interested spectators rode northward for a distance of three miles, where they discovered a large herd of buffaloes quietly browsing. The party then halted, and Buffalo Bill, removing both saddle and bridle from Old Brigham, rode off on his well-trained horse, directing him solely by motions of his hand. Reaching the herd by circling and coming down upon it from the windward quarter, the two rival hunters rushed upon the surprised buffaloes and renewed the slaughter. After killing thirteen of the animals, Buffalo Bill drove one of the largest buffaloes in the herd toward the party, seeing which many among the interested spectators became very much frightened, showing as much trepidation, perhaps, as they would have manifested had the buffalo been an enraged lion. But when the ponderous, shaggy-headed beast came within a few yards of the party Bill shot it dead, thus giving a grand *coup d'état* to the day's sport, which closed with this magnificent exhibition of skill and daring.

The day having now been far spent, and time called, it was found that the score stood thus: Buffalo Bill, sixty-nine; Comstock, forty-six. The former was therefore declared winner, and entitled to the championship as the most skillful buffalo-slayer in America, and crowned forever with the title of "Buffalo Bill."

In referring to the fact that he has the record of having killed far more game than other great hunters, Buffalo Bill, who always speaks most modestly of all his exploits, gives as a reason for his scoring greater numbers of buffalo, bear, deer, elk, antelope, etc., that the huntsmen of years ago were armed with muzzle-loading weapons, while it fell to his lot to get the advantage of late inventions and be armed with the very best of repeating rifles.

The fact that Buffalo Bill makes this statement in favor of others shows how willing he is to give credit where credit is due.

CHAPTER XVIII

Scout, Guide, and Indian Fighter

After the great buffalo-killing match the name of Buffalo Bill became familiar all over the country, and his exploits were topics people never grew tired of discussing. All his great battles with the Indians, valuable services as a scout, and hairbreadth escapes were told and retold, not only at the fireside, but around the camp-fires.

In the spring of 1868 a violent Indian war broke out in Kansas, and General Sheridan, in order to be on the field, made his headquarters at Hays City. Sending for Buffalo Bill General Sheridan appointed him chief of scouts. From that time on Buffalo Bill acted as scout and guide in all the principal military operations upon the part of the frontier.

He was also appointed chief of scouts for the Fifth Cavalry to proceed against the Dog Soldier Indians.[1] The campaigns of the Fifth Cavalry are matters of history, as are also the services of Buffalo Bill, the letters of the commanding officers speaking for themselves.

During his services as scout he served directly under General Forsyth, Colonel Royall, Gen. E. A Carr, General Hazen, General Penrose, and others.

These officers, who had won fame upon the battlefields of the Civil War, many of them wearing the stars of a general, found themselves ordered to the far frontier—when

48. Buffalo Bill as a Scout.

the South had given up the struggle—to oppose the Indians, who were making desperate efforts to kill off their pale-face foes.

The truth was that the Indians regarded the Civil War with feelings of delight, and as a blessing to them, as they supposed that one side would utterly wipe out the other side, and their victors being weakened by the struggle the redskins could consolidate their forces, and attacking the remaining whites drive them off the face of the earth.

They certainly made a bold effort to do so, and in the war that followed the general officers were glad indeed to have the services of Buffalo Bill as scout, guide, and Indian fighter.

In all the operations of the army upon the frontier Buffalo Bill's identity with them was such that to recount his valuable services would be only to go over the pages of history. The stories of his adventures, scouting expeditions, hunting down desperadoes as a Government officer, and guiding of the armies through trackless wildernesses have been told and retold until every school-boy is familiar with them, and the name of no one man is better known than that of Buffalo Bill.

Early in September of 1871 a grand hunt was projected by General Sheridan for the purpose of giving a number of prominent gentlemen a buffalo-hunt. James Gordon Bennett of the New York *Herald,* Gen. Anson Stager of the Western Union Telegraph, Lawrence R. and Leonard W. Jerome, and Generals Davis, Fitzhughes, and Rucker, with Surgeon-General Asch,[2] Carrol Livingston, and others, formed the party. Immediately upon their arrival at Fort McPherson General Sheridan sent for Buffalo

Bill, introducing him with flattering remarks to each one of the hunting-party and telling him that he was to be their special guide and scout. The party hunted over a large extent of territory, killing many buffaloes, turkeys, jack-rabbits, and antelopes, and greatly enjoyed their visit to the plains.

In 1872 Buffalo Bill was visited by General Forsyth, who arranged with him a grand buffalo-hunt for the Duke Alexis, who was then visiting this country. Buffalo Bill at once conceived the idea of engaging a large number of Indians to join in the hunt, to make the affair a more pleasurable one for the grand duke. On the day of the hunt Buffalo Bill loaned the grand duke his splendid buffalo horse Buckskin Joe, and riding by his side instructed him in the manner of shooting buffaloes.

That night in camp numbers of glasses of champagne were disposed of in drinking to the great success of the Grand Duke Alexis as a buffalo-hunter. It was soon after the Alexis hunt that Buffalo Bill received an invitation from James Gordon Bennett, August Belmont, and others of equal prominence to visit the East. At the earnest solicitation of General Sheridan Bill accepted the invitation, and thus it was that he entered upon the life so different from that in which he had passed his earlier years.

Attending the theater one night to see a frontier play bearing his own name—J. B. Studley[3] taking the character of Buffalo Bill—he conceived the idea of going upon the stage and playing himself, and thus it was that he became an actor, winning fame and fortune through his enterprises. Having introduced upon the stage Indians as actors, Buffalo Bill decided upon reproducing in miniature

49. General Miles and Buffalo Bill Viewing the
Hostiles' Village in the Last Indian War.

scenes in wild life upon the frontier, and from this sprung the Wild West, the greatest exhibition ever known.

During his life as an actor and his career as the head of the Wild West exhibition Buffalo Bill obeyed every call to the frontier whenever there was any trouble among the Indians, and at once resumed his duties as scout, guide, and Indian fighter, winning added laurels thereby and conclusively proving that through his life in cities his heart, brain, and hand had not lost their cunning or courage and the nobility of his nature had not suffered through contact with the world, nor had he been spoiled by applause and praise.

After the massacre of Custer's band there was great activity in military movements in the Northwest, and as chief of scouts under Merritt, Crook, and other generals Buffalo Bill's career was a most brilliant one. During the last Indian campaign Buffalo Bill's valuable services were publicly recognized by Gen. Nelson A. Miles, one of our greatest Indian fighters, and who so quickly crushed the Indians in their late rising, when Sitting Bull lost his life.

Buffalo Bill is one of the few famous scouts who has justly won the renown which encircles his name. His exploits have been so numerous, involving a display of such extraordinary daring and magnificent nerve, that language can not exaggerate them. General Sheridan often asserted that Buffalo Bill had "slain as many Indians as any white man that ever lived." It would be no credit to this daring scout if these Indians had fallen without justification; but since they were the victims of legitimate warfare and were slain in the performance of a sworn duty, Buffalo Bill may properly wear the laurels and deserve

50. After the Battle.

the plaudits of civilization—whose effective instrument he has been—for the friendship he has displayed for the red man in times of peace.

As the noted scout is revealing to the eyes of the whole world the scenes in which he has been a participant, there are few indeed who do not care to see the Wild West in miniature as he portrays it with the aid of his Indians and cowboys, and give him praise for his phenomenal success. Having produced the Wild West in all the large cities of America, Buffalo Bill decided, so to speak, to "carry the war into Africa," and the result was that with his partner, Mr. Nate Salsbury,[4] an actor of renown, he invaded first the English capital, then the other capitals of Europe, his enterprise everywhere winning the plaudits of royalty, the press, and the public.

CHAPTER XIX

Buffalo Bill's "Pards" of the Plains

To gain great local and national fame as a plains celebrity in the days of old was not an easy task; rather one of the most competitive struggles that a young man could possibly engage in. The vast, comparatively unknown, even called great, American Desert of twenty-five and thirty years ago was peopled only by the descendants of the sturdy pioneers of the then far West—Illinois, Missouri, Arkansas, Iowa, Minnesota, Kansas, etc.—born, raised, and used to hardships and danger; and attracted only the resolute, determined adventurers of the rest of the world, seeking an outlet for pent-up natures imbued with love of daring adventure. Hundreds of men achieved local, and great numbers national, fame for the possession of every manly quality that goes to make up the romantic hero of that once dark and bloody ground. When it is brought to mind the work engaged in—the carving out of the advance paths for the more domestically inclined settler; of the dangers and excitements of hunting and trapping; of carrying dispatches, stage-driving, freighting cargoes of immense value, guiding successfully the immense wagon-trains, gold-hunting—it is easy to conceive what a class of sturdy, adventurous young spirits entered the arena to struggle in a daily deadly, dangerous game to win the "bubble reputation." When such an army of the best human material battled for supremacy, individual distinction gained by the unwritten law of unprejudiced *popular* promotion possessed a value that made its acquirer a "plains celebrity," stamped indelibly with an *honored title* rarely possessed unless fairly, openly, and justly won—a prize so pure that its ownership, while envied, crowned the victor with the friendship, following, and admiration of the contestants. Thus Boone, Crocket, Carson, Beale, Fremont, Cody, Bridger, Kinman,[1] Hickok, Cosgrove,[2] Comstock, Frank North,[3] and others will live in the romance, the poetry, and history of their distinctive work forever. The same spirit and circumstances have furnished journalists innumerable, who in the West imbibed the sterling qualities they afterward used to such effect—notably, Henry M. Stanley, who (in 1866) saw the rising sun of the young empire that stretches to the Rockies; General Greely, of Arctic fame, and the equally scientific explorer, Lieutenant Schwatka,[4] passed their early career in the same school, and often followed the trail, led by Buffalo Bill; Finerty[5] (formerly of the Chicago *Times*); "Modoc" Fox[6] and O'Kelly[7] (of the New York *Herald*), 1876; while of late years[8] the scribblers were initiated to their baptism of fire by Harries (of Washington *Star*), McDonough (New York *World*), Bailey (of *Inter Ocean*), brave young Kelley (of the Lincoln *Journal*), Cressey (of the Omaha *Bee*), Charlie Seymour (Chicago *Herald*), Allen (of the New York *Herald*), Robert J. Boylan (of *Inter Ocean*), present in the battle, who were honored by three cheers from "Old White Top" Forsyth's gallant Seventh Cavalry, the day after the battle of "Wounded Knee," as they went charging over

51. Wild Bill.

Wolf Creek—to what came near being a crimson day—to the fight "down at the mission." That there are still "successors to every king" is assured by the manly scouts so prominent in the last Indian war in such men as Frank Grouard, now the most celebrated of the present employed army scouts; of "Little Bat," true as steel and active as the cougar; Philip Wells, Louis Shangrau, "Big Baptiste," and John Shangrau;[9] while the friendly Indians furnish such grand material for any future necessity as No Neck, Major Sword, Red Shirt, and Yankton Charley.[10]

"Wild Bill" (J. B. Hickok)

It is a noticeable coincidence that nearly all of the famous frontier characters are natives of the West, and J. B. Hickok, better known as Wild Bill, was not an exception to the rule.

Born in La Salle County, Illinois, in 1837, his earliest desire was for horses and firearms. At the age of fourteen he had become known as a wolf-killer, for at that time the country where he lived was overrun by them.

Acquiring a rudimental education he started out to earn his living, and began as a tow-path driver on the Illinois & Michigan Canal.

Longing for fields of adventure he went into Kansas, where he soon made a name in the border war then going on there.

It was in Kansas that he was given the name of "Bill," though just why no one seems to know; and afterward his daring and adventurous career got for him the added cognomen of "Wild Bill," a name that he certainly made famous.

52. Texas Jack.

Serving upon the frontier as wagon-boss, pony-rider, stage-driver, and then drifting into the position of guide and Government scout, Wild Bill made a name for himself in each occupation he followed.

It was while serving as train-boss of one of Russell & Majors wagon-trains that Wild Bill met and befriended Buffalo Bill, then a mere boy; and the friendship thus begun ended only with the death of Hickok, at Deadwood, at the hands of the assassin Jack McCall.

A soldier, scout, and spy during the Civil War, Wild Bill returned to scouting at its close, the frontier becoming his home.

Constantly he was thrown in the company of Buffalo Bill, and when the latter decided to go upon the stage he determined that his companions in the enterprise should be Wild Bill and Texas Jack, and they accompanied him to the East.

A dead shot, an enemy to fear, Wild Bill was as brave as a lion and as tender-hearted as a woman, and he will go down in history as a true hero of the border.

"Texas Jack" (J. B. Omohundro)

Known in his native State, Virginia, as John B. Omohundro, the subject of this sketch won the sobriquet of "Texas Jack" after service as a ranger in the Lone Star State.

Reared in a part of Virginia where every man rode a horse, and born a natural hunter, while his parents were able to gratify his desire to become a skilled horseman and expert shot, Jack Omohundro at an early age became noted among his comrades as a fearless rider and a dead shot.

When the Civil War broke out, though but a boy, Jack

enlisted in the Confederate cavalry, and during the four years saw much hard service and was a participant in many battles.

Becoming connected with the headquarters of a Texas general he was made a scout, and as such rendered valuable services to the Confederate army.

Allied with Texans he went with them to Texas at the close of the war, going to the frontier, where he joined a company of rangers.

From ranger, in which capacity he saw much service against the Indians, he turned to cattle-herding, becoming first a cowboy and afterward a rancher.

Going northward into Kansas in charge of a large herd of cattle Texas Jack met, at a frontier post, Buffalo Bill.

A warm friendship at once sprung up between the two, which ended only with the death of the gallant Texan some years ago at Leadville, Colo.

It was through the agency of Buffalo Bill that Texas Jack entered the service of the Government as a scout and won distinction as such, and also as guide and Indian fighter.

As a scout he was respected by army officers for his skill and courage, and he became the warm friend of "White Beaver" (Dr. Frank Powell), Maj. Frank North, and Wild Bill, joining the latter, with Buffalo Bill, in the theatrical enterprise which Buffalo Bill continued until he originated the Wild West exhibition.

Dr. D. Frank Powell ("White Beaver")[11]

The life of "White Beaver" (Dr. D. Frank Powell) bears all the colors and shades of an idyllic romance. His character

53. Dr. D. Frank "White Beaver" Powell.

stands out upon the canvas of human eccentricities in striking originality, and never finds its counterpart save in stories of knight-errantry, when hearts, names, and titles were the prizes bestowed for daring deeds evolved from generous sentiments. His has been the tenor of uneven ways, with characteristics as variable as the gifts in Pandora's box. A born plainsman, with the rough, rugged marks of wild and checkered incident, and yet a mind that feeds on fancy, builds images of refinement, and looks out through the windows of his soul upon visions of purity and fields of elysian. A reckless adventurer on the boundless prairies, and yet in elegant society as amiable as a school-girl in the ball-room; evidencing the polish of an aristocrat, and a cultured mind that shines with vigorous luster where learning displays itself. A friend to be valued most in direst extremity, and an enemy with implacable, insatiable, and revengeful animosities. In short, he is a singular combination of opposites, and yet the good in him so predominates over his passions that no one has more valuable friendships and associations than these strange complexities attract to him. He is an ideal hero, the image which rises before the ecstatic vision of a romancer, and he impresses himself upon the millions who know his reputation as a brave and chivalrous gentleman.

A description of White Beaver is not difficult to give, because of his striking features; those who see him once are so impressed with his bearing that his image is never forgotten. He is almost six feet in height, of large frame and giant muscular development; a full round face, set off by a Grecian nose, a handsome mouth, and black eyes of penetrating brilliancy. His hair is long and hangs over his shoulders in raven ringlets. In action he is marvelously quick, always decisive, and his endurance almost equals that of a steam-engine. His appearance is that of a resolute, high-toned gentleman, conscious of his power, and yet his deference, I may say amiability, attracts every one to him. He is, in short, one of the handsomest as well as most power-ful men among the many great heroes of the plains.

In addition to his other qualifications peculiarly fitting him for a life on the plains, he is an expert pistol and rifle shot; in fact, there are perhaps not a half-dozen persons in the United States who are his superiors; his precision is not so great now as it once was, for the reason that during the past three or four years he has had but very little prac-tice; but even now he would be regarded an expert among the most skillful. For dead-center shooting at stationary objects he never had a superior. His eyesight is more acute than an eagle's, which enables him to distinguish and hit the head of a pin ten paces distant, and this shot he can perform now nine times out of ten. Any of his office em-ployees will hold a copper cent between their fingers and let him shoot it out at ten paces, so great is their confi-dence in his skill; he also shoots through finger-rings held in the same manner. One very pretty fancy-shot he does is splitting a bullet on a knife-blade; he also suspends objects by a hair, and at ten paces cuts the hair, which of course he can not see, but shoots by judgment. Several persons have told me that they have seen him shoot a fish-line in two while it was being dragged swiftly through the water.

White Beaver and Buffalo Bill have been bosom friends and fellow-plainsmen since boyhood. History records no love between two men greater than that of these two foster-brothers.

Maj. Frank J. North

This gallant officer was universally recognized as one of the best executive leaders and bravest men that ever faced the dangers of the plains.

Although born in the State of New York (March 10, 1840), he was by virtue of his training a thorough Westerner. While still a boy his father moved from New York to near Columbus in the State of Nebraska, and very soon thereafter was frozen to death at Emigrant Crossing, on Big Papillion Creek,[12] while searching for wood for his suffering family. After a short connection with McMurra, Glass, and Messenger, the party of trappers, he returned to Columbus and turned his hand to anything that offered.

In 1860, at the age of twenty years, he procured employment with Agent De Puy, at the Pawnee Indian Reservation,[13] While there he studied and became thoroughly proficient in the Pawnee language, and in the following year was engaged as interpreter by Mr. Rudy,[14] son-in-law of the Indian Commissioner.

In 1864, when the Sioux war broke out, he was commissioned by General Curtis[15] to organize the Pawnee Scouts. He formed a company of seventy-seven young warriors, and was made first lieutenant. To Major North belongs the honor of making the first enlistment of Indians for regular Government service. In October following Lieutenant North supplemented his first enlistment by another of 100 Pawnee warriors, who were equipped as regular cavalry, and he was promoted to the rank of captain.

In January, 1865, Captain North, with forty of his Pawnee braves, started in pursuit of the Sioux, who had been committing terrible outrages in the neighborhood of Julesburg. Death and destruction marked the trail of the Sioux, and Captain North arrived at Julesburg just in time to rescue its inhabitants. Still pursuing, he caught up with a party of twenty-eight of the red devils, and not one of them escaped his vengeance. This was a part of Red Cloud's forces,[16] and only a few days before they had suddenly attacked Lieutenant Collins and fourteen men and massacred the entire party.[17]

Shortly after this he became the hero of one of the most daring fights ever recorded. During the pursuit of a party of twelve Cheyennes, with the intention of punishing them for atrocities committed in the neighborhood of Fort Sedgwick,[18] his impetuous ardor was so great that it led him far in advance of his followers. He suddenly realized that he was at least a mile ahead of his men. After bringing down one of the fleeing Cheyennes he turned to rejoin his command. Seeing him alone the Indians started in pursuit, and his horse having been killed he was compelled to continue his retreat on foot. After having gone some distance he remembered he had left two loaded revolvers in the holsters on his saddle, and notwithstanding the danger he boldly returned for them, and with them fought the Cheyennes single-handed for nearly half an hour longer, until relieved by Lieutenant Small.

In 1865–66, after the Pawnees were mustered out of service, Captain North was appointed post trader at the Pawnee Reservation.

In the March following, under orders from General Auger, he raised a battalion of 200 Pawnees, who were equipped for cavalry service and taken to Fort Kearny, he being commissioned a major. This battalion guarded construction trains on the Union Pacific Railroad until it reached Ogden.

Upon the completion of the road Major North retired to a ranch on Dismal River, near North Platte, where he

54. Sitting Bull.

went into the cattle-raising business. He was then a great sufferer from asthma, and had abandoned all hope of relief.

Buffalo Bill and Major North met for the first time at Fort McPherson, and served together in several campaigns. They became very warm friends, and afterward partners in the cattle business under the firm name of Cody & North.

Major North, besides being a remarkable Indian fighter and a phenomenally brave man, was a thorough gentleman, of generous and noble instincts, an honest friend, and popular with all classes. His death a few years ago at North Platte was deeply and sincerely regretted by the many who had known and loved him well. To none did the news cause more sincere regret than to his old "pard" and partner, Buffalo Bill.

Sitting Bull[19]

Though nearly a score of years have gone by since the battle of the Little Big Horn, where the gallant Custer and his brave band were slain, the name of Sitting Bull is recalled by all; and a sigh of relief went up all along the border when the news came that the noted chief had started upon the trail for the happy hunting-grounds.

Those who condemn the Indian for his red deeds should remember that it is his education to be a savage, to kill and burn and pillage; that the greatest slayer of mankind, in the opinion of the red men, is the greatest hero.

Thus, considering that the Indian has his story to tell as well as the white man, the mantle of charity should be drawn over their deeds.

Sitting Bull was not a chief in the true sense of the word, but was the Moses of his people.

He had unlimited influence with his tribe, and among other tribes as well; and, a mighty medicine-man, he claimed as well to be a prophet.

The career of Sitting Bull was eventful and remarkable.

He was a leader and schemer, and when Generals Terry, Crook, and Gibbon were sent to capture him he showed great generalship in all that he did.

He checked the advance of General Crook, slaughtered Custer, and escaped into Canada, where he and his people were safe.

In 1877 a part of Sitting Bull's tribe surrendered to General Miles, who pressed them so hard they could not escape into Canada.

In 1880 others of the tribe surrendered to General Miles at Fort Keogh,[20] and later Sitting Bull and others surrendered to keep from starving. They were transferred to Standing Rock Agency.[21]

Sitting Bull received tempting offers to go East on exhibition, but refused all except one from Buffalo Bill—whom he knew as a deadly foe in warfare and a good friend in times of peace—and so went with some of his people to join the Wild West, with which he remained for a year.

The killing of Sitting Bull is still fresh in the minds of the people, and his taking off has been condemned by many.

At the time of his death Buffalo Bill, Surgeon Frank Powell, Pony Bob Haslam,[22] and others were on their way to his camp to demand his surrender. Had Buffalo Bill not been halted by the command of the President and had reached Sitting Bull's camp, the great chief would not have been slain; and probably Cody's influence would have been strong enough to have changed to a more peaceful settlement the *émeute*[23] that culminated in Wounded Knee and Pine Ridge.

"Oklahoma Payne" (Capt. D. L. Payne), the Cimarron Scout[24]

David L. Payne, known throughout the West as Captain Payne, of the Oklahoma Colony Company, was born in Grant County, Indiana, December 30, 1836. In 1858, with his brother, he started West, intending to engage in the Mormon War, but reached there too late. He settled in Doniphan County, Texas. His commercial pursuits there not resulting in success he turned hunter, and so became thoroughly acquainted with the topography of the great Southwest. Afterward a scout, he was often engaged in that capacity by the Government and by private expeditions. In this way he became acquainted with Kit Carson, Wild Bill, Buffalo Bill, California Joe, General Custer, and others of national reputation.

During the Civil War he served as a private in the Fourth Regiment, which was afterward merged into the Tenth. In the fall of 1864 he was elected to the Kansas Legislature. Upon its adjournment he again enlisted, and his command was detailed for duty at Washington City. His service in the volunteer army covered a period of eight years, his last position being captain of Company H, Nineteenth Kansas Cavalry, from October, 1868, to October, 1869. During these eight years he held the positions of postmaster at Fort Leavenworth, member of the Legislature, and sergeant-at-arms of the Kansas Senate.

At the close of the war Captain Payne returned to the life of the plains, and in the spring of 1868 he accompanied

55. Brigadier-General George A. Custer.

General Custer in an expedition against the Cheyennes, during which he, with two others, was detailed as special messenger to Fort Hays to secure assistance, and in that capacity encountered great dangers and privations.

In 1870 he removed to Sedgwick County, Kansas, near Wichita, and in the following year was again elected to the Legislature. In 1879 he became interested in a movement for the occupation and settlement of a district in the Indian Territory which is known as Oklahoma (beautiful land). In 1880 he organized a colony for the purpose of

56. Nate Salsbury.

entering upon and settling these lands, but was stopped by a decision of Carl Schurz,[25] then Secretary of the Interior, to the effect that these lands were open to settlement only to negroes or Indians. Owing to the arrest of Captain Payne by the United States authorities the colony disbanded.

However historians may differ as to the wisdom or legality of Captain Payne's so-called Oklahoma invasion and the court's decisions upon the subject, the fact remains that his name is held high in honor and esteem by the older citizens of the now flourishing Oklahoma—a monument to his forethought.

Nathan Salsbury

Now to one who if not a "pard" of the plains is a partner in the Wild West.

Mr. Nate Salsbury, the partner of Buffalo Bill in his business enterprise of the Wild West, and his devoted friend, was born in Freeport, Ill., his parents being in humble circumstances. Nate Salsbury began to work for a living at an early age, his ambition being to win fame and fortune by becoming a self-made man. As there was little to bind his affections to the home of his nativity, when the war broke out with all the patriotism of an American stirring in his bosom, he enlisted as a private in the Fifteenth Illinois Regiment, though but a boy in years.[26] His career as a boy soldier won for him praise and promotion, and he was wounded in battle on three different occasions.

Made a prisoner by the Confederates, he was incarcerated in Andersonville prison, where he remained for seven months.

Being at length exchanged, he returned to his home and began the study of law. A few months of office work and attendance at school, as well, impressed him with the idea that the legal profession would still have a fairly large membership, even though his name was not added to the list. Abandoning his intention of becoming a lawyer, and while attending school he was selected for a part in an amateur theatrical performance. From the time that he made his first bow to an audience before the footlights as an amateur, he was seized with the irresistible desire to become an actor. With Nate Salsbury to decide was to act, and going to Grand Rapids, Mich., with only a few dollars in his pocket, he received a position which, though humble, gave him a start in professional life. After a short season there he went East and secured a position in the Boston Museum Company, where his histrionic talent was quickly recognized by the management. His success at this theater soon attracted to him the attention of managers of other cities, and he accepted the position of leading man at Hooley's Theater in Chicago. His progress was thenceforth rapid. His popularity grew apace and his salary was added to with every engagement. There was too much originality in Nate Salsbury to allow of his remaining a member of a stock company, so he conceived and constructed a comedy entertainment to which he gave the title of "The Troubadours."

From the first production of "The Troubadours" the fame and fortune of Nate Salsbury were assured. His play of "Patchwork" followed, then his most successful comedy, "The Brook," which added largely to his riches and his name as an actor.

Mr. Salsbury went with his Troubadours in a trip around the world, everywhere receiving deserved praise, and he was the first dramatic manager who made this hazardous tour with his own company.

The tour took the Troubadours—after going all over the United States, playing from Maine to Texas, the Carolinas to California—through Australia, India, Scotland, England, Ireland, and Wales, wherever the English tongue was spoken.

Meeting Buffalo Bill and learning from him his intention of giving Wild Western exhibitions, Mr. Salsbury became a partner in the Wild West, and took the active management of that gigantic aggregation, withdrawing from the stage to do so.

During the tour of Buffalo Bill abroad, at many dinners and assemblages Mr. Nate Salsbury's oratorical powers, mimic skills, ready wit, recitative talent, and facility of expressing sentiment delighted all who heard him, and invariably made an impression that will long keep his memory green, while the reputation of Americans for oratory was well sustained by the prairie-born boy soldier.

As a proof of Mr. Salsbury's nerve under trying circumstances, he was about to go upon the stage at Denver when he received a dispatch from his partner, Buffalo Bill, which told him that the Wild West steamer on the Mississippi had collided with another boat and sunk. Buffalo Bill telegraphed, "The whole outfit at the bottom of the Mississippi River. What do you advise?" Without an instant's hesitation Nate Salsbury wrote on a telegraph blank this answer, "Go to New Orleans, reorganize, and open on your date," and this Buffalo Bill did.

Some years ago Mr. Salsbury invested heavily in the cattle business in Montana, and to-day owns one of the most valuable ranches in the Northwest. It was during his visit to his ranch that he saw the practicability of an exhibition such as the Wild West, and readily joined Buffalo Bill in the enterprise. A man of brains, a strict disciplinarian, a genial gentleman, with genius to originate and ability to accomplish, generous and courageous, Nate Salsbury stands to-day unrivaled as an executive of great amusement enterprises, and he thoroughly deserves the fortune and fame that he has won.

Indian Names of States

Massachusetts, from the Indian language, signifying the "country about the great hills."[27]

Connecticut was Mohegan, spelled originally "Quon-eh-ta-cut," signifying "a long river."[28]

Alabama comes from the Indian word signifying "the land of rest."[29]

Mississippi derived its name from that of the great river, which is in the Natchez tongue "The Father of Waters."[30]

Arkansas is derived from the word Kansas, "smoky waters," with the French prefix of "ark," a bow.[31]

Tennessee is an Indian name, meaning "the river with a big bend."[32]

Kentucky is also an Indian name, "Kin-tuk-ae," signifying "at the head of the river."[33]

Ohio is the Shawnee name for "the beautiful river."[34]

Michigan's name was derived from the lake, the Indian name for fish-weir or trap, which the shape of the lake suggested.[35]

Indiana's name came from that of the Indians.

Illinois's name is derived from the Indian word "Illini" (men) and the French affix "ois," making "tribe of men."[36]

Wisconsin's name is said to be the Indian name for a wild, rushing channel.[37]

Missouri is also an Indian name for "muddy," having reference to the muddiness of the Missouri River.[38]

Kansas is an Indian word for "smoky water."[39]

Iowa signifies, in the Indian language, "the drowsy ones,"[40] and Minnesota, "a cloudy water."[41]

57. Ready for the Trail.

CHAPTER XX

Border Poetry

BILL CODY

William E Annin,[1] Omaha Bee.
Washington, D.C., February 28, 1891

You bet I know him, pardner, he ain't no circus fraud,
He's Western born and Western bred, if he has been late abroad.
I knew him in the days way back, beyond Missouri's flow,
When the country round was nothing but a huge Wild Western
    Show;
When the Injuns were as thick as fleas, and the man who ven-
    tured through
The sandhills of Nebraska had to fight the hostile Sioux.
These were hot times, I tell you; and we all remember still
The days when Cody was a scout, and all the men knew Bill.

I knew him first in Kansas in the days of '68,
When the Cheyennes and Arapahoes were wiping from the slate
Old scores against the settlers, and when men who wore the blue,
With shoulder-straps and way-up rank, were glad to be helped
    through
By a bearer of dispatches, who knew each vale and hill
From Dakota down to Texas, and his other name was Bill.

I mind me too of '76, the time when Cody took
His scouts upon the Rosebud, along with General Crook;

When Custer's Seventh rode to their death for lack of some
    such aid
To tell them that he sneaking Sioux knew how to ambuscade.
I saw Bill's fight with Yellow Hand, you bet it was a "mill";
He downed him well at thirty yards, and all the men cheered Bill.

They tell me that the women folk now take his word as laws;
In them days laws were mighty skerce, and hardly passed with
    s***ws;
But many a hardy settler's wife and daughter used to rest
More quietly because they knew of Cody's dauntless breast;
Because they felt, from Laramie way down to old Fort Sill,
Bill Cody was a trusted scout, and all their men knew Bill.

I haven't seen him much of late; how does he bear his years?
They says he's making ducats now, from shows and not from
    "steers"
He used to be a judge of "horns," when poured in a tin cup,
And left the wine to tenderfeet, and men who felt "way up";
Perhaps he cracks a bottle now, perhaps he's had his fill;
Who cares, Bill Cody was a scout, and all the world knows Bill.

To see him in his trimmins, he can't hardly look the same,
With laundered shirt and diamonds, as if "he run a game."
He didn't wear biled linen then, or flash up diamond rings;
The royalties he dreamed of then were only pasteboard kings;
But those who sat behind the queens were apt to get their fill,
In the days when Cody was a scout, and all the men knew Bill.

BUFFALO CHIPS,[2] THE SCOUT, TO BUFFALO BILL

(The following verses on the life and death of poor old Buffalo Chips are founded entirely on facts. His death occurred on September 8, 1876, at Slim Buttes. He was within three feet of me when he fell, uttering the words credited to him below.—Capt. Jack Crawford,[3] Poet Scout.)

The evenin' sun war settin', droppin' slowly in the west,
An' the soldiers, tired an' tuckered, in the camp would find that rest
Which the settin' sun would bring 'em, for they'd marched since
    break o' day,
Not a bite to eat 'cept horses as war killed upon the way.
For ye see our beans an' crackers an' our pork were outen sight,
An' the boys expected rashuns when they struck our camp that
    night;
For a little band had started for to bring some cattle on,
An' they struck an Indian village, which they captured just at dawn.

Wall, I were with that party when we captured them ar' Sioux,
An' we quickly sent a courier to tell old Crook the news.
Old Crook! I should say gen'l, cos he war with the boys,
Shared his only hard-tack, our sorrows, and our joys;
An' that is one thing startin—he never put on style;
He'd greet the scout or soldier with a social kinder smile.
An' that's the kind o' soldier as the prairy likes to get,
An' every man would trump Death's ace for Crook or Miles, you bet.

But I'm kinder off the racket, cos these gener'ls get enough
O' praise 'ithout my chippin', so I'll let up on that puff;
Fer I want to tell a story 'bout a mate of mine as fell,
Cos I loved the honest fellar, and he did his dooty well.
Buffalo Chips we call'd him, but his other name war White;
I'll tell ye how he got that name, an' reckon I am right.
You see a lot of big-bugs an' officers came out
One time to hunt the buffaler an' fish fer speckled trout.

Wall, little Phil,[4] ye've heerd on him, a dainty little cuss
As rode his charger twenty miles to stop a little muss;
Well, Phil he said to ter Johnathin, whose other name war White,
"You go an' find them buffaler, an' see you get 'em right."
So White he went an' found 'em, an' he found 'em sech a band
As he sed would set 'em crazy, an' little Phil looked bland;
But when the outfit halted, one bull was all war there.
Then Phil he call him "Buffalo Chips," an' swore a little swear.

Wall, White he kinder liked it, cos the gener'l called him Chips,
An' he us'ter wear two shooters in a belt above his hips.
Then he said, "Now, look ye, gener'l, since ye've called me that
    ar' name,
Jist around them little sandhills is yer dog-gone pesky game!
But when the hunt war over, an' the table spread for lunch,
The gener'l called for glasses, an' wanted his in punch;
An' when the punch was punished, the gener'l smacked his lips,
While squar' upon the table sot a dish o' *buffalo chips*.

The gener'l looked confounded, an' he also looked for White,
But Johnathin he reckon'd it war better he should lite.
So he skinned across the prairy, cos ye see he didn't mind
A *chippin'* any longer while the gener'l saw the *blind*;
Fer the gener'l would *a raised him*, if he'd jist held up his hand,
But he thought he wouldn't *see him*, cos he didn't hev the sand;
An' he rode as fast—aye, faster—than the gener'l did that day,
Like lightin' down from Winchester some twenty miles away.

Wall, White he had no cabin, an' no home to call his own,
So Buffaler Bill he took him an' shared with him his home.
An' how he loved Bill Cody! By gosh! it war a sight
Ter see him watch his shadder an' foller him at night;

Cos Bill war kinder hated by a cussed gang o' thieves,
As carried pistols in that belts, an' bowies in that sleeves.
An' Chips he never left him, for fear he'd get a pill;
Nor would he think it mighty hard to die for Buffalo Bill.

We us'ter mess together, that ar' Chips an' Bill an' me,
An' ye oughter watch his movements; it would do ye good ter see
How he us'ter cook them wittles, an' gather lots o' greens,
To mix up with the juicy pork an' them unruly beans.
An' one cold chilly mornin' he bought a lot o' corn,
An' a little flask o' likker, as cost fifty cents a horn.
Tho' *forty yards* war nowhar, it was finished soon, ye bet;
But, friends, I *promised some one*, and I'm strong teetotal yet.

RATTLIN' JOE'S PRAYER[5]

(By Capt. Jack Crawford)

Jist pile on some more o' them pine knots,
An' squat yoursel' down on this skin,
An', Scotty, let up on yer growlin'—
The boys are all tired o' yer chin.
Allegheny, jist pass round the bottle,
An' give the lads all a square drink,
An' as soon as yer settled I'll tell ye
A yarn as 'll please ye, I think.

'Twas eighteen hundred an' sixty,
A day in the bright month o' June,
When the angel o' death from the diggin's
Snatched "Monte Bill"—known as McCune.
Wal, Bill war a favorite among us,
In spite o' the trade that he had,
Which war gamblin'; but—don't you forget it—

He of'en made weary hearts glad.
An', pards, while he lay in that coffin,
Which we hewed from the trunk o' a tree,
His face war as calm as an angel's,
An' white as an angel's could be.

An' thar's whar the trouble commenced, pards.
Thar war no gospel-sharps in the camps,
An' Joe said, "We can't drop him this way,
Without some directions or stamps."
Then up spoke old Sandy McGregor,
"Look'ee yar, mates, I'm reg'lar dead stuck,
I can't hold no hand at religion,
An' I'm 'feared Bill's gone out o' luck.
If I knowed a darn thing about prayin',
I'd chip in an' say him a mass;
But I ain't got no show in the layout,
I can't beat the game, so I pass."

Rattlin' Joe war the next o' the speakers,
An' Joe war a friend o' the dead;
The salt water stood in his peepers,
An' these are the words as he said,
"Mates, ye know as I ain't any Christian,
An' I'll gamble the Lord don't know
That thar lives sich a rooster as I am;
But thar once war a time long ago
When I war a kid; I remember,
My old mother sent me to school,
To the little brown church every Sunday,
Whar they said I was dumb as a mule.
An' I reckon I've nearly forgotten

Purty much all that I ever knew.
But still, if ye'll drop to my racket,
I'll show ye jist what I kin do.

"Now, I'll show you *my* bible," said Joseph,
"Jist hand me them cards off that rack;
I'll convince that this *are* a bible,"
An' he went to work shufflin' the pack.
He spread out the cards on the table,
An' begun kinder pious-like, "Pards,
If ye'll jist cheese yer racket an' listen,
I'll show ye the pra'ar-book in cards.

"The 'ace'; that reminds us of one God;
The 'deuce' of the Father an' Son;
The 'tray' of the Father, an' Son, Holy Ghost,
For ye see all them three are but one.
The 'four-spot' is Matthew, Mark, Luke, an' John;
The 'five-spot' the virgins who trimmed
Their lamps while yet it was light of the day;
And the five foolish virgins who sinned.
The 'six-spot,' in six days the Lord made the world,
The sea, and the stars in the heaven;
He saw it war good w'at he made, then he said,
'I'll jist go the rest on the "seven."'
The 'eight-spot' is Noah, his wife, an' three sons,
An' Noah's three sons had their wives;
God loved the hull mob, so bid 'em emb-ark—
In the freshet he saved all their lives.
The 'nine' were the lepers of Biblical fame,
A repulsive and hideous squad.
The 'ten' are the holy commandments, which came

To us perishin' creatures from God.
The 'queen' war of Sheba in old Bible times,
The 'king' represents old King Sol.
She brought in a hundred young folks, gals an' boys,
To the king in his government hall.
They were all dressed alike, an' she axed the old boy
(She'd put up his wisdom as bosh)
Which war boys an' which gals. Old Sol said, 'By Joe,
How dirty their hands! Make 'em wash!'
An' then he showed Sheba the boys only washed
Their hands and a part o' their wrists,
While the gals jist went up to their elbows in suds.
Sheba weakened an' shook the king's fists.
Now the 'knave,' that's the devil, an' God, if ye please,
Jist keep his hands off'n poor Bill.
An' now, lads, jist drop on yer knees for a while
Till I draw, and perhaps I kin fill;
An' Havin' no Bible, I'll pray on the cards,
Fur I've showed ye they're all on the squar',
An' I think God'll cotton to all that I say,
If I'm only sincere in the pra'r.
Jist give him a corner, good Lord—not on stocks,
Fur I ain't such a durned fool as that,
To ax ye fur anything worldly fur Bill,
Kase ye'd put me up then fur a flat.
I'm lost on the rules o' yer game, but I'll ax
Fur a seat fur him back o' the throne,
And I'll bet my hull stack thet the boy'll behave
If yer angels jist lets him alone.
Thar's nothin' bad 'bout him unless he gets riled,
The boys'll all back me in that;

But if any one treads on his corns, then you bet

He'll fight at the drop o' the hat.

Jist don't let yer angels run over him, Lord;

Nor shut off all to once on his drink;

Break him in kinder gentle an' mild on the start,

An' he'll give ye no trouble, I think.

An' couldn't ye give him a pack of old cards

To amuse himself once in a while?

But I warn ye right hyar not to bet on his game,

Or he'll get right away with yer pile.

An' now, Lord, I hope that ye've tuck it all in,

An' listened to all thet I've said.

I know that my prayin' is just a bit thin,

But I've done all I kin for the dead.

An' I hope I hain't troubled yer lorship too much,

So I'll cheese it by axin' again

Thet ye won't let the 'knave' git his grip on poor Bill.

Thet's all, Lord—yours truly—Amen."

Thet's Rattlin' Joe's prayer, old pardners,

An'—what! You all snorin'? Say, Lew—

By thunder! I've talked every rascal to sleep,

So I guess I hed best turn in, too.

BUFFALO BILL AND YELLOW HAND

(By Hugh A. Wetmore,[6] Editor, People's Press)

You may talk' bout duels requirin' sand,

But the slickest I've seen in any land

Was Buffalo Bill's with Yellow Hand.

Thar wa'n't no seconds to split the pot,
No noospaper buncombe, none o' the rot
Your citified, dudefied duels 'as got.

Custer was not long into his shroud
When a bunch o' Cheyennes quit Red Cloud
To j'in the cranky Sittin' Bull crowd.

It looked somewhat like a crazy freak,
But Merritt's cavalry made a sneak
To head the reds at Big Bonnet Creek.

Bill an' some soljers was on one side,
For which Bill was actin' as chief an' guide,
When he git this call from the copper-hide:

"I know ye, Long Hair," yells Yellow Hand,
A-ridin' out from his pesky band
(A reg'lar bluff o' the Injun brand).

"You kill heap Injun, I kill heap white;
My people fear you by day or night;
Come, single-handed, an' you me fight."
"I'll go ye!" quick as a thunder-clap
Says Bill, who jest didn't care a rap;
"Stan' by, an' watch me an' the varmint scrap."

They was then 'bout fifty yards apart,
When without a hitch they made a start
Straight for each other, straight as a dart.

The plug which was rid by that Cheyenne
Was plugged by a slug from Bill's rifle, an'
Bill's hoss stumbled—now 'twas man to man!

Or man to devil, 'f you like that best.
But in them days, in the sure-enough West,
All stood as equals who stood the test.

They next at twenty steps blazed away,
An' had they ben equal both had ben clay,
But Bill was best, an' he win ther day.

It's a good shot to hit a Injun's heart,
For obvious reasons. Bill wa'n't scart,
An' found the center without a chart.

When they see Bill claim the tommyhawk
An' feathers an' beads wore by the gawk,
The other Injuns begin to squawk.

It all happened so dad-gasted quick,
The opposition must 'a felt sick;
But to my taste the duel was monstrous slick.

The other Injuns made for Bill,
But the soljers met 'em on the hill,
An' convinced 'em they had best keep still.

When Yellow Hand, Senior, heared the news
He offered ponies 'f Bill 'd let loose
Them trophies—but Bill he wa'n't no goose.

With this remark I'll close my letter:
"Thar's nought a Injun can do—no matter
What—but a white man can do it better."

CHAPTER XXI

From Prairie to Palace

In olden times, when a great leader of an "army with banners" was about to depart for a foreign country, bent on conquest, great was the outpouring of the people; loud sounded the drum and fife, and gay bunting flirted with the joyous breeze; salvos of artillery and great shouting rent the air, and songs were sung in honor of the mighty host decked in all the glittering panoply of war. All this in anticipation of the spoils of conquest to be brought back by the victor—human prisoners, coffers of gold, or blood-bought titles to war-won territory. How different in spirit, in action, and in expression was the assemblage that bade "God speed" to Gen. W. F. Cody on his departure as commander of the little heterogeneous army that sailed from Columbia's shores. Yet no leader ever started on a mission possible of such rich achievement; none ever embarked upon a voyage destined to be so thoroughly and completely a tour of conquest and of glory. His project included neither the shedding of blood, the conquest of territory, nor the enslaving of prisoners. His was the mission of peace; the awakening of the Old World to the contemplation of fresh truths in the picturesque history of the New. Columbus had told old Spain of the savages that greeted him on his landing upon the shores of the

58. The Prairie Home of Buffalo Bill.

New World; the Pilgrim Fathers had sent messages of their terrible struggles with their bitter Indian foes; but General Cody took with him great chieftains who called him friend. As evidences and traditions of the past, and for the delectation of peasant and prince "across the water," they danced their war-dance and sounded their war-whoop. But to the thoughtful it must have been a grander sight to see them, in the hours not devoted to duty, grouped in friendly conclave around the man who, appearing first among them as a foe, they had learned at last to understand and appreciate as their friend indeed. What a lesson to power, what an exemplification of the true spirit that moved the founders of the great American Republic! No compulsion was used by this hero of the plains to enforce the attendance of these bronzed warriors on his journeys; but trusting to his word alone as the guerdon of their safety, they willingly, gladly, went into a far country among scenes and people strangely new to them.

How appropriate that such an army, under such a leader, and on such a peaceful and glorious invasion, should carry into and plant in sturdy England, sunny France, historic Spain, mighty Germany, and poetic Italy the flag that proclaims to all the world that "all men are, and by right ought to be, free and equal."

Before following the Wild West of America in a mimic display across the seas into foreign lands, it may be well to here consider something that this wonderful man among men has done in the way of educating our own and other people into knowing what the Indian really is.

Glancing now over the history of the Indians, we recall how cruel has been their mode of warfare, and massacres innumerable rise up before us, from the red scene in the Wyoming Valley[1] to the death of the gallant Custer and his brave 300 boys in blue.[2]

Yet, reared upon the frontier, amid scenes of courage, and learning from actual experience all the redskin could become as a foe, Buffalo Bill yet accorded to them the rights that others would not allow.

If fighting them, he yet would befriend them in time of need and was never merciless to them in defeat.

Winning fame as scout, guide, and Indian fighter, Buffalo Bill was seized upon as a hero for the pen of the novelist, and volumes have been written founded upon his deeds of daring.

Then, like a meteor, he flashed upon the people of the East, impersonating upon the stage one other than himself, living over before the footlights his own life.

Men who have criticised Buffalo Bill as an actor forget wholly that he is the only man who is *playing himself.*

He plays his part as he knows it, as he has acted it upon many a field, acting naturally and without bombast and forced tragic effect.

Be the motive what it may, love of lucre or the gratification of pride, the fact still remains that in his delineation of border life Buffalo Bill educated the people to seeing the hated and ever-dreaded red men in another light.

He was their friend in peace, not their foe always because once upon their trail; and he brought the red man before the public in a way never witnessed before.

Buffalo Bill never was a man-killer, and there was nothing of bravado in his nature and not a tinge of the desperado.

Brought face to face with the stern reality that either his foe or himself must die, when it was in the discharge of duty or self-defense William Cody never quailed in the face of death, and acted, as his conscience dictated, for the right.

But his stage experience gave William Cody the thought of producing border life upon a grander scale than could be done within the walls of a theater, and from this sprang the Wild West exhibitions that have delighted the world.

Conceiving the idea of presenting border life as it was before vast audiences, he at once carried the thought into execution, and Buffalo Bill's Wild West became the center of attraction wherever it appeared.

After several times swinging around the circle in this country, the Wild West crossed the ocean in a steamship chartered to carry the vast aggregation, and landed upon the shores of England.

Behold the result! Opening in London before vast

audiences, the queen,[3] the Prince of Wales,[4] and other royal personages of high rank flocked to see the man and those he had brought with him into the very heart of the English metropolis.

There, upon the soil of the mother country, before tens of thousands of Britishers, the Wild West held sway for months, while the hero of the plains, the prairie boy, found himself honored by royalty, a welcome visitor across the threshold of palaces, fêted by men whose names were known the wide world over.

Bearing the stars and stripes in his hand, mounted upon his finest charger, Buffalo Bill saluted the queen, who rose, and bowed in salutation to the American flag, borne by so fit a representative of his country.

Nor did the triumphal march of the Wild West end here, for Buffalo Bill sought other lands to conquer, and bore the stars and stripes into France, Spain, Italy, Germany, Austria, Belgium, and elsewhere, presenting the American flag before more peoples than it had ever been seen by during its existence of a century.

Traveling through Europe with three railway trains of seventy-five cars, carrying over three hundred people, with the horses of our plains, the buffaloes, and wild steers, the Wild West was the observed of all observers, and crowned heads everywhere gave Buffalo Bill, his cowboys, and Indians a welcome, even his holiness the pope granting them an audience.

Living in their own camp, eating American food, the people of the Wild West did much to educate foreigners into a taste for American hams, corn meal, and other luxuries; and it was through the sending of so much corn to

Cody's commissary that Colonel Murphy[5] of the Department of Agriculture won the name of "Corn-meal Murphy."

From this explanatory sketch the reader can readily see how it was that Buffalo Bill went from the prairie to the palace.

For the benefit of those of my readers who are interested in the study of physiognomy, I submit the following physiognomical study of Colonel Cody by Prof. A. I. Oppenheim, B. P. A., of London:[6]

"The length from the opening of the ear to the outer corner of the eye shows great intellectual capacity and quickness of comprehension. The forehead is broad, square, and practical. The deep setting of the eyes in their sockets denotes great shrewdness and keenness of perception. The fullness under the eye means eloquence and the faculty of verbal expression. The downward projection of the outer corner of the eyebrows means contest—he never gives in. The unevenness of the hair of the eyebrows shows hastiness of temper and irritability when under restraint, but the straightness of the eyebrows themselves denotes truthfulness and sincerity. The height of the facial bone generally indicates great intensity and strong powers of physical endurance. The ridge in the center of the nose means relative defense, protection, quixotism, taking up other people's cudgels and fighting their battles for them. The thinness of the bridge of the nose denotes generosity and love of spending money. Colonel Cody might make many fortunes, but he would never succeed in amassing one. The length of the nostrils shows activity; the manner in which they dilate and curl, pride; and their size denotes courage and fearlessness. The transparency of the eyelids and the fineness of the eye-lashes is indicative of a keenly sensitive, sympathetic, and benevolent nature. Though a large-sized man, and a great warrior, his heart is as tender as a woman's. The angle of the jaw denotes determination and strength of purpose, but the narrowness of the lower part of the face suggests a complete absence of coarseness or brutality. The length of the throat shows a marvelous independence of spirit and love of fresh air and exercise. The wavy lines in the forehead mean hope and enthusiasm; the two perpendicular ones between the eyes, love of equity and justice."

To-day Buffalo Bill stands as a typical plainsman, the last of a race of men whose like will never be seen again.

The trackless wilderness, the arid deserts, mountains, and plains are to-day as an open book through the work of just such pioneers of the star of empire as is Buffalo Bill.

They have solved the mysteries of the unknown land of the setting sun as it was half a century ago, and then sprang into existence as educators, and having done their work well are awaiting the last call to that great terra incognita beyond the river of death.

Their like will never be seen again on this earth, for there are no new lands to explore.

As Columbus was the pilot across the seas to discover a new world, such heroes as Boone, Fremont, Crockett, Kit Carson, and last, but by no means least, Cody, were the guides to the New World of the mighty West, and their names will go down in history as

"Among the few, the immortal names
That were not born to die."

CHAPTER XXII

The Wild West at Sea

The Wild West visited many of the principal cities of this country, played a winter season in New Orleans, a summer season at Staten Island, and the winter of 1886–87 in Madison Square Garden in New York. But with the immortal bard who wrote "ambition grows with what it feeds on," Colonel Cody and Mr. Salsbury had an ambition to conquer other nations. The importance of the undertaking was fully realized, but nothing daunted by all that would have to be undergone to reach a foreign land and give exhibitions, the owners of the Wild West boldly made the venture.

The writer went abroad and arranged to play a season of six months in London, as an adjunct of the American exhibition. All arrangements being made, the Indians were secured, the representative types of the Sioux, Cheyennes, Kiowas, Pawnees, and Oglalas, and a number of prominent chiefs.

Having collected a company of more than two hundred men and animals, consisting of Indians, cowboys, Mexican riders, rifle-shots, buffaloes, Texas steers, burros, broncos, racing-horses, elk, bear, and an immense amount of paraphernalia such as tents, wagons, stage-coach, arms, ammunition, costumes, and all equipage necessary, the steamship State of Nebraska, Captain Braes, was chartered. The State of Nebraska, loaded with the Wild West, set sail from New York, Thursday, March 31, 1887. The piers were crowded with thousands of good friends who went down to wave adieux and to wish the Wild West a pleasant voyage and success.

As the steamship State of Nebraska pulled out of the dock the cowboy band played "The Girl I Left Behind Me" in a manner that suggested more reality than empty sentiment in the familiar air. Before starting on the trip a number of the Indians had expressed grave fears about trusting themselves upon the mighty ocean, fearing that a dreadful death would soon overtake them, and it required much persuasion at the last moment to induce them to go on board.

Red Shirt explained that these fears were caused by a superstitious belief that if a red man attempted to cross the ocean he would be seized of a malady that would first prostrate the victim and then slowly consume his flesh, until at length the very skin itself would drop from his bones, leaving nothing but the skeleton, and this even would never find burial. This weird belief was repeated by the chiefs of several tribes to the Indians who had joined the Wild West, so there was little reason for wonder that the poor children of the forest should hesitate to submit themselves to such an experiment. On the day following the departure from New York the Indians began to grow weary, and becoming seasick they were both treacherous and rebellious. Their fears were greatly intensified as even Red Shirt, the bravest of his people, looked anxiously toward the hereafter, and began to feel his flesh to see if it was really diminishing. The hopelessness stamped upon the faces of the Indians was pitiful to behold, and but for the endeavors of Buffalo Bill to cheer them up and relieve their forebodings there is no knowing what might have happened. But for two days the whole company, Indians, cowboys, and all, did little other active service than to feed the fishes.

On the third day all began to grow better, and the Indians were called into the salon and given a sermon by Buffalo Bill; Red Shirt also, having lost his anxiety, joining in the oratory.

After the seasickness was over, Mr. Salsbury, as singer and comedian, took an active part in amusing all on board. The seventh day of the voyage a fierce storm swept over the sea, and the ship was forced to lay to, and during its continuance the stock suffered greatly; but only one horse died on the trip. At last the steamship cast anchor off Gravesend, and a tug-boat loaded with custom-house and quarantine officers boarded to make the usual inspection. The English government, through its officials, extended every courtesy. A special permit was given for the animals to land, and the people started for the camp.

The arrival of the City of Nebraska had been watched for with great curiosity, as a number of yachts, tug-boats, and other craft surrounding it testified. A tug was soon seen flying the Stars and Stripes, and as it came nearer the strains of "The Star Spangled Banner," rendered by the band on her deck, floated across the water. As the welcome strains ended, the cowboy band on the Nebraska responded with "Yankee Doodle." When the tug came alongside, the company on board proved to be the directors of the American exhibition in London, with Lord Ronald Gower[1] heading a distinguished committee and representatives of the leading journals of England.

As Buffalo Bill landed with the committee three cheers were given, and cries rang out of "Welcome to old England," giving pleasing evidence of the public interest that had been awakened through the coming of the Wild West. A special train with saloon carriages was waiting to convey the party to London, and leaving behind them the old Kentish town, in an hour after they arrived at Victoria Station.

Entering the headquarters of the exhibition[2] Buffalo Bill and those who accompanied him found a bounteous repast set, and a generous welcome was accorded them. After brief social converse a visit was made to the grounds, where hundreds of busy workmen were hastening the completion of the arena, the grand-stand, and stabling for the cattle. When it is taken into consideration that these operations were dealing with an expenditure of over one hundred and thirty thousand dollars, the greatness of the enterprise can be understood. An arena of more than a third of a mile in circumference, flanked by a grand-stand filled with seats and boxes to accommodate 20,000 persons, sheltered stands for 10,000 more, the standing-room being 10,000, will give an idea of the size of the Wild West exhibition grounds.

The interest evinced by the British workmen in the coming of the Wild West people was as a straw indicating which way the wind blew, or intended to blow. On the following morning, when the tide was at its flood, the City of Nebraska steamed up the river, the trip being a pleasure to all on board. With the assistance of the horse-men, each looking after his own horse, the unloading was begun and carried on with a rapidity that astonished even the old dock-hands and officials. Through the courtesy of the custom-house people there was hardly a moment's delay in the debarkation; but although landing in London, the Wild West was still twelve miles away from its city camp. Loading the entire outfit on two trains, it was speedily delivered at the Midland Railway Depot adjoining the grounds, and by 4 o'clock on the same afternoon the horses and other animals had been stabled, watered, and fed, and the camp equipage and bedding distributed. The camp cooks were preparing the evening meal, tents were going up, stoves being erected, tables spread and set in the open air, tepees erected, and by six o'clock a perfect canvas city had sprung up in the heart of West End London.

Upon the flag-staff the starry banner had been run up and was floating in the breeze, and the cowboy band rendering the national airs of America, amid the shouts and cheers of thousands who lined the walls, streets, and housetops of the surrounding neighborhood. This was most gratifying to the new-comers, and in answer to the hearty plaudits of the English, Colonel Cody ordered the band to play "God Save the Queen," and the Wild West was at home in London.

The first camp meal being necessarily eaten in full view of the crowd, the dining-tents not being ready, was a novel sight to them, from the motley population of Indians, cowboys, scouts, Mexicans, etc. The meal was finished by 7 o'clock, and by 9 o'clock the little camp was complete, and its tired occupants, men, women, and children, were reposing more snugly, safely, and peacefully than they had done in many weeks.

Trivial as these details may appear at first sight, the rapidity with which the Wild West had transported its materials from dock to depot, and depot to ground, had an immense effect upon the people of London. A number of notable visitors present, especially the representatives of the press, expressed great astonishment at the enterprise of the Americans, and communicated that feeling throughout London.

"The Yankees mean business" was the expression heard upon all sides. As the Wild West was not to open its exhibition for several days after its arrival, Colonel Cody and Mr. Salsbury had an opportunity of meeting many distinguished persons in England, who called upon them, and who afterward proved most friendly and hospitable. Among these prominent persons was Mr. Henry Irving,[3] who had witnessed the Wild West performance at Staten Island, and paved the way in a great measure for its success in London by speaking in the kindest terms to a representative of the great dramatic organ, *The Era.* It may not be amiss to here quote his remarks. Mr. Irving said in *The Era:*

"I saw an entertainment in New York, the like of which I had never seen before, which impressed me immensely. It is coming to London. It is an entertainment in which the whole of the most interesting episodes of life on the extreme frontier of civilization in America are represented with the most graphic vividness and scrupulous detail. You have real cowboys with bucking horses, real buffaloes, and great hordes of steers, which are lassoed and stampeded in the most realistic fashion imaginable. Then there are real Indians, who execute attacks upon coaches driven at full speed. No one can exaggerate the extreme excitement and 'go' of the whole performance. It is simply immense, and I venture to predict that when it comes to London it will take the town by storm."

Among other early callers upon the Wild West, and who gave their influence and friendly aid in London, were genial John L. Toole,[4] Miss Ellen Terry,[5] Mr. Justin Mc-Carthy,[6] United States Minister Phelps,[7] Consul-General Gov. Thomas Waller,[8] Deputy Consul Moffat,[9] Mr. Henry Labouchère, M. P.,[10] Miss Mary Anderson,[11] Mrs. Brown-Potter,[12] Mr. Charles Wyndham,[13] Lord Ronald Gower, Sir Cunliffe Owen,[14] Lord Henry Paget,[15] Lord Charles Beresford,[16] the Grand Duke Michael of Russia,[17] Lady Monckton,[18] Sir Francis Knollys private secretary to the Prince of Wales;[19] Colonel Clarke,[20] Colonel Montague,[21] Lady Alice Bertie[22] (whom the Indians afterward named the "Sunshine of the Camp"), Lord Strathmore,[23] Lord Windsor,[24] Lady Randolph Churchill,[25] Mrs. John W. Mackay,[26] and a host of distinguished American residents in London, who also visited the camp before the regular opening of the Wild West, and by their expressions of friendship gave encouragement for success in the future.

The sight of the Indians, cowboys, American girls, and Mexicans, with Buffalo Bill as chief, was most attractive to Londoners, while the English love of horsemanship, feats of skill, and fondness for sports presaged an appreciative community. The press was also most generous, the column of the papers teeming daily with information so eulogistic that the Wild Westerners were afraid they would never be able to come up to expectations.

Fifty large scrap-books, filled to repletion with press notices, now form a conspicuous part of Colonel Cody's library at Scout's-Rest Ranch.[27] The London *Illustrated News*, in connection with two pages of illustration, is drawn upon for the following extract:

"It is certainly a novel idea for one nation to give an exhibition devoted exclusively to its own frontier history, or the story enacted by genuine characters of the dangers and hardships of its settlement, upon the soil of another country 3,000 miles away. Yet this is exactly what the Americans will do this year in London, and it is an idea worthy of that thorough-going and enterprising people. We frankly and gladly allow that there is a natural and sentimental view of the design which will go far to obtain for it a hearty welcome in England. The progress of the United States, now the largest community of the English race on the face of the earth, though not in political union with Great Britain, yet intimately connected with us by social sympathies; by a common language and literature; by ancestral traditions and many centuries of common history; by much remaining similarity of civil institutions, laws, morals, and manners; by the same forms of religions; by the same attachments to the principles of order and freedom, and by the mutual interchange of benefits in a vast commerce, and in the materials and sustenance of their staple industries, is a proper subject of congratulation; for the popular mind in the United Kingdom does not regard, and will never be taught to regard, what are styled 'imperial' interests—those of mere political dominion—as equally valuable with the habit and ideas as domestic life of the aggregate of human families belonging to our own race. The greater numerical proportion of these, already exceeding sixty millions, are inhabitants of the great American Republic, while the English-speaking subjects of Queen Victoria number a little above forty-five millions, including those in Canada and Australasia and scattered among the colonial dependencies of this realm. It would be unnatural to deny ourselves the indulgence of a just gratification in seeing what men of our own blood, men of our own mind and disposition in all essential respects, though tempered and sharpened by more stimulating conditions, with some wider opportunities for exertion, have achieved in raising a wonderful fabric of modern civilization, and bringing it to the highest prosperity, across the whole breadth of the Western Continent, from the Atlantic to the Pacific Ocean. We feel sure that this sentiment will prevail in the hearts of hundreds of thousands of visitors to Buffalo Bill's American camp, about to be opened at the west end of London; and we take it kindly of the great kindred people of the United States that they now send such a magnificent representation to the motherland, determined to take some part in celebrating the jubilee of her majesty the queen,[28] who is the political representative of the people of Great Britain and Ireland."

The tone of this article strikes the same chord as the whole of the comments of the English press. It divested the Wild West of its attributes as an entertainment simply, and treated the visit as an event of first-class international importance, and a link between the affections of the two kindred nations such as had never before been forged.

59. European Celebrities—Visitors at the Wild West, London.

CHAPTER XXIII

A Royal Welcome

While in the midst of extensive preparations for their opening, the proprietors of the Wild West received an intimation
that the ex-premier, the Rt. Hon. W. E. Gladstone, M. P.,[1]
proposed honoring them with a preliminary call. The date
fixed for the visit was the 25th of April, and shortly after 1
o'clock p.m. on that day the distinguished visitor arrived
at Earl's Court with Mrs. Gladstone, and accompanied by
the Marquis of Lorne (husband of the Princess Louise),
attended by Lord Ronald Gower and Mr. Waller (Consul-
General of the United States), escorted by Nate Salsbury.

The cowboy band welcomed the visitors with the strains
of "Yankee Doodle," and they were presently introduced
to Colonel Cody, who in turn presented to them the den-
izens of the encampment. The Grand Old Man was soon
engaged in conversation with Red Shirt, to whom Colonel Cody had explained that Mr. Gladstone was one of the
great white chiefs of England. Red Shirt was much puzzled by Mr. Gladstone's inquiring, through an interpreter, if he thought the Englishman looked enough like the
American for him to believe that they were kinsmen and
brothers. Red Shirt created quite a laugh by replying that
"he wasn't quite sure about that." It would be hard to picture the astonishment of the visitors when the Indians, in

60. A Redskin Village in a Paleface City—London.

full war-paint, riding their swift horses, dashed into the
arena from an ambuscade, and the enthusiasm grew immense when Colonel Cody placed himself at the head of
the whole body and wheeled them into line for a general salute. It was a real treat to see the ex-premier enjoying himself like a veritable school-boy when the lasso, the
feats of shooting, and the bucking-horses were introduced;
and when the American cowboys tackled the incorrigi-
ble bucking-horses he sometimes cheered the animal and
sometimes the man. At the conclusion of the exhibition
Mr. Gladstone expressed himself as having been greatly
entertained and interested, and spoke in warm and affect-
ing terms of the instrumental good work the Wild West
had come to do. In a brilliant little speech he proposed

"success to the Wild West Show," which aroused the enthusiasm of all present. His demeanor on this and other occasions when he met the Americans made clear to them the reason of the fascination he exercises over the masses of his countrymen.

Then for Colonel Cody commenced a long series of invitations to breakfasts, dinners, luncheons, midnight layouts, and other attentions by which London society delights to honor a distinguished foreigner. In addition to many receptions tendered him, he was made an honorary member of most of the best clubs, notably the Reform Club,[2] where he was presented to the Prince of Wales, the Duke of Cambridge,[3] and many prominent gentlemen. He was afterward a guest at a civic lunch at the Mansion House, with the Lord Mayor and Lady Mayoress;[4] a dinner at the Beaufort Club,[5] where that fine sportsman the Duke of Beaufort[6] occupied the chair; and a memorable evening at the Savage Club,[7] with Mr. Wilson Barrett[8] (who had just returned from America) presiding, and an attendance comprising such great spirits as Mr. Henry Irving, John L. Toole, and others great in literary, artistic, and histrionic London. At the United Arts Club[9] he was entertained by the Duke of Teck,[10] and at the St. George's Club[11] by Lord Bruce,[12] Lord Wolmer,[13] Lord Lymington,[14] Mr. Christopher Sykes,[15] Mr. Herbert Gladstone,[16] and others. Subsequently he dined at Mr. Irving's, Lady McGregor's,[17] Lady Tenterden's,[18] Mrs. Charles Mathews'[19] (widow of the great actor), Mrs. J. W. Mackay's, Lord Randolph and Lady Churchill's, Edmund Yates',[20] and at Great Marlow.[21] These are but a very few of the many invitations he was called upon to accept during this visit. When Mr. and Mrs.

Labouchère gave their grand garden production of "A Midsummer Night's Dream" Colonel Cody was an honored guest. He also accompanied Lord Charles Beresford in the Coaching Club Parade in Hyde Park,[22] and was prevented by press of business from accepting an invitation to a mount with the Honorable Artillery Company of London[23] (the oldest volunteer in the kingdom), in the parade in honor of her majesty the queen's birthday.

Considering the fact that the Indians were all new from the Pine Ridge Agency[24] and had never seen the exhibition, and that 100 of the ponies came direct from the plains of Texas and had never been ridden or shot over, it is a wonder how Colonel Cody, with these social demands made upon his time, succeeded in forming so good an exhibition on the opening day.

During all this fashionable hurly-burly Colonel Cody received the following letter:

Marlborough House,

Pall Mall, S. W., April 26, 1887

Dear Sir: I am desired by the Prince of Wales to thank you for your invitation. His royal highness is anxious I should see you with reference to it. Perhaps, therefore, you would kindly make it convenient to call at Marlborough House.

Would it suit you to call at 11.30 or 5 o'clock either tomorrow (Wednesday) or Thursday? I am, dear sir,

Yours faithfully,
(Signed) Francis Knollys,
Private Secretary

This resulted in an arrangement to give a special and exclusive performance for H.R.H. the Prince and Princess of Wales, although everything was still incomplete, the track unfinished, and spoiled by rainy weather and the hauling on of vast timbers. The ground was in unspeakably bad condition. The Prince of Wales being busily occupied in arranging matters for the queen's jubilee had but limited latitude in regard to time, so postponement was out of the question. The royal box was handsomely rigged out with American and English flags, and the party conducted into the precincts of the Wild West was a strong one numerically as well as in point of exalted rank: The Prince and Princess of Wales, with their three daughters, Princesses Louise, Victoria, and Maud, led the way;[25] then came the Princess Louise and her husband, the Marquis of Lorne;[26] the Duke of Cambridge; H. S. H. of Teck and his son;[27] the Comtesse de Paris;[28] the Crown Prince of Denmark;[29] followed by Lady Suffield[30] and Miss Knollys, Lady Cole,[31] Colonel Clarke, Lord Edward Somerset,[32] and other high-placed attendants on the assembled royalties.

Colonel Cody was introduced by the Prince of Wales to the princess, and introductions to the other exalted personages followed, in which Nate Salsbury and the writer were included. This was one of many meetings between his royal highness and Colonel Cody, and before leaving London the prince presented to the colonel a very handsome diamond copy of his crest—the three ostrich feathers mounted in gems and gold—as a breastpin.

When the prince gave the signal the Indians, yelling like fiends, galloped out from their ambuscade and swept round the enclosure like a whirlwind. The effect was instantaneous and electric. The prince rose from his seat and leaned eagerly over the front of the box, and the whole party seemed thrilled at the spectacle. From that moment everything was all right; everybody was in capital form and the whole thing went off grandly. At the finish an amusing incident occurred. Our lady shots, on being presented, cordially offered to shake hands with the princess. Be it known that feminine royalty offers the left hand, back uppermost, which the person presented is expected to reverently lift with the finger-tips and to salute with the lips. However, the princess got over the difficulty by taking their proffered hands and shaking them heartily.

Then followed an inspection of the Indian camp and a talk between the prince and Red Shirt. His royal highness expressed through the interpreter his great delight at what he had seen, and the princess personally offered him a welcome to England. "Tell the great chief's wife," said Red Shirt with much dignity, "that it gladdens my heart to hear her words of welcome." While the ladies of the suite were petting John Nelson's half-breed papoose,[33] the prince visited Colonel Cody's tent and while there seemed much interested in the gold-mounted sword presented to Colonel Cody by the generals of the United States Army. Despite the muddy state of the ground, the prince and his party made an inspection of the stables, where 200 bronco horses and other animals were quartered. He particularly gratified Colonel Cody by demanding a full, true, and particular history of Old Charlie—then in his twenty-first year—who had carried his owner through so much arduous work on the plains and who once bore him over a flight of 100 miles in nine hours and forty minutes when chased by hostile Indians.

61. Royal Visitors to the Wild West, London.

At seven o'clock the royal visit, and our fist full performance in England, terminated by the prince presenting the contents of his cigarette-case to Red Shirt.

A walk around the principal streets of London at this time would have shown how, by anticipation, the Wild West had "caught on" to the popular imagination. The windows of the London bookseller were full of editions of Fenimore Cooper's novels, "The Pathfinder," "The Deerslayer," "The Last of the Mohicans," "Leather Stocking,"[34] and, in short, all that series of delightful romances which have placed the name of the American novelist on the same level with that of Sir Walter Scott.[35] It was a real revival of trade for the booksellers, who sold thousands of volumes of Cooper, where twenty years before they had sold them in dozens, while Colonel Prentiss Ingraham's[36] realistic "Border Romances of Buffalo Bill" had a tremendous sale. There is no doubt that the visit of the Wild West to England set the population of the British Islands to reading, thinking, and talking about their American kinsmen to an extent theretofore unknown. It taught them to know more of the mighty nation beyond the Atlantic, and consequently to esteem it better than at any time within the limits of modern history.

The Wild West having made its début in London, the following comment of the *Times* and letters from General Sherman will be appreciated by the reader:

The American exhibition, which has attracted all the town to West Brompton for the last few months, was brought yesterday to an appropriate and dignified close. A meeting of representative Englishmen and Americans was held, under the presidency of Lord Lorne, in support of the movement for establishing a Court of Arbitration for the settlement of disputes between this country and the United States. At first sight it might seem to be a far cry from the Wild West to an International Court. Yet the connection is not really very remote. Exhibitions of American products and scenes from the wilder phases of American life certainly tend, in some degree at least, to bring America nearer to England. They are partly cause and partly effect. They are the effect of increased and increasing intercourse between the two countries, and they tend to promote a still more intimate understanding. Those who went to be amused often stayed to be instructed. The Wild West was irresistible. Colonel Cody suddenly found himself the hero of the London season. Notwithstanding his daily engagements and his punctual fulfillment of them, he found time to go everywhere, to see everything, and to be seen by all the world. All London contributed to his triumph, and now the close of his show is selected as the occasion for promoting a great international movement, with Mr. Bright,[37] Lord Granville,[38] Lord Wolseley,[39] and Lord Lorne for it sponsors. Civilization itself consents to march onward in the train of "Buffalo Bill." Colonel Cody can achieve no greater triumph than this, even if he some day realizes the design attributed to him of running the Wild West show within the classic precincts of the Coliseum at Rome.

This association of the cause of international arbitration with the fortunes of the American Wild West is not without its grotesque aspects. But it has a serious import, nevertheless. After all, the Americans and the English are one stock. Nothing that is American comes altogether amiss to an Englishman. We are apt to think that American life is not picturesque. We have been shown one of its most picturesque aspects. It is true that Red Shirt would be as unusual a phenomenon in Broadway as in Cheapside. But the Wild West, for all that, is racy of the American soil. We can easily imagine Wall Street for ourselves; we need to be shown the cowboys of Colorado. Hence it is no paradox to say that Colonel Cody has done his part in bringing America and England nearer together.—Editorial from the *London Times*, November 1, 1887.

The following letters were received by Buffalo Bill from Gen. W. T. Sherman soon after the opening of the Wild West in London.

Fifth Avenue Hotel,

New York, May 8, 1887

Dear Cody: I was much pleased to receive your dispatch of May 5th announcing the opening of the Wild West in old London, and that your first performance was graced by the presence of the Prince and Princess of Wales. I had penned a short answer to go by cable, but it fell so far short of my thoughts that I tore it up and preferred the old-fashioned letter, which I am sure you can afford to await. After your departure in the State of Nebraska I was impatient until the cable announced your safe arrival in the Thames, without the loss of a man or animal during the voyage. Since that time our papers have kept us well "posted," and I assure you that no one of your host of friends on this side of the water was more pleased to hear of your safe arrival and of your first exhibition than myself. I had, in 1872, the honor and great pleasure of meeting the Prince of Wales and the Princess Alexandra on board our fleet in Southampton Bay, and was struck by the manly, frank character of the prince, and the extreme beauty and grace of the princess. The simple fact that they honored your opening exhibition assures us all that the English people will not construe your party as a show, but a palpable illustration of the men and qualities which have enabled the United States to subdue the 2,000 miles of our wild West continent, and make it the home of civilization. You and I remember the time when we needed a strong military escort to go from Fort Riley in Kansas to Fort Kearny on the Platte; when emigrants to Colorado went armed and organized as soldiers, where now the old and young, rich and poor, sweep across the plains in palace cars with as much comfort as on a ride from London to Edinburgh. Your exhibition better illustrates the method by which this was accomplished than a thousand volumes of printer matter. The English people always have, and I hope always will love pluck and endurance. You have exhibited both, and in nothing more than your present venture, and I assure you that you have my best wishes for success in your undertaking.

Sincerely Your Friend,

W. T. Sherman.

Fifth Avenue Hotel,

New York, June 29, 1887.

Hon. Wm. F. Cody,

London, England

Dear Cody:

* * * In common with all your countrymen, I want to let you know that I am not only gratified, but proud of your management and general behavior; so far as I can make out, you have been modest, graceful, and dignified in all you have done to illustrate the history of civilization on this continent during the past century.

I am especially pleased with the graceful and pretty compliment paid you by the Princess of Wales, who rode in the Deadwood coach while it was attacked by the Indians and rescued by the cowboys. Such things did occur in our days, and may never again.

As near as I can estimate, there were *in 1865 about nine and a half millions of buffaloes* on the plains between the Missouri River and the Rocky Mountains. All are now gone—killed for their meat, their skins and bones.

This seems like desecration, cruelty, and murder, yet they have been replaced by twice as many *neat* cattle. At that date there were about 165,000 *Pawnees, Sioux, Cheyennes, Kiowas, and Arapahoes*, who depended on these buffaloes for their yearly food. They, too, are gone, and have been replaced by twice or thrice as many white men and women, who have made the earth to blossom as the rose, and who can be counted, taxed, and governed by the laws of nature and civilization. This change has been salutary, and will go on to the end. You have caught one epoch of the world's history, have illustrated it in the very heart of the modern world—London—and I want you to feel that on this side the water we appreciate it.

This drama must end; days, years, and centuries

follow fast; even the drama of civilization must have an end.

All I aim to accomplish on this sheet of paper is to assure you that I fully recognize your work and that the presence of the queen, the beautiful Princess of Wales, the prince, and British public, are marks of favor which reflect back on America sparks of light which illuminate many a house and cabin in the land where once *you guided me honestly and faithfully in 1865–66 from Fort Riley to Kearney in Kansas and Nebraska.*

Sincerely your friend,

W. T. Sherman

CHAPTER XXIV

A Visit from Queen Victoria

"By command of her majesty the queen."—It must be understood that the queen never requests, desires, or invites even her own prime minister, to her own dinner-tables, but "commands" invariably. A special performance was given by the Wild West, the understanding being that he majesty and suite would take a private view of the performance. The queen, ever since the death of her husband nearly thirty years ago, has cherished an invincible objection to appearing before great assemblages of her subjects. She visits her parliament seldom, the theaters never. Her latest knowledge of her greatest actors and actresses has been gained from private performances at Windsor, whither they have been "commanded" to entertain her, and that at very infrequent intervals. But, as with Mahomet and the mountain, the Wild West was altogether too colossal to take to Windsor, and so the queen came to the Wild West—an honor which was unique and unexampled in its character. When this visit was announced the public would hardly believe it, and if bets had been made at the clubs, the odds on a rank outsider in the Derby would have been nothing to the amount that would have been bet that it was a Yankee hoax. The news that her majesty would arrive at 5 o'clock and would require to see everything in an hour was in the nature of an astounding surprise to the management of the Wild West; but they determined to do the very best in their power, and that settled it. A dais for her majesty was erected and a box specially constructed draped with crimson velvet and decorated with orchids, leaving plenty of accommodation for the attendant noblemen, and all was made as bright and cheerful as possible.

With royal punctuality the sovereign lady and her suite rolled up in their carriages, drove around the arena in state, and dismounted at the entrance to the box. The august company included, besides her majesty, their royal highnesses Prince and Princess of Battenberg,[1] the Marquis of Lorne, the dowager Duchess of Atholl,[2] and the Hon. Ethel Cadogan,[3] Sir Henry and Lady Ponsonby,[4] Gen. Lynedoch Gardiner,[5] Col. Sir Henry Ewart,[6] Lord Ronald Gower, and a collection of uniformed celebrities and brilliantly attired fair ladies, who formed a veritable parterre of living flowers around the temporary throne.

During the introduction of the performers of the exhibition a remarkable incident occurred which is worthy of being specially recorded. As usual in the entertainment the American flag, carried by a graceful, well-mounted horseman, was introduced, with the statement that it was "an emblem of peace and friendship to all the world." As the standard-bearer, who on this occasion was Col. William F. Cody himself, waved the proud emblem above his head, her majesty rose from her seat and bowed deeply and impressively toward the banner. The whole court party rose, the ladies bowed, the general present saluted, and the English noblemen took off their hats. Then there arose from the company such a genuine, heart-stirring American yell as seemed to shake the sky. It was a great event. For the first time in history since the Declaration of Independence a sovereign of Great Britain had saluted the star-spangled banner—and that banner was carried by Buffalo Bill. It was an outward and visible sign of the extinction of that mutual prejudice, sometimes almost amounting to race hatred, that had severed the two nations from the times of Washington and George III to the present day. The hatchet was buried at last, and the Wild West had been at the funeral.

The queen not only abandoned her original intention of remaining to see only the first acts, but saw the whole thing through, and wound up with a "command" that Buffalo Bill should be presented to her, and her compliments were deliberate and unmeasured. Mr. Nate Salsbury and Chief Red Shirt, the latter gorgeous in his war paint and splendid feather trappings, were also presented. The chief's proud bearing seemed to take with the royal party immensely, and when he quietly declared that "he had come a long way to see her majesty, and felt glad," and strolled abruptly away, the queen smiled appreciatively, as one who would say, "I know a real duke when I see him." After inspecting the papooses the queen's visit came to an end, with a last "command," expressed through Sir Henry Ponsonby, that a record of all she had seen should be sent on to Windsor.

While receiving generous attention from the most prominent English people, Colonel Cody was by no means neglected by his own countrymen, many of whom were frequent visitors to the Wild West Show, and added by their presence and influence much to the popularity of both the show and Colonel Cody himself. Hon. James G. Blaine,[7] accompanied by his family, spent several hours in Colonel Cody's tent, and was a frequent visitor to the show. So also were Hon. Joseph Pulitzer,[8] Chauncey M. Depew,[9] Lawrence Jerome,[10] Murat Halstead,[11] General Hawley,[12] Simon Cameron,[13] and many other distinguished Americans.

When the Hon. James G. Blaine visited the Wild West in London, accompanied by his wife and daughters, his carriage was driven through the royal gate to the grounds, and he was received by the English people as though he had been one of the royal highnesses.

The Wild West band played the "Star Spangled Banner," the air so loved by all true Americans being received by the English audience rising, and standing while Mr. Blaine and party alighted from their carriage and were escorted to the box set aside for them.

When the distinguished party were seated the band played "Way Down in Maine" and "Yankee Doodle." After the entertainment, when Mr. Blaine took his departure, he was given three rousing cheers by the English, a tribute which he gracefully acknowledged and appreciated fully.

So many prominent Americans, acquaintances of Colonel Cody, were in London at that time that it was determined to give them a novel entertainment that would serve the double purpose of regaling their appetites while affording an illustration of the wild habits of many Indian tribes. In accordance with this resolution Gen. Simon Cameron—as the guest of honor—and about one hundred other Americans, including those named above, were invited to a rib-roast breakfast prepared by the Indians after the manner of their cooking when in their native homes.

The large dining-tent was gorgeously festooned and decorated for the occasion, and all the invited guests responded to the summons and arrived by 9 o'clock in the morning. Before the tent a fire had been made, around which were grouped a number of Indian cooks. A hole had been dug in the ground and in this a great bed of coals was now made, over which was set a wooden tripod from which was suspended several ribs of beef. An Indian noted for his skill as a rib-roaster attended to the cooking by gently moving the meat over the hot coals for nearly half an hour, when it was removed to the quarters and there jointed ready to be served. The guests were much interested in the process of cooking and were equally anxious to sample the product of Indian culinary art. The whole of the Indian tribes in camp breakfasted with the visitors, squatting on straw at the end of the long dining-tent. Some dozen ribs were cooked and eaten in this primitive fashion, civilized and savage methods of eating confronting each other. The thoroughly typical breakfast over, excellent speeches, chiefly of a humorous nature, were made by the honored guest General Cameron, Colonel Cody, and others of the party. The breakfast was supplemented by an Indian dance, and thus ended the unique entertainment.

On the 20th of June a special morning exhibition of the Wild West was, by further "command" from her majesty, given to the kingly and princely guests of Queen Victoria upon the occasion of her jubilee. This was the third entertainment given to royalty in private, and surely never before in the history of the world had such a gathering honored a public entertainment. The gathering of personages consisted of the King of Denmark,[14] the King of Saxony,[15] the King and Queen of the Belgians[16] and the King of Greece,[17] the Crown Prince of Austria,[18] the Prince and Princess of Saxe-Meiningen,[19] the Crown Prince and Princess of Germany,[20] the Crown Prince of Sweden and Norway,[21] the Princess Victoria of Prussia,[22] the Duke of Sparta,[23] the Grand Duke Michael of Russia,[24] Prince George of Greece,[25] Prince Louis of Baden,[26] and last, but not least, the Prince and Princess of Wales with their family, besides a great host of lords and ladies innumerable.

A peculiar circumstance of the visit of Queen Victoria to the Wild West exhibition may be mentioned here. It was at the time of the queen's jubilee, and there had gathered in London the largest and grandest assemblage of royalty ever before known in the world's history, to do honor to the queen's reign of half a century.

It was the day before her majesty had appointed to meet all the royal personages that she came face to face with them, all gathered together to do honor to the American entertainment of Buffalo Bill's Wild West; an honor indeed to the famous scout, and which was commented upon by the Prince of Wales, who referred to the great number of distinguished people present, and that it was made possible by the fact that peace reigned upon earth with all nations who were there represented.

On this occasion the good old Deadwood coach, "baptized in fire and blood" so repeatedly on the plains, had the honor of carrying on its time-honored timbers four kings and the Prince of Wales. This elicited from his royal highness the remark to Colonel Cody, "Colonel, you never held four kings like these before," to which Colonel Cody promptly and aptly replied, "I've held four kings, but four kings and the Prince of Wales makes a royal flush, such as no man ever held before." At this the prince laughed heartily.

After this interesting gathering Colonel Cody received from Marlborough House the following letter of thanks:

Marlborough House, Pall Mall, S.W.

Dear Sir: Lieut.-Gen. Sir Dighton Probyn,[27] comptroller and treasurer of the Prince of Wales's household, presents his compliments to Colonel Cody, and is directed by his royal highness to forward him the accompanying pin as a souvenir of the performance of the Wild West which Colonel Cody gave before the Prince and Princess of Wales, the kings of Denmark, Belgium, Greece, and Saxony, and other royal guests, on Monday last, to all of whom, the prince desires Sir Dighton Probyn to say, the entertainment gave great satisfaction.

London, June 22, 1887

This souvenir pin bore the crest and motto of the Prince of Wales, and readers will perhaps be familiar with the story of how this crest and motto (*Ich dien*, "I serve") were wrested from the King of Bohemia at Cressy by the Black Prince, son of Edward III, of England.[28]

Few men have had such honors bestowed upon them as has Buffalo Bill, for he can also point with pride to a superb diamond crest presented him by Queen Victoria, the elegant pin from the Prince of Wales, while from Prince George of Prussia[29] he received a magnificent gold tankard of mosaic pattern.

Other royal personages have also made him the recipient of many costly gifts, while persons in private life have shown their appreciation of the record he has won in many ways.

The prince and princess and their sons and daughters were frequent visitors to the Wild West during its stay in London. Upon one occasion his royal highness determined to try the novel sensation of a ride in the old stage, and notwithstanding some objection on the part of her royal husband, the princess also booked for inside passage and took it smilingly, seeming highly delighted with the experience. On one occasion the royal lady startled the managers of the show by an intimation that she would that evening attend the performance *incognito*. The manager whose duty it was to receive her declared himself in a "middling tight fix" as to where and how to seat her. Upon her arrival, in answer to the question if she desired any particular position, the lady replied, "Certainly, yes. Put me immediately among the people. I like the people." The manager, with great thoughtfulness, ushered her into one of the press boxes, with Colonel Montague, Mrs. Clark, and her brother the Prince of Denmark. Later, to his surprise, several of the newspaper boys came into the adjoining box, and in order to avert the latter's suspicion of who the lady occupant of the box was, the manager was compelled to address the royal lady and her escort as "Colonel and Mrs. Jones, friends of mine from Texas." The princess took the joke with becoming gravity, and

afterward confessed the evening was one of the pleasan-
test and funniest she had ever spent in her life.

And so, amid the innumerable social junketings, roast-
ings, and courtly functions, added to hard work, the London
experiences of the Wild West drew to a successful close.

CHAPTER XXV

The Home Trail

From London the Wild West visited Birmingham, where it occupied the Aston Lower Grounds; thence to Manchester—"Cottonopolis," as it is endearingly called by its inhabitants—where the winter season was opened. In the short space of two months the largest theater ever seen in the world was here erected by an enterprising firm of Manchester builders, together with a commodious building attached to it for the accommodation of the troupe, whose tents and tepees were erected under its shelter. The whole of the structure was comfortably heated by steam and illuminated by electric light. This building was built on the great race-course, where several times in the course of each year it is not uncommon for 80,000 or 100,000 persons to assemble; and the buildings in which Ormonde, Ben d'Or, Robert the Devil, and a thousand other world-famed equine wonders had taken their rest and refreshment, were now appropriated to the comfort of the broncos, mustangs, and other four-footed coadjutors of the Wild West.

The first performance given in Manchester was complimentary, and the entire beauty, rank, and fashion of Manchester and the surrounding towns were invited guests. The mayors, town councils, corporation officials, prominent merchants and manufacturers, bishops and clergy of all denominations, and an able-bodied horde of pressmen came down in their thousands. From Liverpool, across country through Leeds and York to Hull and New Castle, and from Carlisle, as far south as Birmingham, everybody of consequence was present, and the immense building was filled to its utmost capacity. The consequence was that from the opening day, and despite the dreary winter weather, the well-lighted, well-warmed "Temple of Buffalo Bill and Thespis"[1]—as somebody called it—was constantly crowded with pleasure-seeking throngs. Incidentally it may be mentioned that the scores of requisitions from the heads of schools and charitable institutions for reduced rates for "their little waifs," was always met by the management of the Wild West with a courteous invitation for the little ones to attend the Wednesday afternoon performances free of charge. During their stay in "Cottonopolis" the members of the Wild West were welcomed with the same ungrudging and overwhelming hospitality that had marked their visit to the capital. While here Colonel Cody was publicly presented with a magnificent rifle by the artistic, dramatic, and literary gentlemen of Manchester, and the event having got wind in London, the élite of the metropolitan *literati*, headed by Sir Somers Vine[2] and including representatives of all the great American journals, secured a special train and ran up to Manchester some hundred strong to grace the ceremony with their presence. The presentation took place in the arena, and afterward Colonel Cody invited the whole crowd of local celebrities and London visitors to a regular camp dinner, with fried oysters, Boston pork and beans, Maryland chicken, and other American dishes, and a real Indian "rib-roast" as the *piece de resistance*. The banquet was held in the race-course pavilion. Among the guests were the Mayor of Salford, a number of civil dignitaries from both Manchester and the neighboring borough, United States Consul Moffat of London and Consul Hale[3] of Manchester, the latter of whom made the speech of the evening. This dinner was certainly an entirely original lay-out to the visitors, and the comments of the English guests upon the novel and to them outlandish fare they were consuming were highly amusing to the American members of the party. To the Englishmen corn-cake, hominy, and other American *fixings* were a complete revelation, and the rib-roast, served in tin platters and eaten in the fingers, without knives or forks, was a source of huge wonderment. The American flag was rarely ever toasted more heartily by Englishmen than on that occasion, and for a week afterward the press of the country were dilating on the strange and savage doings at the Wild West camp.

The afternoon of Good Friday, the consent of the directors of the Manchester race-track having been obtained, a series of open-air horse races and athletic sports was performed by the members of the company—red and white—which included hurdle-races, bareback horsemanship, etc. Notwithstanding very inclement weather during the earlier part of the day, an attendance of nearly 30,000 was recorded, and weather cleared up and kept fine during the progress of the sports.

During this visit to Manchester the Freemasons of the district treated Colonel Cody with marked hospitality, and he was a frequent visitor at their lodges. A mark of especial honor from this occult and powerful body was a public presentation to him of a magnificent gold watch in the name of the Freemasons of England. The season in Manchester was a grand success in every way, and the people had begun to regard the institution as a permanency among them; but their engagements in the land of the stars and stripes were as fixed and unalterable as the laws of the Medes and Persians, and on Monday evening, May 1st, was given the last indoor representation in Manchester. The occasion was a perfect ovation. On Tuesday afternoon a benefit was tendered Colonel Cody by the race-course people. An outdoor performance was given, and despite the unfavorable weather the turn-stiles showed that nearly 50,000 people had paid admission to the grounds. Thus ended the Wild West performances in Manchester.

On Friday morning, May 4th, at 11 a.m., amid the cheers, well-wishes, and handshaking of a vast crowd, the Wild West left Manchester by special train for Hull, where the last performance in England was given on the afternoon of Saturday, May 5th, and at nine o'clock on that evening the entire effects of the monster aggregation were aboard the good ship Persian Monarch, upon which vessel, under the command of the brave, gallant, and courteous Captain Bristow, the Wild West left for New York the next morning at 3 o'clock. On the homeward voyage Colonel Cody's favorite horse Charlie died. For fifteen years he had ridden Charlie in sunshine and in storm, in days of adversity as well as prosperity, and to this noble animal's fleetness of foot Colonel Cody owed his life on more than one occasion when pursued by Indians.

During the night of May 19th, the Persian Monarch arrived off New York harbor, and by daylight of the 20th steamed up toward Staten Island, where they were to debark.

The arrival of this vessel, outside of the company's reception, was an event of future commercial importance to the port of New York, from the fact of her being the first passenger-ship of her size, draught, and class to effect a landing (at Bechtel's wharf) directly on the shores of Staten Island, thus demonstrating the marine value of some ten miles of seashore of what in a few short years must be a part of the greater New York.

Upon the arrival of this giant combination at its home, it would seem that a long and undisturbed rest would have been natural and consequent. Such, however, was not to be the case. The master-mind concluded that it would be well to show to his own countrymen what manner of exhibition it was that had accomplished such wonderful results on its visit to Albion. A summer season was inaugurated at Erastina, S.I., and New York followed. In this latter city Colonel Cody originated, at Madison Square Garden, the now popular and much-copied idea of leviathan spectacle. Visits respectively to Philadelphia, Baltimore, and Washington followed, and this remarkable exhibition closed, at the Richmond, Va., exposition, a wonderful and uninterrupted season which had begun two years and seven months before at St. Louis, Mo. Faithful to his promises, and following his invariable custom, Colonel Cody saw that all his people, from the Texan cowboy and the Mexican Vaquero to the Sioux warrior of Dakota, had safe and pleasant conduct to their homes. The realistic story of America had been told in the mother country, and the interest of Continental Europe had also been awakened. The returning red man, cowboy, and Mexican had had experiences and learned lessons the value of which it is impossible to compute, and the influence of which must perforce permeate their entire lives and broaden their thought and moral nature, leading to results of unbounded possibilities. The cowboy by the camp-fire of his prairie home, the Vaquero among his companions in Mexico's mountains, and the red man in his lodge and with his people, had wonderful tales to tell during the winter nights of their well-earned resting-spell.

CHAPTER XXVI

Swinging Around Europe

This man of many parts, this unique exemplification of the possibilities of human intellectual and physical development and progress, had now passed through successive, and with all truth it can be said, successful, gradations from the illiterate urchin of the rough cabin on the plains to a great practical educator; and the lessons taught in his magnificently illustrated lectures had for their object the welding together of human interests and the enlarging of the mutual sympathies of nations. I am aware that the selfish, captious, and narrow-minded may see in the exhibitions and travels of the Wild West under Colonel Cody's leadership simply a scheme for personal aggrandizement or for the accumulation of great wealth. With the same foundation for truth, might not these same unworthy motives be attributed to the magnetic Edison,[1] whose discoveries and inventions have startled the world into a wondering recognition of electric power? to Stanley, through whose terrible trials, weary wanderings, and persevering persistency the heart of Africa has been laid bare to scientific and humane investigation? to Humboldt and scores of other world-instructors? Such unworthy commentators, to whose eyes all advancement in knowledge is veneered with a base coating of selfish aims, are unworthy of serious consideration.

In pursuance of a resolve made during his visit to England in 1887, Colonel Cody, in the spring preceding the Paris Exposition, set all of his able lieutenants and coadjutors to work preparing another Wild West for a trip to the French capital, thence through Continental Europe, and, after another visit to Old England, back to dear America. Under the spell of their leader's energetic and systematic direction, these trusted assistants soon had all things in complete readiness, and once again on board the majestic Persian Monarch, and under the care of that able seaman and popular officer Captain Bristow, the Wild West was launched upon "the briny," for Paris bound.

The Wild West camp in Paris was pitched on immense grounds near the Porte Maillot, and the welcome extended to the Americans by the people of the sister republic was hearty, spontaneous, and grand. It was said that the audience which assembled on the occasion of the opening exhibition equaled any known in the record of *premières* of that brilliant *capitale des deux mondes*.[2] Early in the performance the vast audience became thoroughly enthusiastic, and every act attracted the closest attention and the most absorbing interest. It was evident that the novel and starling display had won the fullest approval of the experienced sight-seers of the gay capital; and in France audiences rarely if ever take the middle ground. With them approval or commendation comes promptly and is quickly manifested, and the immediate triumph of the Wild West was a subject of hearty congratulation. As in England upon his first appearance there Colonel Cody was welcomed by those highest in authority and honor, so in France the initial performance was graced by the presence of notables of the republic. President Carnot and wife,[3] the members of his cabinet, and families; two American ministers, Hon. Whitelaw Reid,[4] Hon. Louis MacLean; the Diplomatic Corps, officers of the United States Marine, and other prominent personages were among the auditors. It was an audience thoroughly representative of science, art, literature, and society, and the Wild West soon became second only in public interest to the great Exhibition itself. Colonel Cody soon became the recipient of especial social courtesies, the first of which was a breakfast given in his honor on May 29th by the Vicomtesse Chandon de Briailles,[5] at which the *haut ton*[6] of Paris was present. In recognition of the courtesy of the Minister of War in granting the Wild West the use of a large tract of land in the military district, Colonel Cody invited fifty soldiers of the garrison of Paris to visit the show each day, a courtesy that was duly appreciated.

Among the many incidents that occurred in Paris may be noted the fact that Isabella, ex-Queen of Spain,[7] with her companions enjoyed a ride in the famous old Deadwood stagecoach.

Altogether the Wild West's visit to Paris, which lasted seven months, was a most thorough and emphatic success, and closed in a blaze of glory.

It may seem strange to claim that the Wild West abroad was an incentive to the introduction of American subjects for art illustration; but the facts strongly warrant the assertion.

It became a fad to introduce curious and *bijouterie*[8] from the American plains and mountains. Buffalo robes of Indian tanning, bear-skins embroidered with porcupine

62. Rosa Bonheur's Painting, "Buffalo Bill on Horseback."

quills, and mats woven in redskin camps became fashionable; while lassos, bows and arrows, Mexican bridles and saddles, and other things from the American borderland became most popular as souvenirs.

Nor was this all, for the artists took a turn at producing American scenes, characters, and animals, and the Indian and cowboy were chiseled in marble. Busts were made of Buffalo Bill, the illustrated papers were full of pictures of the Wild West and its characters, and the comic papers were constantly caricaturing Cody and his people, some of their work being remarkably clever and artistic in execution.

Invited to the studios of artists in Rome, Berlin, Paris, and elsewhere, Buffalo Bill extended the courtesies of his camp to many whose names are known the world over by their works. The Wild West became a central place of attraction to artists as well as to military men and statesmen, and often painters and sculptors were seen going about the camp looking for subjects for their brush and chisel.

Having accepted an invitation from Rosa Bonheur to visit her at her elegant chateau, Buffalo Bill in turn extended the hospitalities of his camp to the famous artist, who day after day visit it and made studies for her pleasure, giving much time to sittings for a painting of Colonel Cody.

The result was the superb painting that attracted so much comment abroad, and which she presented to the great frontiersman, who prizes it above all the souvenirs he has in his charming home at North Platte, where it holds the place of honor.

The painting represents Buffalo Bill mounted upon his

63. Indians Under the Shadow of St. Peter's, Rome.

favorite horse, and it is needless to say that where both
man and animal are portraits, it is a work of art coming
from such a hand as that of Rosa Bonheur. The fact of
uniting man and beast in a painting, giving each equal
prominence, was never before done, I believe, by this great
artist, yet her hand did not lose its cunning in departing
from the rule of her life, as all can testify who have seen
this superb picture.

With America as a vast and grand field for the brushes
of English and European artists, there is little doubt that
hereafter the foreign academies will possess many works
on American scenes and characters; and with the example thus set them our own artists will find in their own
country material enough to prevent their going to other
lands to get artistic inspiration.

After a short tour in the south of France in the fall,

a vessel was chartered at Marseilles, the Mediterranean crossed at Barcelona, landing the first band of Americans with accompanying associates, scouts, cowboys, Mexican horses of Spanish descent, and wild buffaloes, etc., on the very spot where on this return to Spain landed the world's greatest explorer Christopher Columbus. Here the patrons were demonstratively eulogistic, the exhibition seeming to delight them greatly, savoring as it did of an addenda to their national history; recalling after a lapse of 400 years the resplendent glories of Spanish conquests under Ferdinand and Isabella, of the sainted hero Cristobal Colon (1492), Columbus in America (1890), "Buffalo Bill" and the native American in Spain!

Recrossing the Mediterranean via Corsica and Sardinia (encountering a tremendous storm), Naples (the placid waters whose noble bay gave a welcome refuge) was reached, and in the shadow of old Vesuvius, which in fact formed a superbly grand scenic background, another peg in history was pinned by the visit of the cowboy and Indian to the various noted localities that here abound; the ruins of Herculaneum, Pompeii,[9] and the great crater of "the burning mountain" striking wonder and awe as well as giving geological and geographical knowledge to the stoical "red man."

Then the "famed of the famous cities" of the world, Rome, was next visited, to be conquered through the gentle power of intellectual interest in, and the reciprocal pleasure exchanged by, its unusual visitors; the honor being given to "the outfit," as an organization, of attending a dazzling fête given in the Vatican by his holiness Pope Leo XIII,[10] and of receiving the exalted pontiff's blessing. The grandeur of the spectacle, the heavenly music, the

64. Camped in the Coliseum.

entrancing singing, and impressive adjuncts produced a most profound impression on the astonished children of the prairie. The Wild West in the Vatican!

The company were photographed in the Coliseum, which stately ruin seemed silently and solemnly to regret that its famed ancient arena was too small for this modern exhibition of the mimic struggle between that civilization born and emanating from 'neath its very walls, and a primitive people who were ne'er dreamed of in Rome's world-conquering creators' wildest flights of vivid imaginings.

Strolling through its arena, gazing at its lions' dens, or lolling lazily on its convenient ruins, hearing it interpreted history of Romulus, of Cæsar, and of Nero,[11] roamed this band of Wild West Sioux (a people whose history in barbaric deeds equals, if not excels, the ancient Romans'), now hand-in-hand in peace and firmly cemented friendship with the American frontiersman, once gladiatorial antagonists on the Western plains. They, listening to the tale, on the spot, of those whose "morituri te salutant"[12] was the short prelude to a savage death, formed a novel picture in a historical frame. The Wild West in the Coliseum!

The following extracts from cablegrams sent to the New York *Herald* by its special correspondent, tell of interesting occurrences that happened during the visit of the Wild West to the historic city of Rome:

Rome, March 4, 1890

All Rome was to-day astir over an attempt of Buffalo Bill's cowboys with wild horses, which were provided for the occasion by the Prince of Sermoneta.[13]

Several days past the Roman authorities have been busy with the erection of specially cut barriers for the purpose of keeping back the wild horses from the crowds.

The animals are from the celebrated stud of the Prince of Sermoneta, and the prince himself declared that no cowboy in the world could ride these horses. The cowboys laughed over this surmise and then offered at least to undertake the mount one of them, if they might choose it.

Every man, woman, and child expected that two or three people would be killed by this attempt.

The anxiety and enthusiasm was great. Over 2,000 carriages were ranged round the field and more than 20,000 people lined the spacious barriers. Lord Dufferin[14] and many other diplomatists were on the terrace, and among Romans were presently seen the consort of the Prime Minister Crispi,[15] the Prince of Torlonia,[16] Madame Depretis,[17]

65. The Arena in Verona.

Princess Colonna,[18] Gravina Antonelli, the Baroness Reugis, Princess Brancaccio,[19] Grave Giannotti,[20] and critics from among the highest aristocracy.

In five minutes the horses were tamed.

Two of the wild horses were driven without saddle or bridle in the arena. Buffalo Bill gave out that they would be tamed. The brutes made springs into the air, darted hither and thither in all directions, and bent themselves into all sorts of shapes—but all in vain.

In five minutes the cowboys had caught the wild horses with the lasso, saddled, subdued, and bestrode them. Then the cowboys rode them round the arena, while the dense crowds of people applauded with delight.

BUFFALO BILL IN VENICE
(BY TELEGRAPH, NEW YORK HERALD)
Venice, April 16, 1890

Buffalo Bill and his Wild West have made a big show in Venice. This evening the directors have a special invitation on the Grand Canal, where the whole troupe will be shown. Colonel Cody is taken by the Venetian prefect in his own private residence. No one can think them ordinary artistes after they have seen the gathering of different Indians in gondolas, or seen the wonderful sight which presents itself at the Venetian palace and in the little steamboats that ply between the pier of St. Mark[21] and the railway station.

Thousands of Venetians assembled yesterday in Verona, where the company of the municipal authorities of justice have allowed the use of the amphitheater, or the so-called arena, one of the most interesting structures of Italy, and a rival of the Coliseum of Rome itself.

Forty-five thousand persons can conveniently find sitting-room in this arena, and for standing-room there is also extensive space. As his royal highness Victor Emanuel[22] was on a visit here once, 60,000 people were accommodated in it. It is, perhaps, interesting to know that this building is the largest in the world, although the Wild West Show quite filled it.

The amphitheater (arena) was built in the year 290 A. D., under Diocletian,[23] and is known in Germany as the Home of the Dietrich of Bern.[24] It is 106 feet high, 168 meters long, and 134 meters broad (the arena itself is 83 meters long, 48 meters broad); the circumference is 525 meters. In the surrounding amphitheater (entering by the west side through arch No. 5, admission 1 franc, Sunday free), are five- and-forty rows of steps 18 inches high, 26 inches broad, built of gray, or rather reddish-yellow, limestone, where nearly 20,000 spectators can find places, and where many more people can see by standing on the wooden benches behind them. From an inscription on the second story it will be remembered that Napoleon I[25] visited this place in 1805. The restoration of the building was by recommendation of that emperor. A wonderful view is obtained from the higher steps.

THE WILD WEST AT THE VATICAN—BUFFALO BILL'S INDIANS AND COWBOYS AT THE ANNIVERSARY CEREMONY OF LEO XIII.

New York Herald, March 4, 1890—(From our Special Correspondent)

Rome, March 3rd

One of the strangest spectacles ever seen within the walls of the Vatican was the dramatic entry of Buffalo Bill at the head of his Indians and cowboys this morning, when the ecclesiastical and secular military court of the Holy See assembled to witness the twelfth annual thanksgiving of Leo XIII, for his coronation. In the midst of the splendid scene, crowded with the old Roman aristocracy and surrounded by walls immortalized by Michael Angelo and Raphael,[26] there suddenly appeared a host of savages in war-paint, feathers, and blankets, carrying tomahawks and knives.

A vast multitude surged in the great square before St. Peter's early in the morning to witness the arrival of the Americans. Before half-past nine o'clock the Ducal Hall, Royal Hall, and Sistine Chapel of the Vatican were packed with those who had influence enough to obtain admittance. Through the middle of the three audiences the pathway was bordered with the brilliant uniforms of the Swiss Guards, Palatine Guards, papal gendarmes, and private chamberlains. The sunlight fell upon the lines of glittering steel, nodding plumes, golden chains, shimmering robes of silk, and all the blazing emblems of pontifical power and glory.

The Wild West Make Their Entrée

Suddenly a tall and chivalrous figure appeared at the entrance, and all eyes were turned toward him. It was Col. W. F. Cody, "Buffalo Bill." With a sweep of his great sombrero he saluted the chamberlains, and then strode between the guards with his partner, Mr. Nate Salsbury, by his side.

Rocky Bear[27] led the Sioux warriors, who brought up the rear. They were painted in every color that Indian imagination could devise. Every man carried something with which to make big medicine in the presence of the great medicine man sent by the great spirit.

Rocky Bear rolled his eyes and folded his hands on his breast as he stepped on tiptoe through the glowing sea of color. His braves furtively eyed the halberds and two-handed swords of the Swiss Guards.

The Indians and cowboys were ranged in the south corners of the Ducal Hall. Colonel Cody and Mr. Salsbury were escorted into the Sistine Chapel by chamberlains, where they were greeted by Miss Sherman, daughter of General Sherman. A princess invited Colonel Cody to a place in the tribune of the Roman nobles.

He stood facing the gorgeous Diplomatic Corps, surrounded by the Prince and Princess Borghese, the Marquis Serlupi, Princess Bandini, Duchess di Grazioli, Prince and Princess Massimo, Prince and Princess Ruspoli and all the ancient noble families of the city.[28]

66. Pope Leo XIII.

The Papal Blessing

When the Pope appeared in the *sedia gestatoria*, carried above the heads of his guards, preceded by the Knights of Malta[29] and a procession of cardinals and archbishops, the cowboys bowed, and so did the Indians. Rocky Bear knelt and made the sign of the cross. The pontiff leaned affectionately toward the rude groups and blessed them. He seemed to be touched by the sight.

As the papal train swept on the Indians became excited, and a s***w fainted. They had been warned not to utter a sound, and were with difficulty restrained from whooping. The Pope looked at Colonel Cody intently as he passed, and the great scout and Indian fighter bent low as he received the pontifical benediction.

After the thanksgiving mass, with its grand choral accompaniment and now and then the sound of Leo XIII's voice heard ringing through the chapel, the great audience poured out of the Vatican.

Among the many verses written of and to the noted scout, the following may be given as a poet's idea of his visit to Rome:

BUFFALO BILL AND THE ROMANS

I'll take my stalwart Indian braves
Down to the Coliseum,
And the old Romans from their graves
Will all arise to see 'em;
Pretors[30] and censors will return
And hasten through the Forum,
The ghostly Senate will adjourn
Because it lacks a quorum.

And up the ancient Appian way[31]
Will flock the ghostly legions,
From Gaul unto Calabria,
And from remoter regions;
From British bog and wild lagoon,
And Libyan desert sandy,
They'll all come, marching to the tune
Of "Yankee Doodle Dandy."

Prepare the triumph car for me
And purple throne to sit on,
For I've done more than Julius C.—
He could not down the Briton!
Cæsar and Cicero[32] shall bow,
And ancient warriors famous,
Before the myrtle bandaged brow
Of Buffalo Williamus.

We march, unwhipped, through history—
No bulwark can detain us—
And link the age of Grover C.
And Scipio Africanus.[33]
I'll take my stalwart Indian braves
Down to the Coliseum,
And the old Romans from their graves
Will all arise to see 'em.

Artistic Florence, practical Bologna, grand and stately Milan, and unique Verona were next added to the list. Verona's superb and well-preserved Arena, excelling in superficial area the Coliseum and bolding 45,000 people, was especially granted for the Wild West's use. The Indians were taken by Buffalo Bill to picturesque Venice, and there shown the marvelous results of the ancient white man's energy and artistic architectural skill. They were immortalized by the camera in the ducal palace, St. Marc's Piazza, and in the strange street vehicle of the Adriatic's erstwhile pride—the gondola; contributing another interesting object lesson to the distant juvenile student members of their tribe, to testify more fully to their puzzled senses the fact of strange sights and marvels whose existence is to be learned in the breadth of knowledge.

67. Buffalo Bill and His Indians in Venice.

Moving via Innsbruck through the beautifully scenic Tyrol, the Bavarian capital, Munich, with its naturally artistic instincts, gave a grand reception to the beginning of a marvelously successful tour through German land, which included Vienna (with an excursion on the "Blue Danube"), Berlin, Dresden, Leipzig, Magdeburg, Hanover, Brunswick, Hamburg, Bremen, Dusseldorf, Cologne, along the Rhine past Bonn, Coblentz, "Fair Bingen on the Rhine," to Frankfort, Stuttgart, and Strasburg. These historic cities, with all their wealth of legendary interest, art galleries, scientific conservatories, educative edifices, cathedrals, modern palaces, ancient ruins, army maneuverings, fortifications, commercial and varied manufacturing and agricultural industries, and the social, genial, friendly, quiet customs of its peoples, should form good instruction to the rugged rovers of the American plains—heirs to an empire as much more vast in extent and resources as is the brightness of the diamond—after the skill expended by the lapidary—in dazzling brilliancy to the rude, unpolished stone before man's *industry* lends value to its existence.

At Strasburg the management decided to close temporarily this extraordinary tour and winter the company. Although in the proximity of points contemplated for a winter campaign (southern France and the Riviera), this was deemed advisable on account of the first and only attack from envious humanity that the organization had encountered. This matter necessitated the manly but expensive voluntary procedure of taking the Indians to America to meet face to face and deny the imputations of some villifiers, whom circumstances of petty political "charity" and "I-am-ism" and native buoyancy permit at times to float temporarily on the surface of a cosmopolite community, and to whose ravings a too credulous public and press give hearing.

The quaint little village of Benfield furnished an ancient nunnery and a castle with stables and good range. Here the little community of Americans spent the winter comfortably, being feasted and fêted by the inhabitants, whose esteem they gained to such an extent that their departure was marked by a general holiday, assisting hands, and such public demonstrations of regret that many a rude cowboy when once again careering o'er the pampas of Texas will rest his weary steed while memory reverts to the pleasant days and whole-souled friendships cemented at the foot of the Vosges Mountains in disputed Alsace-Lorraine.

In Alsace-Lorraine! whose anomalous position menaces the peace not only of the two countries interested but of the civilized world; whose situation makes it intensely even sadly interesting as the theater of that future human tragedy for which the ear of mankind strains day and night, listening for detonations from the muzzles of the acme of invented mechanisms of destruction. The lurid-garbed Angel of Devastation hovers, careering through the atmosphere of the seemingly doomed valley, gaily laughing, shrieking exultingly, at the white-robed Angel of Peace as the latter gloomily wanders, prayerful, tearful, hopelessly hunting, ceaselessly seeking, the return of modern man's boasted newly created gods—Equity, Justice, Reason!

What a field for the vaunted champions of humanity, the leaders of civilization! What a neighborhood wherein to sow the seeds of "peace and earth and good-will to men." What a crucible for the universal panacea, arbitration! What a test of the efficacy of prayer in damming up the conflicting torrents of ambition, cupidity, passion, and revenge, which threaten the color crimson the swift current of the Rhine, until its renown as the home of wealth and luxury be eclipsed by eternal notoriety as the Valley of Death!

CHAPTER XXVII

The Last Indian War

Leaving the temporary colony under the charge of his di-
rector-partner Mr. Nate Salsbury (whose energy found occupation in attending to the details of the future), Colonel
Cody and the Indians departed for America, arriving safely, and after refuting satisfactorily, by the Indians themselves, the base slanders that emanated in the imagination
of notoriety-seeking busy-bodies, proceeded to the seat
of the Indian difficulties in the distant State of Dakota.

State of Nebraska

Executive Department

General W. F. Cody.

Lincoln January 6th, 1891.

Rushville. Nebraska

My Dear General. As you are a member of my Staff,
I have detailed you for special service; the particular
nature of which, was made known during our
conversation.

You will proceed to the scene of the Indian troubles,
and communicate with General Miles.

You will in addition to the special service refered to
please visit the different towns, if time permit, along the

68. State of Nebraska certificate.

line of the Elkhorn Rail-Road, and use your influence to quiet excitement and remove apprehensions upon the part of the people.

Please call upon General Colby,[1] and give him your views as to the probability of the Indians breaking through the cordon of regular troops; your superior knowledge of Indian character and mode of warfare, may enable you to make suggestions of importance.

All Officers and members of the State Troops, and all others, will please extend to you every courtesy.

In testimony whereof.

[signed] John M, Thayer,

Governor

In this campaign against the Indians Buffalo Bill rendered valuable services and was ordered to the command of General Colby of the National Guard of the State of Nebraska, and to report to General Miles, the commander-in-chief.

His authority for going to the front is shown by the accompanying appointment and order from the governor.

Had the Indian uprising broken out into a general war, Buffalo Bill would have had the opportunity to show the world what he could do as a general officer, handling a number of men in action; but fortunately the splendidly conceived and executed maneuvers of General Miles, the commander-in-chief, prevented the outbreak from extending to all the tribes, and put down the rebellious savages with little bloodshed, thus saving a long and cruel war upon the frontier.

The letter given herewith from General Miles, at the conclusion of the campaign, shows the appreciation by General Miles of Buffalo Bill's services, and which met the general approbation of the press of the country, many correspondents being upon the field; while Colonel Cody's telegrams to the New York *Herald* and *Sun* give a most thorough explanation of the situation.

AS BUFFALO BILL SEES IT—HE THINKS IT LOOKS LIKE PEACE IN THE INDIAN COUNTRY

Buffalo Bill telegraphs to the New York Herald
from Pine Ridge Agency:

Pine Ridge Agency, Dak.

IN THE FIELD, VIA COURIER TO TELEGRAPH

New York Herald: Your request for my opinion of the Indian situation is, by reason of the complications and the changeable nature of the red man's mind and action, a puzzler. Every hour brings out a new opinion. Indian history furnishes no similar situation.

———————

In the Field, Pine Ridge, S.D., January 11, 1891

Brig. General W. F. Cody,

Nebraska National Guard, Present

Sir: —I am glad to inform you that the entire body of Indians are now camped near here (within a mile and a half). They show every disposition to comply with the orders of the authorities. Nothing but an accident can prevent peace being re-established, and it will be our ambition to make it of a permanent character. I feel that the State troops can now be withdrawn with safety, and desire through you to express to them my thanks for the confidence they have given your people in their isolated homes.

Like information has this day been given General Colby.

Very respectfully yours,
[signed] Nelson A. Miles
Major General Commanding

You must imagine about five thousand Indians, an unusual proportion warriors, better armed than ever known before, hemmed in by a cordon, about sixteen miles in diameter, composed of over three thousand troops, acting like a slowly closing drag-net. This mass of Indians is now influenced by a percentage as despairingly desperate and fanatical as the late Big Foot party under

Short Bull and Kicking Bear.[2] It contains also restrained neutrals, frightened and disaffected Oglalas, hampered by the powerful Brulés, backed by renegades and desperadoes from all other agencies. There are about twenty-five hundred acting and believed to be friendly Indians in and around the agency.

Such is the situation General Miles and the military confront. Any one of this undisciplined mass is able to precipitate a terrible conflict from the most unexpected quarter. Each of the component quantities is to be watched, to be measured, to be just to. In fact it is a war with a most wily and savage people, yet the whites are restrained by a humane and peaceful desire to prevent bloodshed and save a people from themselves. It is like cooling and calming a volcano. Ordinary warfare shows no parallel. General Miles seems to hold a firm grip on the situation. The Indians know him, express confidence in his honor, truth, and justice to them, and they fear his power and valor as well.

As the matter now stands, he and they should be allowed, untrammeled even by suggestion, to settle the affair, as no one not on the spot can appreciate the fearfully delicate position. The chaff must be sifted from the wheat, and in this instance the chaff must be threshed.

At the moment, as far as words go, I would say it will be peace, but the smoldering spark is visible that may precipitate a terrible conflict any time in the next few days. However it ends, more and prompt attention should be paid in the future to the Sioux Indians—his rights, his complaints, and even his necessities. Respect and consideration should also be shown for the gallant little army, for it is the Indian and soldier who pay the most costly price in the end. I think it looks like peace, and if so the greater the victory.

———————

W. F. CODY ("BUFFALO BILL")

The Situation in the Indian Country a Marvel of Military Strategy

Col. W. F. Cody ("Buffalo Bill"), who is at Pine Ridge, telegraphs the following for the New York *Sun*, which expresses his views of the present critical situation:

The situation to-day, so far as military strategy goes, is one of the best-marked triumphs known in the history of Indian campaigns. It speaks for itself, for the usual incidents to an Indian warfare, such as raids on settlers and widespread devastation, have been wholly prevented. Only one white man has been killed outside the military circle. The presiding genius and his able aids have acted with all the cautious prowess of the hunter in surrounding and placing in a trap his dangerous game, at the same time recognizing the value of keeping the game imprisoned for future reasons. I speak, of course, of the campaign as originally intended to overawe and pacify the disaffected portion of the Oglalas, Wassaohas,[3] and Brules, the Big Foot affair at Wounded Knee Creek being an unlooked-for accident.

The situation to-day, with a desperate band corralled and the possibility of any individual fanatic running amuck, is most critical, but the wise measure of holding them in a military wall, allowing them time to

69. Cody with daughters Arta(r) and Orra.

quiet down and listen to the assurances of such men as Young-Man-Afraid-of-His-Horses,[4] Rocky Bear, No Neck, and other progressive Indians, relieves the situation, so that unless some accident happens the military end of the active warfare seems a complete, final, and brilliant success, as creditable to General Miles's military reputation as it is to the humane and just side of his character.

Neither should praise be withheld from Generals Brooke, Carr, Wheaton,[5] Henry, Forsyth, and the other officers and men of the gallant little army, who stood much privation. In every instance when I have heard them speak they have expressed great sympathy for their unhappy foe and regrets for his impoverished and desperate condition. They and the thoughtful people here are now thinking about the future. In fact the Government and nation are confronted by a problem of great importance as regards remedying the existing evils.

The larger portion of the Oglala Sioux have acted nobly in this affair, especially up to the time of the stampede. The Wassaohas and Brules have laid waste the reservation of the Oglalas, killed their cattle, shot their horses, pillaged their houses, burned their ranches; in fact, poor as the Ogalalas were before, the Brules have left nothing but the bare ground, a white sheet instead of a blanket, with a winter at hand, and the little accumulations of thirteen years swept away. This much, as well as race and tribal dissensions and personal enmity, have they incurred for standing by the Government. These people need as much sympathy and immediate assistance as any section of country when great calamities arouse the sympathy of the philanthropist and the Government. This is now the part of the situation that to me seems the most remarkable. Intelligent and quick legislation can now do more than the bullet.

William F. Cody ("Buffalo Bill")

CHAPTER XXVIII

Back to Europe

After peace was restored Buffalo Bill secured Government authority and selected a band of Indians—composed equally of the "active friendly," headed by Chiefs Long Wolf, No Neck, Yankton Charley, Black Heart, and the "band of hostages" held by the military under Gen. Nelson A. Miles at Fort Sheridan, and headed by the redoubtable Short Bull, Kicking Bear, Lone Bull, Scatter, and Revenge[1]— for a short European tour, and they left Philadelphia in the chartered Red Star steamer Switzerland. The significance of this fact should *still* forever the tongue of those who, without rhyme, truth, or reason, have tried to stain a fair record, which has been justly earned; and by its very prominence, perhaps, difficult to maintain.

Coming direct from the snow-clad hills and blood-stained valley of the *Mauvaise Terre* of last winter's central point of interest, it can not be denied that an added chapter to Indian history, and the Wild West's province of truthfully exhibiting the same, is rendered more valuable to the student of primitive man, and to the ethnologist's acquaintance with the strange people whose grand and once happy empire plethoric in all its inhabitants needed) has been (rightfully or wrongfully) brought thoroughly and efficiently under the control of our civilization, or (possibly more candidly confessed) under the Anglo-Saxon's commercial necessities. It occurs to the writer that our boasted civilization has a wonderful adaptability to the good soils, the productive portions, and the rich mineral lands of the earth, while making snail-like pace and intermittent efforts among the frigid haunts of the Esquimaux, the tangled swamps of Africa, and the bleak and dreary rocks of Patagonia.

A sentimental view is thus inspired, when long personal association has brought the better qualities of the Indian to one's notice, assisting somewhat to dispel the prejudices engendered by years of savage, brutal wars, conducted with a ferocious vindictiveness foreign to our methods. The savageness of Indian warfare is born in the victim, and probably intensified by the instinctive knowledge of a despairing weakness that renders desperate the fiery spirit of expiring resistance, which latter (in another cause) might be held up for a courage and tenacity as bright as that recorded in the pages dedicated to the heroes of Thermopylæ.[2]

After all, in what land, in what race, nationality, or community can be found the vaunted vestal home of assured peace? And where is human nature so perfected that circumstances might not waken the dormant demon of man's innate savageness?

But then again the practical view of the non-industrious use of nature's cornucopia of world-needed resources and the inevitable law of the *survival of the fittest* must bring the "flattering unction to the soul" of those to whom the music of light, work, and progress is the charm, the gauge of existence's worth, and to which the listless must hearken, the indolent attend, the weak imbibe strength from—whose ranks the red man must join, and advancing with whose steps march cheerily to the tune of honest toil, industrious peace, and placid fireside prosperity.

Passing through the to them marvelous experience of the railroad and its flying express train; the sight of towns, villages, cities, over valley, plain, and mountains to the magic *floating house* (the steamer); sadly learning, while struggling with the *mal de mer*,[3] the existence of the "big waters," that tradition alone had bruited to incredulous ears, was passed the first portion of a tempestuous voyage. Its teachings were of value in bringing to the proud spirits of the self-reliant Dakotans the terrible power of nature, and of white man's marvelous skill, industry, and ability in overcoming the dangers of the deep; the reward of patience being found in a beautifully smooth approach to land. The Scilly Islands and a non-fog-encumbered journey up the English Channel—unusually bright with sunshine; the grand panorama of England's majestic shores, her passing fleet of all kinds of marine architecture, the steaming up the river Scheldt, with its dyked banks and the beautifully cultivated fields, opened to the marveling nomad his first edition of Aladdin, and landed him—wonderingly surprised at the sight of thousands of white men peacefully greeting his arrival—in the busy commercial mart of Antwerp.

After introducing the Indians to hotel life for the first time, a tour of the city was made, among the notable points visited being the cathedral, which grand edifice aroused their curiosity; the grand picture, Rubens's "Descent from the Cross,"[4] bringing to the minds of all—white men, "friendlies," and "hostiles"—the "Messiah craze"; an interest intensified by the fact that the æsthetic-looking Short Bull and some of the others had been the leading fanatical believers (probably even apparently conscientious), promoters, and disciples of the still mysterious religious disease that lately agitated the Indian race in America. In fact, after the death of Sitting Bull the central figures of this strange belief were Short Bull as the religious leader and Kicking Bear as the war chief. Grouped together with Scatter, Revenge, and others, in moody contemplation of this subject, was the late defier of a mighty nation of 65,000,000 people, nearly all of whom teach or preach the truthfulness of the picture's traditions. A man in two short months transported from the indescribably desolate, almost inaccessible natural fortresses of the Bad Lands (*Mauvaise Terre*) of Dakota to the ancient city of Antwerp, gazing spellbound on the artistic reproduction by the renowned artist of the red man's late dream, "The Messiah." Respect for his thoughts and the natural stoical nature of the Indian leaves to future opportunity an interesting interrogative of what passed through the mind of the subtle chief. Suffice it to say that surprise at the white man's many-sided character and the greatness of his resources in the past and present was beginning to the dawn more and more of the new tourists. Arriving the next day at Strasburg, introduction to the cowboys, the camp life, the cathedral, the great clock, the fortifications, etc., was followed by the delight of each brave on receiving his pony, and once more with his trusty friend the horse, the Oglala and Brule in a few days felt as though "Richard were himself again."

Joining more heartily than was expected in the mimic

scenes of the Wild West, soon the ordinary routine of daily duties seemed a pleasant diversion. A grand reception in Strasburg, the tour resumed to Carlsruhe, Mannheim—including a visit to Heidelberg Castle, Mayence, Wiesbaden, Cologne (the Rhine legends of Lurline, etc., giving interest to the *Peau Rouge*,[5] en route), Dortmund, Duisburg, Crefeld, and Aix-la-Chapelle, terminated a tour of Germany filled with the most pleasant recollections. The tomb of Charlemagne (Carlo Magno)![6] The history of this great warrior was interpreted to attentive ears, a lesson being instilled by the relation that after all his glory, his battles, triumphs, and conquests in which he defeated the dusky African prototypes of the present visitors to his tomb, peace brought him to pursue knowledge, to cultivate the arts and sciences, and that after a hundred years of entombment his body was found by Otto the Saxon[7] sitting erect upon a granite throne, the iron crown upon his head, imperial scepter in right hand, while his left rested on an open volume of Holy Scriptures, the index finger pointed to the well-known passage, "What will it profit a man if he gain the whole world and lose his own soul?" Here by the grave of the founder of Christianity stood the latest novitiates to its efforts, who may yet, in following its teaching, it is hoped, make such progress through its aid and education as to furnish one of their race capable of holding the exalted chieftainship, the presidency in their native land—the Empire of the West. Who can say? Why not?

Belgium—Brussels its Paris—brings vividly to mind, in its semblance of language, people, habits, beauty, wealth, culture, and appreciation, remembrance of our delightful sojourn in the capital of (how truly named) *la belle France*.[8]

70. Earl's Court, London.

Visit Waterloo![9] From Pine Ridge to historic Waterloo!
The courteous treatment and repeated visits and kindly
interest of that most amiable lady the queen—an enthusiastic horsewoman—her pleasant reference to London in
the Jubilee year, combined to increase the gratitude the
Wild West voyagers felt for the treatment everywhere received in Europe since, in 1887, the Wild West invaded old
England and pitched their tents in the world's metropolis, London. So after a short season in Antwerp the motley cargo set sail across the North Sea to make a farewell
visit to their cousins of the isle, revel in a common language (bringing a new pleasure to the ear), hoping to deserve and receive a continuance of that amicable appreciation of their humble efforts that the past seemed to justify.

Returning to England was next to going home to the
wild Westerners, after wandering through foreign lands,

71. Grave of the Indian Chief Long Wolf, at
West Brompton Cemetery, London.

and they were welcomed as though indeed "cousins" in the real sense of the word.

A tour was made which was most extensive, for exhibitions were given in Leeds, Birmingham, Liverpool, Manchester, Sheffield, Stoke-on-Trent, Nottingham, Leicester, Cardiff, Bristol, Portsmouth, Glasgow, and then back to London, where Colonel Cody gave a special entertainment in the grounds of Windsor Castle before the queen and her invited guests.

It was upon this occasion that Buffalo Bill was honored with the presentation of an elegant souvenir from the queen, while Mr. Salsbury and the writer were also remembered with handsome gifts from her majesty.

Conclusion

Thus concluded the second tour in Europe. The Wild West had been received and treated with marked kindness by every nation, every city, and by persons of every rank and of every station—press, public, and officials. Every one had shown a willingness to lend a helping hand and displayed a fraternal interest and general appreciation toward them and their country's flag, so that returning home it is a pleasant duty to record the same, believing that in presenting their rough pictures of a "history almost passed away" some moiety of good may have been done in simplifying the work of the historian, the romancer, the painter, and the student of the future, and in exemplifying in themselves and their experiences the fact that "travel is the best educator," and that association and acquaintanceship dispel prejudice, create breadth of thought, and enhance appreciation of the truism that "one touch of nature makes the whole world akin."

APPENDIX

Col. W. F. Cody (Buffalo Bill) and the London Workingmen's Association

On Saturday evening, October 1, 1892, a conference of delegates from the various branches of the London Workingmen's association was held at the Wild West, when an illuminated address was presented to Col. W. F. Cody.

The chair was occupied by Mr. George Potter, president of the association, who was supported by Mr. Fred Whetstone, vice-president; Mr. F. Wigington, treasurer; Mr. Robert Wilson, secretary. There was a large attendance.

Colonel Cody was accompanied by Maj. John M. Burke and Mr. Nate Salsbury.

Mr. George Potter, in presenting the address which congratulated Buffalo Bill on the splendor of his show, its value from an education standpoint, and the success which had attended his visit, now fast drawing to a close, said that those whom he represented admired the colonel's pluck and appreciated his indomitable courage. He had taught us a lesson which would not be forgotten, and Buffalo Bill would ever be a household word with us. (Loud cheers.) Mr. Potter and those with him expressed the hope that after Buffalo Bill had visited the World's Fair at Chicago and settled down in his own country to dwell among his own people, he would enjoy the remainder of his life in contentment, prosperity, and peace. (Loud cheers.)

Mr. Potter then read the following address:

Col. W. F. Cody:

Sir: The members of the London Workingmen's Association, representing large bodies of workingmen, have a friendly word to say at a time when your visit to this country is fast drawing to a close.

They desire to approach you in spirit of congratulation and to place on record their thorough appreciation of the enterprise and ability displayed by you in the conception and creation of the brilliant realistic spectacle known as the Wild West, fully realizing its magnitude and its value from an educational standpoint as a vivid picture of past life on the American frontier.

To those whose domestic cares and necessities prevent them enjoying the luxury of travel and its acknowledged advantages in forming proper ideas of foreign peoples and strange races, your enterprise has brought not only entertainment for the moment, but has enabled thousands to enjoy more fully the books, histories, paintings, and sculpture that come under their observation. This alone is something of future value to every nation you have visited (among all classes), as well as the fraternal feeling of the general brotherhood of man that your introduction of national and racial differences in one body for mutual instruction produces.

Neither the costly outlay through which these results have been effected by the difficulties of presenting the best specimens of these primitive peoples, nor the talent displayed by the performers, could have secured the enormous audiences, had not careful attention been paid to fidelity of depiction, the mastery of detail, and ample provision for the comfort of the public.

That the marked success of the undertaking is in a large measure due to your own personal supervision affords an additional ground for offering our meed of congratulation to you as a workingman.

With this we couple our sincere hope that upon your future retirement you may find, in well-earned repose, no reason to regret your visits to England of 1887 and 1892; and you may rest assured you carry with you the good wishes of the millions whom you have so liberally entertained.

We are, on behalf of the association,
George Potter, President,
Fred Whetstone, Vice-President,
F. Wigington, Treasurer,
Robert Wilson, Secretary.
14 Fetter Lane, London.
October 1, 1892

Mr. Fred Whetstone (late chairman of the Amalgamated Society of Engineers), in supporting the address, expressed a wish from the bottom of his heart that the colonel would have a safe and glorious passage and a successful career in Chicago. (Loud cheers.)

Colonel Cody said he deeply felt the honor they had bestowed upon him in the kindly expressions contained in the address they had presented him with that evening. To deserve their good-will was a source of satisfaction greater than mere words could express. (Cheers.) He hoped that time and opportunity would enable him to extend to them an American hospitality in his own land, where sunshine and prosperity met men in every walk of life. (Cheers.) He hoped they would excuse him, for he was very ill, but presently he would try to come up smiling, whether he felt it or not. (Loud cries of "Bravo.")

The delegates than sat down to a substantial tea, after which the following toasts were proposed:

Mr. Robert Wilson (secretary to the association) in a very interesting speech proposed "Health and Prosperity to Mr. Nate Salsbury." This was seconded by Mr. T. P. Lind of the East End organizations and supported by Mr. Thomas Cornish, mining engineer. The toast was accepted with loud cheers and accompanied with musical honors.

Mr. Nate Salsbury, who was most enthusiastically received, responded in a powerful and eloquent speech, in which he referred to the friendly feelings that existed between the peoples of England and America, and concluded by expressing his pleasure at being present that evening.

Mr. F. Wigington (of the lightermen and watermen of the River Thames) proposed "Health and Prosperity to Maj. John M. Burke," which was seconded by Mr. Thomas Armstrong (patternmakers), supported by Mr. H. Le Fevre (president of the Balloon Society), and carried with acclamation.

Major Burke, who was received with great cordiality, responded in a humorous and interesting speech, which was heartily received.

During the evening each member was presented with a portrait of Buffalo Bill, bearing his autograph; after which they witnessed a performance of the Wild West Show, and altogether enjoyed a most pleasant entertainment.

AN EPISODE SINCE THE RETURN FROM EUROPE

When abroad Buffalo Bill heard so many officers of the army of France, England, and other countries ask about the Wild West of America, its game and wonderful scenery, that he extended an invitation to a number of gentlemen of rank and title to join him, with others from this country, on an extended expedition to the Grand Cañon of the Colorado, and thence on through Arizona and Utah to Salt Lake City on horseback.

Various causes prevented many from accepting the invitation, but a number assembled at Scout's Rest Ranch, the home of Colonel Cody at North Platte, Neb., and started upon the long and adventurous trail of a thousand miles in the saddle. The following are those who went on the expedition:

Col. W. F. Cody (Buffalo Bill); Col. Frank D. Baldwin,[1] U. S. Army; Col. W. H. MacKinnon,[2] Grenadier Guards, England; Maj. St. John Mildmay,[3] Grenadier Guards; Col. Allison Nailor,[4] Washington, D.C.; Maj. John M. Burke (Arizona John); Col. Prentiss Ingraham, Washington D.C.; Hon. George P. Everhart, Chicago, Ill.; Elder Daniel Seigmiller, Utah; Elder Junius Wells,[5] Utah; Robert H. Haslam (Pony Bob); Horton S. Boal,[6] Nebraska; Edward Bradford, Denver, Colo.; William B. Dowd, New York; John Hance,[7] Guide of Grand Cañon of the Colorado.

72. Buffalo Bill's Lasso to the Rescue.

Going by rail to Denver, then down into New Mexico to Flagstaff, Arizona, the party found there a wagon outfit and horses, with an escort of nearly half a hundred Mormon scouts, guides, and cowboys.

They took the trail to the Grand Cañon of the Colorado, hunting as they went along, then by a long flank movement through the Navajo Country, they crossed at Lee's Ferry, thence going on to the Kaibal Mountains, viewing the grandest scenery on earth, and enjoying the sport of hunting bear, mountain lions, mountain sheep, elk, deer, antelope, turkey, ducks, and catching fine trout and other fish.

Caught in several blizzards on the mountains, and following unknown trails, many perilous adventures were met with on the expedition, but fortunately no life was lost, though one adventure well nigh proved fatal to Major Mildmay of the Grenadier Guards, giving an opportunity to Colonel Cody to show his nerve in sudden danger and his skill with a lasso as well, for, but for his quick act, horse and rider would have run over a precipice a couple of thousands feet down to the valley below.

The expedition left the trail at Salt Lake City and returned via Wyoming and Colorado, back to the East, thus ending Colonel Cody's last trail upon the frontier, though if there should occur another border war, he would at once be found at his old post.

The End.

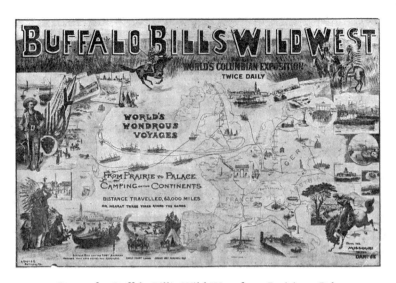

73. Poster for Buffalo Bill's Wild West from Prairie to Palace.

NOTES

Editor's Introduction

1. *New York Morning Telegraph*, March 18, 1911.

2. New York passenger list for the *Henry Kneeland*, July 27, 1833 (from Liverpool, England).

3. New York passenger lists for the *Orbit*, December 26, 1833 (from Kingston, Jamaica); for the *Barque Bradshaw*, June 16, 1834 (from Liverpool, England). U.S. Federal Census, 1840, for Brandy Wine Hundred, New Castle, Delaware.

4. Delaware state marriage records, 1838, and records of the Roman Catholic Archdiocese of Wilmington, Delaware, available at http://www.lalley.com, accessed April–June 2011.

5. U.S. Federal Census, 1850 and 1860, for First Ward, New Castle, Delaware.

6. U.S. Federal Census, 1870, for First Ward, New Castle, Delaware. Also resident at the same address are Thomas Burk, a twenty-seven-year-old pork butcher (presumably the brother identified as "Thomas M Burke" and to whom the author refers in an article in the *National Republican* on July 14, 1875) and his Ireland-born wife, Julia Burk. Delaware state marriage records for 1868 show Julia's maiden surname as Lambert.

7. Sandra K. Sagala, *Buffalo Bill on Stage* (Albuquerque: University of New Mexico Press, 2008), 44; and Nellie S. Yost, *Buffalo Bill: His Family, Friends, Fame, Fortune, and Failures* (Chicago: Sage Press/Swallow Books, 1979), 72.

8. Sarah J. Blackstone, *Buckskins, Bullets, and Business: A History of Buffalo Bill's Wild West* (New York: Greenwood 1986), 99, 101, and 142nn14–15.

9. Jack Rennert, *100 Posters of Buffalo Bill's Wild West* (New York: Darien House, 1976), 6.

10. Dexter W. Fellows and A. A. Freeman, *This Way to the Big Show—The Life of Dexter Fellows* (New York: Viking , 1936), 17.

11. Fellows and Freeman, *This Way to the Big Show*, 17–18.

12. Fellows and Freeman, *This Way to the Big Show*, 20–21.

13. Fellows and Freeman, *This Way to the Big Show*, 21.

14. Lew Parker, *Odd People I Have Met* (n.p., n.d.), 86.

15. Parker, *Odd People I Have Met*, 88.

16. Sarah J. Blackstone, *The Business of Being Buffalo Bill: Selected Letters of William F. Cody 1879–1917* (New York: Greenwood, 1988), 82–83. Burke's "How Koolah" is his attempt at the Lakota *hau kola*, which is a standard greeting between male friends.

17. Fellows and Freeman, *This Way to the Big Show*, 163.

18. Richard White, "When Fredrick Jackson Turner and Buffalo Bill Cody Both Played Chicago in 1893," in *Does the Frontier Experience Make America Exceptional?* ed. Richard W. Etulain (Boston: Bedford/St Martin's, 1999).

19. Richard White, "Fredrick Jackson Turner and Buffalo Bill," in *The Frontier in American Culture*, ed. Richard White and Patricia Nelson Limerick (Berkeley: University of California Press, 1994), 7–55, 9.

20. Frederick J. Turner, "The Significance of the Frontier in American History," in *Report of the American Historical Association for 1893* (Chicago: American Historical Association, 1893), 199–227.

21. White, *Fredrick Jackson Turner and Buffalo Bill*, 55.

22. William F. Cody, *The Life of Hon. William F. Cody, Known as Buffalo Bill: The Famous Hunter, Scout and Guide. An Autobiography.* Hartford: Frank E. Bliss, 1879; rpt. Lincoln: University of Nebraska Press, 1978). Don Russell, *The Lives and Legends of Buffalo Bill* (Norman: University of Oklahoma Press, 1960), 268.

23. Russell, *Lives and Legends of Buffalo Bill*, xvii.

24. Joy S. Kasson, *Buffalo Bill's Wild West: Celebrity, Memory and Popular History* (New York: Hill & Wang, 2000), 31.

25. John M. Burke, *From Prairie to Palace—The Lost Biography of Buffalo Bill*, edited by Tim Connor (Spokane: Marquette, 2005).

26. Burke, *From Prairie to Palace*, 11. Jason Berger had previously explored the importance of Burke as an innovative figure in "celebrity brand management" in "Buffalo Bill's Wild West and John M. Burke—Exploring the Origins of Celebrity Brand Management," *Journal of Promotion Management* 7, nos. 1 & 2 (2002): 225–52.

Compiler's Preface

1. Burke has a tendency to exaggerate. As discussed in the introduction to this edition, he first met William F. Cody in the first week of September 1873, which is twenty rather than thirty years before this volume was published.

2. Thomas Hart Benton (1782–1858) was a U.S. senator for Missouri from 1821 to 1851. He was a key proponent of western expansion and played a crucial role in the development of the movement that would be termed "Manifest Destiny." Benton was also an important backer of the various expeditions undertaken by his son-in-law, John C. Frémont.

3. Edward Fitzgerald "Ned" Beale (1822–1893) was a colorful public figure and a former U.S. naval officer who served with the army in the Mexican-American War of 1846–1848. Beale was appointed by President Buchanan in 1857 to survey and construct a wagon road from Fort Defiance, New Mexico, to the Colorado River on the border between California and Arizona. This road would become an important part of the overland trail for emigrants in the mid-nineteenth century and parts of it continue to be in use today, being followed by Interstate 40, U.S. Route 66, and the Santa Fe Railway.

4. John Charles Frémont (1813–1890) was known as "The Pathfinder" for the crucial role that his four major expeditions between 1842 and 1848 played in the opening of the West. Frémont was also a prominent military figure in both the Mexican-American War of 1846–1848 and the Civil War and as a political figure in the early development of the Republican Party.

5. James "Jim" Bridger (1804–1881) was one of the foremost mountain men, trappers, scouts, and guides in the West between the 1820s and the 1850s.

6. Christopher "Kit" Carson (1809–1868) was such a key influence

on William F. Cody that Cody named his only son in Carson's honor. A mountain man and trapper through the 1830s, Carson acted as guide to John Charles Frémont on his first two expeditions, fought in the Mexican-American War of 1846–1848 and the Civil War, and was a prominent figure in the Indian Wars on the southern plains and the Southwest.

7. William F. Cody had been claiming the rank of colonel from about 1887 and it was by that rank that friends and associates usually referred to him. In 1889, however, and essentially at his own request, he was appointed as an honorary *aide-de-camp* to Nebraska governor John Thayer, with the rank of brigadier general in the National Guard of the State of Nebraska.

1. Introductory

1. *The Arabian Nights* is a collection of Middle Eastern and South-Asian folktales that date from the Islamic Golden Age of the eighth to the thirteenth century. The stories have been influential in the development of European and American adventure stories, particularly fairy-tales for children, since the eighteenth century.

2. Isaac Cody (1811–1857) was William F. Cody's father.

3. Friedrich Wilhelm Heinrich Alexander Freiherr von Humboldt (1767–1835) was a Prussian nobleman, naturalist, and explorer whose accounts of his numerous expeditions to the Americas are generally regarded as offering the first modern scientific descriptions of much of South America and the American West.

4. Sir Henry Morton Stanley (1841–1904) was a renowned journalist, explorer of Africa, and politician. Stanley was born to an unmarried mother in Denbigh, Wales, and adopted the name by which he is best known when he moved to the United States in 1859. He fought for the Confederacy in the Civil War before turning to journalism and embarking on his famous quest to find David Livingstone, the Scots missionary in Africa. After his expeditions to Africa in the 1870s and 1880s, Stanley returned to Britain and entered politics as a Liberal member of Parliament. He was made a Knight Grand Cross of the Order of Bath by Queen Victoria in 1899.

5. Sir Charles Wentworth Dilke, Second Baronet, PC (1843–1911), was a prominent intellectual, reformist, and liberal politician whose

best-known written work was *Greater Britain: A Record of Travel in English Speaking Countries During 1866 and 1867* (London: MacMillan, 1868). Dilke's political aspirations were ruined by his involvement in a scandalous divorce case, known as the "Crawford Scandal," in 1876. Although he spent much of the rest of his life attempting to exonerate himself of the charge that he had perjured himself in court, he did find time to publish *Problems of Greater Britain* (London: MacMillan, 1890), a follow-up volume to his earlier work.

6. The story of Aladdin and his magic lamp is generally associated with the *Arabian Nights* but it did not in fact form part of the original collection. Along with the other well-known stories *The Seven Voyages of Sinbad* and *Ali Baba and the Forty Thieves*, it was an eighteenth-century French interpolation in the translation by Antoine Galland, *Les mille et une nuits* (Paris: Garnier Flammarrion, 1965 [first edition, 1704]).

7. Washington Irving (1783–1859) was an American writer and diplomat. He is best known for his short stories *The Legend of Sleepy Hollow* and *Rip Van Winkle*, but he also wrote nonfiction, including biographies of George Washington and Christopher Columbus, and he served as the U.S. minister to Spain from 1842 to 1846.

2. The Scout

1. Richard Irving Dodge (1827–1895), a career soldier who served in the U.S. Army from the age of twenty-one until four years before his death, acted as *aide-de-camp* to Gen. William Tecumseh Sherman between 1881 and 1882. From 1851 Dodge served mainly in the West and was the author of a number of published accounts of his time there.

2. William Tecumseh Sherman (1820–1891) was one of the best-known military figures of the nineteenth century who played a crucial role in the Union victory in the Civil War, famously developing tactics that are often seen as the forerunner of twentieth-century "total war." Sherman was subsequently a key figure in the Indian Wars and assumed overall command of the army when Ulysses S. Grant was elected president.

3. Philip Henry Sheridan (1831–1888), a second-generation Irish American career soldier, played a key role in both the Civil War and the Indian Wars. His own memoirs were published in two volumes as *Personal*

Memoirs of P. H. Sheridan (New York: Charles L. Webster, 1888), and the key study of his role in the Indian Wars is Paul A. Hutton's *Phil Sheridan and His Army* (Lincoln: University of Nebraska Press, 1985).

4. Grand Duke Alexei Alexandrovich Romanov (1850–1908), fourth son of Tsar Alexander II of Russia, made an official visit to the United States in 1870–1871 that included a hunting expedition to the plains in January 1871 with William F. Cody as one of his guides.

5. William Selby Harney (1800–1889) was a controversial military figure who fought in the Blackhawk War (1832), the first Seminole War (1835–1842), the Mexican-American War (1846–1848), the first Sioux War (1854–1855), and the Mormon Uprising (1857–1858) before being retired from the service in 1863 after having been relieved of his command of the Department of the Missouri by President Abraham Lincoln.

6. George Alexander "Sandy" Forsyth (1837–1915) served in the U.S. Army from 1861 to 1890, through the Civil War and the Indian Wars, eventually retiring with the rank of colonel.

7. Wesley Merritt (1834–1910) served in the U.S. Army from 1861 to 1910, through the Civil War, Indian Wars, and Spanish-American War of 1898, during which he served as military governor of the Philippines. Merritt was superintendent of the U.S. Military Academy at West Point from 1882 to 1887. He retired with the rank of brigadier general in 1900.

8. James Sanks Brisbin (1837–1892) was an educator and newspaper editor before serving as an officer in the Union Army during the Civil War, rising to the rank of brevet brigadier general. After the war Brisbin remained in the service with the rank of lieutenant colonel, holding command positions with the Second, Ninth, First, and Eighth Cavalry regiments until his death in 1892. He was a prolific writer who authored several books and regularly published articles in a range of magazines, including two accounts of his service in the West.

9. William Hemsley Emory (1811–1887), a West Point graduate and career soldier, served as a first lieutenant with Kearney's 1846 expeditionary force that explored the Southwest. As a major, Emory commanded Forts Washita and Arbuckle in Indian Territory from 1858 through the Civil War; he attained the rank of general and was in command of reconstruction in Louisiana in the immediate postbellum period.

10. John Gibbon (1827–1896) served with distinction in the U.S. Army from 1847 to 1891 and through the Civil War and Indian Wars, then retired with the rank of major general. A general of the famous "Iron Brigade" of the Union Army of the Potomac, Gibbon served during the Great Sioux War of 1876–1877 and in the pursuit of Chief Joseph's Nez Perce Indians in 1877.

11. A promising legal career seemed to beckon for Yale Law School graduate Alfred Howe Terry (1827–1890) when he was appointed as clerk of the Superior Court of Newhaven, Connecticut, at the tender age of twenty-one. At the outbreak of the Civil War, however, he raised a regiment of volunteers for the Union Army, fought with distinction in the Eastern theater throughout the war, and subsequently opted to stay in the military, rising to the rank of major general in 1886, when he assumed command of the Division of the Missouri. Terry was involved in negotiating the Fort Laramie Treaty of 1868, he commanded the Dakota Column in the summer 1876 campaign of the Great Sioux War, and he served as an envoy to Canada in October 1877 in an attempt to negotiate Sitting Bull's return to the United States.

12. Ranald Slidell Mackenzie (1840–1889) graduated at the head of the class of 1862 from West Point Military Academy and served with distinction through the Civil War and Indian Wars, where he saw action in the 1874 Red River War on the Southern Plains and in the Great Sioux War of 1876–1877. In 1882 he was promoted to brigadier general and assigned to the Department of Texas. He suffered from mental illness that resulted from a head injury caused by a fall from a wagon at Fort Sill, Oklahoma, and was retired from the service in 1884.

13. Eugene Asa Carr (1830–1910) graduated from West Point Military Academy in 1850 and was deployed to the Southwest, then gained his first combat experience fighting Apaches in the Diablo Mountains in 1854. He served through the Civil War, winning the Medal of Honor in the battle of Pea Ridge in March 1862. During the Indian Wars he fought on the southern plains, in the Great Sioux War of 1876–1877, and in the Apache Wars of the 1880s, notably commanding at both the battle of Summit Springs in 1869 and at Warbonnet Creek in 1876, the two incidents which William F. Cody dramatized as the killing of chiefs Tall

Bull and Yellow Hand in the Wild West. Carr retired from the service in 1893 with the rank of brigadier general.

14. Winfield Scott Hancock (1824–1886) served with distinction in the U.S. Army for over four decades and was the Democratic nominee for president in 1880. He fought in the Mexican-American War of 1846–1848, through the Civil War—earning the nickname "the Thunderbolt of the Army of the Potomac"—and saw two periods of service in the West in 1866–1867 and 1869–1872.

15. George R. Crook (1828–1890) graduated from West Point Military Academy at the bottom of the class of 1852 but nevertheless went on to a distinguished military career. He fought through the Civil War, serving as both a brigade and division commander, and in the Indian Wars against Bannock, Shoshone, and Paiute people in 1864–1868 and in the Great Sioux War of 1876–1877. His command was defeated at the Battle of the Rosebud on June, 17, 1876, but he obtained notable success in the Apache Wars of the Southwest.

16. John Pope (1822–1892) graduated from West Point Military Academy in 1842 and served with distinction in the western theater of the Civil War before being promoted to command the Army of the Potomac, which he led to defeat in the second Battle of Bull Run/Manassas in August 1862. Thereafter Pope was transferred to the West, where he led an expedition against the Dakota Indians who had been involved in the Great Sioux Uprising of 1862. He subsequently served against the Apaches in the Southwest, retiring from the service in 1886 with the rank of major general.

17. Nelson Appleton Miles (1838–1925) served as an officer through the Civil War, earning the Medal of Honor at Chancellorsville in 1863, in the Indian Wars, and in the Spanish American War of 1898. He volunteered to return to service in 1917 during the First World War but was turned down by President Woodrow Wilson. In the West he fought on the Southern Plains in the early 1870s, in the Great Sioux War of 1876–1877, in the pursuit of the Nez Perces in 1877, against Geronimo and the last non-reservation Apaches into the 1880s, and against the Lakotas during the Ghost Dance trouble of the early 1890s (in which both John M. Burke and William F. Cody had some involvement. Miles was

commanding general of the U.S. Army through the Spanish-American War of 1898.

18. Edward Otho Cresap Ord (1818–1883) graduated from West Point Military Academy in 1839 and fought both in the Second Seminole War of 1835–1842 and in the Civil War. He was appointed commander of the Department of the Platte in 1871 and he was one of the officers who participated in the hunting expedition with Grand Duke Alexis of Russia in January 1871.

19. Christopher Colon Auger (1821–1898) graduated from West Point Military Academy in 1843 and acted as *aide-de-camp* to Generals Hopping and Cushing during the Mexican-American War of 1846–1848. He subsequently gained experience fighting Indians in the Rogue River War in Southern Oregon in 1855–1856 then served briefly as commandant of cadets at West Point in 1861 before transferring to a divisional command in the Army of the Potomac. He was badly wounded at Harper's Ferry in August 1862 and was breveted a major general on the field. He was stationed in Washington DC at the end of the war and was the officer in charge of the escort of President Lincoln's body from the Peterson House to the White House after the president's assassination on the evening of April 14, 1865. Auger commanded the Department of the Platte from 1867 to 1871 and the Department of Texas from 1871 to 1875. He retired from the service in 1885 with the rank of major general.

20. Virginia-born William Bedford Royall (1825–1896) was a career soldier who served as a lieutenant with the Missouri Mounted Volunteers during the Mexican-American War of 1846–1848; in 1855 was commissioned as first lieutenant in the Second U.S. Cavalry. He committed to the Union cause at the outbreak of the Civil War, serving with the Army of the Potomac and holding the rank of major and the brevet rank of colonel by the war's end. He served on the southern plains through December 1875, when he was commissioned lieutenant colonel of the Third Cavalry and commanded his own regiment and five troops of the Second Cavalry in Crook's command during the Great Sioux War of 1876–1877. Royall was promoted to the rank of colonel in 1882 and was retired from the service with the rank of brigadier general in 1887.

21. William Babcock Hazen (1830–1887) graduated from West Point

Military Academy in 1855 and served through the Civil War and subsequently in the West. He was the officer negotiating with Cheyenne Chief Black Kettle in the days before George Armstrong Custer's attack on Black Kettle's village along the Washita River in Oklahoma in November 1868, eventually becoming embroiled in a controversy with Custer over the account of the battle in Custer's *My Life on the Plains* (New York: Sheldon & Company, 1874). Hazen was a military observer during the Franco-Prussian War of 1871, and in 1880 he was appointed brigadier general and chief signal officer of the U.S. Army by President Hayes.

22. Thomas Duncan (1819–1887) fought at the age of thirteen in the Black Hawk War of 1832 before going on to a military career. He fought in the Mexican-American War of 1846–1848 and was stationed in the west during the Civil War, commanding the Third U.S. Cavalry Regiment at Fort Craig, New Mexico, and leading troops at the battle of Valverde in February 1862, an engagement during which he was wounded. He was commander of the Fifth U.S. Cavalry from 1866 and through the first period in which William F. Cody served as a scout for the regiment. He retired from the service due to ill health in 1873 with the rank of lieutenant colonel.

23. William Jackson Palmer (1836–1909) was a civil engineer engaged in railway building at the outbreak of the Civil War when he accepted a commission as colonel in the Union Army. He was captured at the battle of Antietam in 1862 but was back with his regiment the following year after a prisoner exchange; he won the Medal of Honor for actions at the Battle of Nashville in December 1864. He left the service at the end of the war with the brevet rank of major general, moved west, and returned to railway building. He played a key role in the development of the Kansas Pacific Railway from 1867 and his own Denver and Rio Grande Railway from 1870. He is credited with founding the town of Colorado City, subsequently known as Colorado Springs, in 1871.

24. William Henry Penrose (1832–1903) was the son of a regular army captain who abandoned an engineering career at the outbreak of the Civil War when, through his father's connections, he obtained a commission as second lieutenant. By the war's end he had been breveted a brigadier general of both the U.S. Army and the U.S. Volunteers;

he opted to remain in the service, where he served in the West with the Third U.S. Infantry from 1866 to 1888, seeing action against Cheyennes, Kiowas, and Comanches on the southern plains and against Apaches in the Southwest, rising to the rank of lieutenant colonel of the regiment. Penrose was promoted to colonel of the Twentieth Infantry in 1888 and retired from the service with that rank in 1896.

25. George Armstrong Custer (1839–1876) was a Civil War hero and remains perhaps the best-known military figure of the Indian Wars for his exploits on the southern plains in the 1860s and even more so for his defeat and death at Little Bighorn in June 1876. Three figures were crucial in the development of the popular culture perception of the "Custer myth": his first biographer, Fredrick Whittaker; his widow, Elizabeth Bacon Custer, through her three books; and William F. Cody, through his incorporation of *Custer's Last Stand* into the Wild West.

26. Moses Milner (1829–1876) was a mountain man in the early 1840s who acted as a teamster during the Mexican-American War of 1846–1848 and then took part in the California and Montana gold rushes before being appointed as Custer's chief of scouts for the expedition that culminated in the battle of the Washita in 1869. The nickname "California Joe" relates to Milner's participation in the 1849 gold rush. He was romanticized and eulogized by Custer in his account of the campaign. He died in a gunfight at Fort Robinson, Nebraska, in 1876.

27. James Butler Hickok (1837–1876), one of the most notable figures of the American West, was a lawman, gunfighter, marksman, professional gambler, and army scout. He served in the Union Army during the Civil War and gained publicity after the war for his exploits as a scout, marksman, and professional gambler. He was something of a hero to William F. Cody, who based a number of elements of his public image on Hickok. In 1873 Cody invited Hickok to join him and "Texas Jack" Omohundro on stage in their new play, *Scouts of the Plains*. Hickok was shot dead by Jack McCall while playing poker in a Deadwood, South Dakota, saloon in 1876.

28. Sir St. George Gore (1811–1978) was the Eighth Baronet Gore of Magherabegg, a wealthy Irish nobleman and adventurer who made a number of expeditions to the American West between 1824 and 1857. The Gore Range in Colorado is named for him.

29. Windham Thomas Wyndham-Quin, Fourth Earl of Dunraven and Mount-Earl KP PC (1841–1926), was an Irish peer and Conservative politician who first came to the American West in 1872, where he met and befriended "Texas Jack" Omohundro, who acted as a guide and led the earl's party on buffalo and elk hunts. In 1874 Wyndham-Quinn decided to make the whole of Estes Park, Colorado, a game preserve for the exclusive use of himself and his English friends. By stretching the provisions of the Homestead Act and the rights of preemption, Dunraven claimed fifteen thousand acres in present-day Rocky Mountain National Park.

30. James Gordon Bennett Jr. (1841–1918) was a socialite, sportsman, *bon viveur*, and, from 1866, editor of the *New York Herald*, which was founded by his father, a Scots immigrant of the same name. In September 1871 he organized a large-scale hunting expedition to the West, which was extensively covered in the *Herald* and was a major contributing factor to William F. Cody's early fame. In 1877 Bennett was involved in an infamous scandal as a result of which his engagement to socialite Caroline May was broken off, and he lived out most of the rest of his life in Paris, France, attending Buffalo Bill's Wild West when it appeared at the Universal Exhibition there in 1889.

31. Lawrence Rosco Jerome (1820–1888) was a New York socialite and financier who participated in the September 1871 hunting expedition organized by James Gordon Bennett and guided by William F. Cody.

32. Frederic Sackrider Remington (1861–1909) was an artist whose depictions of cowboys, Indians, U.S. cavalrymen, and western landscapes did a great deal to contribute to the development of images of the West in American popular culture. There is no evidence that Cody ever acted as a guide for Remington; nevertheless, the two men were admirers of each other's work, and Remington provided illustrations for Helen Wetmore-Cody's biography of her brother.

33. Henry Augustus Ward (1834–1906) was an American naturalist and geologist who took part in the hunting expedition that was organized for Grand Duke Alexis of Russia in January 1872.

34. Othniel Charles Marsh (1831–1899) was the first professor of paleontology in the United States. William F. Cody acted as guide for Professor Marsh and a group of his students on a fossil-hunting expedition to the West in 1870.

35. John Gerard Heckscher (1837–1908) was a New York socialite and *bon viveur* who served as a first lieutenant in the Twelfth Infantry Regiment in the Civil War. There is nothing in Heckscher's army record to suggest that he held the rank of major. He was a participant in the hunting expedition organized by James Gordon Bennett in 1871. When William F. Cody visited New York in February 1872, Heckscher acted as Cody's guide, introducing him to the Union Club and commissioning a suit of clothes for him from his tailor.

36. George Henry Kingsley (1827–1892), brother of the famous authors Canon Charles Kingsley (1819–1875) and Henry Kingsley (1830–1876), and father of the influential writer and African explorer Mary Henrietta Kinglsey (1862–1900), was personal physician to the Earl of Dunraven and accompanied the earl on his trip to the American West in 1872.

37. Fort McPherson, near the site of present-day North Platte, Nebraska, was originally known as Cantonment McKean when it was founded in 1863. It was renamed on February 26, 1866, in the honor of Maj. Gen. James B. McPherson, who was killed at the battle of Atlanta in July 1864 and was the highest-ranking Union Army officer to lose his life in the Civil War. It was popularly known as Fort Cottonwood due to its location along Cottonwood Creek.

38. George Frederick Price's history of the Fifth Cavalry Regiment covers the period from its organization in 1855 through 1883. George F. Price, *Across the Continent with the Fifth Cavalry* (New York: D. Van Nostrand, 1883).

39. The site of the battle is in the state of Nebraska.

40. This refers to Little Goose Creek, which runs through present day Sheridan, Wyoming, and not Goose Creek that runs by Bozeman, Montana.

41. Buckskin Joe was William F. Cody's favored mount in 1869–1870.

42. Cody nicknamed his 1873 .50-caliber Springfield trapdoor rifle "Lucretia Borgia" after the daughter of Pope Alexander III, the infamous alleged murderess of that name.

43. Robert Edward Lee (1807–1870), Albert Sidney Johnston (1803–1862), William Joseph Hardee (1815–1873), and Earl Van Dorn (1820–1863) were prominent generals in the Confederate Army during the Civil

War. All had previously served as officers in the U.S. Army in either the Fifth Cavalry or its predecessor regiment, the Second Dragoons, as had Union general William Hemsley Emory. George Armstrong Custer never served in the regiment under either designation.

44. Hays City, now simply Hays, Kansas, was the railhead for the Kansas-Pacific Railroad from 1866.

45. Fort Larned, about six miles from present-day Larned, Kansas, on the Pawnee Fork of the Arkansas River, operated as a U.S. military base from 1859 to 1878, having originally been constructed to protect emigrant trains along the Oregon Trail. It was originally known as the Camp on the Pawnee Fork but in 1860 was renamed Fort Larned in honor of Col. Benjamin F. Larned, paymaster general of the U.S. Army.

46. Fort Hays, near present-day Hays, Kansas, was originally named Fort Fletcher, for Gov. Thomas C. Fletcher of Missouri, when it was established in 1865 to protect the stage and freight wagons of the Butterfield Overland Despatch that traveled along the Smoky Hill Trail to Denver, Colorado. After a closure of several months, the fort was renamed Fort Hays and relocated to the site of the current national historic site to be closer to the railroad in October 1866. The name is in honor of Civil War general Alexander Hays, who had been killed in the Battle of the Wilderness in May 1864.

47. Fort Dodge, Kansas, is located approximately five miles East of Dodge City, Kansas, on Highway 400. Fort Dodge, built in 1865, was operated as a military base until 1882. It was named for Gen. Grenville Mellen Dodge (1831–1916), who selected the site for the fort in 1864. In January 1890 the site was deeded to the State of Kansas for use as the Kansas State Soldiers Home.

48. Kansas encompasses four creeks of this name. The one referred to here is "Big Coon Creek," which is crossed by the old Santa Fe Trail in Edwards County, Kansas, about thirty-three miles from the Pawnee Fork of the Arkansas River.

49. Charles King (1844–1933) was the son of Union general Rufus King. He graduated from West Point Military Academy in 1866 and served in the Indian Wars under Crook, retiring from the service in 1879 due to persistent problems arising from an arm wound received in a fight

with Apaches in 1874. King was recalled to the service during the Spanish-American War of 1898 with the rank of brigadier general of Volunteers. He was a prolific writer, producing more than sixty novels in addition to his historical works on army life. He collaborated with William F. Cody in the silent film projects with which he was involved toward the end of his life.

50. Burke is somewhat carried away here as he previously named "Generals" Crittenden, Penrose, Forsyth, and Hayes earlier in the chapter. Although most of the officers named did have experience in the West, William F. Cody did not serve with many of them but was acquainted with almost all of them. The officers mentioned here for the first time are Henry Cary Bankhead (1828–1894), who had a distinguished Civil War career and was commander of Fort Wallace during Cody's time as a scout; James Barnet Fry (1827–1894), who was provost marshal general of the Union Army during the Civil War and was stationed on the Southern Plains in the late 1860s; Jacob Bowman Sweitzer (1821–1881), whose surname is misspelled by Burke as "Switzer" in the original text, served as a brigade commander with the Army of the Potomac through the Civil War and participated in the hunting expedition with Grand Duke Alexis in 1872; Edmund Winchester Rucker (1835–1824), a Confederate cavalry brigade commander under Nathan Bedford Forrest, who had become a prominent industrialist by the time of writing; Edmund Kirby Smith (1824–1893), a West Point graduate who served on the plains before the Civil War, commanded the Confederate Trans-Mississippi Department during the war, and subsequently became a leading industrialist and educator; John H. King (1820–1888), a Civil War hero who subsequently served on the plains; Stewart Van Vliet (1815–1901), a West Point graduate who was reputed to have killed an Indian chief in hand-to-hand combat during the Seminole Wars and served in the first Sioux War of 1855 and as chief quartermaster of the Army of the Potomac in the Civil War; Anson Mills (1834–1924), who served in the Union Army through the Civil War and then in the Indian Wars, fighting at battles of the Rosebud and Slim Buttes in the Great Sioux War of 1876–1877 and retiring from the army with the rank of brigadier general in 1897; John Fulton Reynolds (1820–1863), who fought in the Mexican-American War of 1846–48,

the Rogue River War of 1856, and the Utah War of 1857–58, and who was killed in action at Gettysburg in July 1863. Adolphus Washington Greely (1844–1935) joined the army as a private in 1861, retired as a brigadier general in 1908, and served with distinction through the Civil War but rose to prominence later as an Arctic explorer. Nathan Augustus Monroe Dudley (1825–1910) retired a brevet Major General in 1889 after serving through the Civil War and then in the Indian Wars on the Southern Plains, the South-west and in Montana Territory, being also involved in policing actions during the Lincoln County War of 1878 and on the Crow Reservation in 1887. Edward Richard Sprigg Canby (1817–1873) fought in the Seminole Wars and the Civil War before becoming the only general to be killed by Indians in April 1873 during the Modoc War. James Gilpatrick Blunt (1826–1881), a practicing physician in Kansas at the outbreak of the Civil War, raised a volunteer regiment and fought in the western theater through the war and acted as commander of the District of South Kansas at the war's end. Guy Vernor Henry (1839–1899), a West Point graduate and career army officer who earned the Medal of Honor at Cold Harbor in June 1864 and the brevet rank of brigadier general for gallantry while seriously wounded at the battle of the Rosebud in 1876, went on to fight in the invasion of Puerto Rico during the Spanish-American War and was appointed military governor of Puerto Rico.

3. What Is a Cowboy?

1. William Kidd (1645–1701), Jean Lafitte (1776–1823), and Sir Henry Morgan (1635–1688) were real-life pirates of the Caribbean and the Gulf of Mexico who were much romanticized in popular writing of the nineteenth century. Burke wrongly gives Kidd's surname as "Kyd" in the original text.

2. Daniel Boone (1734–1820) is the famous Scots-Irish Kentucky pioneer who played a key role in the western expansion of the early republic.

3. David Crockett (1786–1836), the much-mythologized Tennessee soldier, frontiersman, and politician, died at the Alamo in 1836.

4. The Riders of the World

1. Ṣalah ad-Din Yusuf ibn Ayyubi (1138–1193), known in English as Saladin, was the sultan of Egypt and Syria who led the Muslim forces

in the Third Crusade (1189–1192) and came to be much mythologized as a chivalric figure.

2. King Richard I of England (1157–1199), known as Richard the Lionheart (in French as *Coeur de Lion*), led the Christian forces in the Third Crusade (1189–1192) and was a much-mythologized and romanticized figure renowned for his purported nobility, chivalry, and bravery.

3. "Mazeppa" is a long narrative poem composed in 1819 by the English Romantic poet George Gordon Byron, the Sixth Baron Byron (1788–1824), better known as Lord Byron. The poem is based on a popular legend about the early life of Ivan Mazepa (1639–1709), a Ukrainian nobleman who became leader of the Ukrainian Cossacks.

4. Hernán Cortés de Monroy y Pizarro (1485–1547), Spanish nobleman and *conquistador*, led a small contingent of Spaniards and their Indian allies to defeat the Aztec rulers of Mexico in 1519–1520 and establish the colony of Nueva España (or New Spain), of which he was appointed first governor.

5. Gaius Julius Caesar (100 BC–44 BC) was a Roman soldier, orator, statesman, and the effective ruler of the empire for the last three years of his life.

6. Gaius Suetonius Tranquillus (ca. 69 AD to ca. 130 AD) was a Roman historian who is best remembered for his *De Vita Caesarum*, known in English as *The Twelve Caesars*.

7. Hernando de Soto (1496–1542) was a Spanish nobleman and *conquistador* who participated in the conquest of Peru in the early 1530s and led an expedition into the territory of the modern-day United States between 1539 and 1542.

8. Marie-Rosalie Bonheur (1822–1899) was a French artist who famously painted William F. Cody on horseback during the Wild West's appearance at the Universal Exhibition in Paris in 1889.

9. Burke is here citing William Shakespeare's 1593 narrative poem, "Venus and Adonis" (lines 265–300), which is based on the legend of the lovers Venus and Adonis from Ovid's *Metamorphoses*.

10. *Pehin hanska* is Lakota for "Long Hair," a name by which both William F. Cody and George Armstrong Custer were known to Lakota-speaking people.

11. Arta Cody (1866–1904) was William F. Cody's eldest daughter.

5. Indian Home Life

1. The word of Algonquin origin commonly used to refer to Indian women at the time this volume was written is now considered to be profoundly offensive to most Indian people and it is therefore not used in this edition.

6. Expert Shooting

1. William Tell, a legendary Swiss hero whose story was first recorded in the late fifteenth century, represents an iconic figure for Swiss nationalists because in the tale he refuses to bow to the authority of the Austrian governor, Gessler, and is required to shoot an apple from the head of his son, Walter, as a punishment.

2. The well-known Bible story from I Samuel 17: 1–58 of how the Israelite boy, David, slew the Philistine giant, Goliath, with a stone from his sling.

7. A Most Famous Ride

1. Civil War veteran Captain Daingerfield Parker (1832–1925) was quartermaster at Fort Larned at the time.

2. In the original text Burke wrongly has "Fort Sarah" for Fort Zarah, which was originally known as Camp Dunlap when it was established two miles east of present-day Great Bend, Kansas, in 1864. It was renamed for Civil War major H. Zarah Curtis, who had been killed in the battle of Baxter Springs in October 1863; the fort was operated as a military post until 1869.

3. Pawnee Rock in present-day Barton County, Kansas, was an important landmark on the Santa Fe Trail.

4. Satanta or White Bear (ca. 1820–1878) was an important member of the Kiowa Koitsenko warrior society, which fought at the first battle of Adobe Walls (1864). In June 1871 Satanta was tried for murder for his involvement in raids on wagon trains along the Warren Wagon Road in Jacksboro, Texas, and then detained in the state penitentiary at Huntsville, where he died in custody. In the original text Burke gives his name as "Santanta."

5. Scotland's national bard, Robert Burns (1759–1796), composed

"Tam o' Shanter," his comic poem of a man on horseback being chased by a witch, in 1790. In the original text Burke makes the common error of spelling the name Tam O'Shanter as if it were an Irish surname. The o' in the original is a contraction for "of."

6. There is currently no place named Ash Grove in Kansas. There is an Ash Creek, which runs more or less parallel to the route of the old Santa Fe Trail between Pawnee Rock and Fort Larned. The name was probably applied to an area along its route.

7. James Maddison Keller (1831–1897), known as "Denver Jim," was an army scout, former Pony Express rider, and companion of William F. Cody in the 1860s.

8. Walnut Creek crosses the Santa Fe Trail near Heizer, Kansas.

9. Sawlog Creek Crossing, located in the northern part of Ford County, Kansas, was originally identified as the South Branch of the Pawnee Fork of the Arkansas River. Its name was changed to Sawlog because of the vast amount of timber that lined its banks and furnished the nearby forts with wood for fuel and construction.

10. Charles G. Cox (1849–1886), a Civil War veteran who was wounded at Cold Harbor in January 1864, went on to serve in the Seventh and Tenth U.S. Cavalries until 1870.

8. Letters of Commendation from Prominent Military Men

1. Richard Coulter Drum (1825–1909) fought in the Mexican-American War of 1846–1848 and the first Sioux War of 1855, leaving an account of the battle at Ash Hollow. He served through the Civil War, reaching the brevet rank of brigadier general, and as adjutant general of the U.S. Army from 1880 to 1889. In the original edition Burke has wrongly transcribed his initials as "S. S."

2. John Milton Thayer (1820–1906) served in the Union Army during the Civil War and attained the brevet rank of brigadier general before going on to become a Republican politician and governor of Nebraska from 1887 to 1891.

3. Gilbert Lafayette Laws (1838–1907) was a Civil War veteran who served as secretary of state of Nebraska from 1886 to 1888. In the original edition Burke wrongly transcribes the surname as "Laur."

9. Buffalo Bill's Boyhood

1. Pierre Terrail LeVieux, Seigneur de Bayard (1473–1524), was a French nobleman and soldier generally known as the Chevalier de Bayard, who came to be known proverbially as the "knight without fear and beyond reproach."

2. William F. Cody's uncle Elijah Cody (1807–1866), Isaac Cody's older brother, was a successful merchant in Weston, Missouri.

3. The site of the current town of Kickapoo, Kansas, in Leavenworth County.

4. Salt Creek Valley, Kansas, is approximately 1.5 miles from the town of Kickapoo, Kansas.

5. Alexander Majors (1814–1900) was a businessman who played a crucial role in the development of Kansas. The freighting company Russell & Majors, owned with his partners, William Hepburn Russell (1812–1872) and William Bradford Waddell (1807–1872), held the contract to haul freight to the army posts along the Santa Fe Trail from 1853. The three men were involved in setting up the short-lived Pony Express service, which ran between St. Joseph, Missouri, and Sacramento, California, from April 1860 to October 1861.

6. The Nebraska-Kansas Act of 1854 effectively nullified the Missouri Compromises of 1820 and 1850, which outlawed slavery in the western territories and thereby divided the nation on the issue of slavery and gave rise to the Bleeding Kansas violence on the Nebraska-Kansas-Missouri frontier in which William F. Cody's father lost his life. It was to be a crucial step on the road to Civil War.

10. Bill Kills His First Indian

1. Fort Kearny was established in the spring of 1848 near the head of the Grand Island of the Platte River, near the site of present-day Kearney, Nebraska. It was originally called Fort Childs, but in 1848 the post was renamed in honor of early western explorer and hero of the Mexican-American War Gen. Stephen Watts Kearny (1794–1848). The fort operated as a military post until 1875. In the original text Burke misspells the name of the fort as "Kearney."

2. Big Sandy Lake was located in present-day Thayer County, Nebraska.

3. The Little Blue River rises near Minden, Nebraska, then flows east-southeast and joins the Big Blue River at Blue Rapids, Kansas. The Oregon Trail and the Pony Express route both ran along the course of the Little Blue.

4. The original Fort Kearny was established in 1846 on the Missouri River at the mouth of Table Creek, near the site of present-day Nebraska City, Nebraska. It operated as an army post for less than two years, until the establishment of Fort Kearny about seventeen miles away on the Platte River.

5. Blue Water Creek, Nebraska, the site where Harney's expeditionary force attacked the Sicangu Lakota village of Wakinyan Cikala (Little Thunder) in September 1855.

6. Burke has 1865 in the original text, rather than the correct year of 1855.

7. The Green River is a tributary of the Colorado River, which rises in Sublette County, Wyoming, and flows through Wyoming, Utah, and Colorado.

8. The Utah War of 1857–1858.

9. Fort Bridger, near the site of the present-day town of the same name in Uinta County, Wyoming, was established as a trading post by Jim Bridger in 1842. It was a staging post for the Pony Express and used as an army base from the time of the Civil War until its abandonment in 1878.

10. Ash Hollow, Nebraska.

11. Cedar Bluffs, in Saunders County, Nebraska, was a key landmark on the Mormon and California Trails.

12. The Jaeger was a single-shot hunting rifle whose name derives from Jäger the German for a huntsman. In the original text Burke wrongly has the name of the weapon as "yager."

11. The Boy Miner

1. Camp Walbach was a short-lived military outpost at the head of Lodgepole Creek in Cheyenne Pass, Wyoming, approximately twenty-five miles northwest of Cheyenne. The camp, named for Gen. John Baptiste de Barth Walbach, Baron de Walbach (1766–1857), an Alsatian aristocrat who served in the U.S. Army but had died the previous year, was operational from September 1858 through April 1859 only.

2. Chugwater Creek is a tributary of the Laramie River, which rises in the nearby mountains and flows into the river near the site of present-day Wheatland, Wyoming.

3. Oak Grove, Missouri, is located in present-day Lafayette County on the Kansas-Missouri border.

4. Grasshopper Falls was the original name of the present-day town of Valley Falls, Kansas.

5. Pike's Peak, in present-day Colorado, was the site of a gold rush from 1859 to 1861.

6. Aurora, in the Aurora Heights east of Denver, Colorado, was no more than a string of mining camps during the gold rush. The nearby city of Aurora did not take the name until 1907, having been founded in 1880 as Fletcher, Colorado.

7. *Ignis fatuus*, Latin for "foolish fire," is used for the phenomenon of ghostly lights seen at twilight over bogs, swamps, and marshes, and is often referred to in folklore by such terms as will-o'-the-wisp, corpse candle, jack-o'-lantern, friar's lantern, and gunderslislik.

8. Black Hawk, Colorado, on the north fork of Clear Creek in Gregory Gulch, is where gold was discovered in May 1859, giving rise to the gold rush.

9. A Jacob's ladder is a mythical ladder to heaven. The term comes from the biblical story in Genesis 28: 10–19.

10. Julesburg, Colorado, was a staging post on the Pony Express route located near the present-day town of that name in present-day Sedgewick County, Colorado. It was named for Jules Beni, an early French trader in the area.

12. Story of the Pony Express

1. Francisco Pizarro González, Marquess (ca. 1471–1541) was the Spanish nobleman, soldier, and *conquistador* who led the overthrow of Inca rule in South America in 1533–1534.

2. Zachary Taylor (1784–1850) was the twelfth president of the United States and had been a brigadier general in the army, fighting in the War of 1812, the Second Seminole War, the Black Hawk War, and the Mexican-American War. Taylor's administration was responsible for the

Missouri Compromise of 1850, which contributed to the nation's western expansion.

3. Winfield Scott (1786–1866) was a soldier and Whig politician who fought in the War of 1812, the Seminole Wars, the Black Hawk War, and the American Civil War. He supervised removal of the Cherokees to the trans-Mississippi region in 1838. He was commanding general of the U.S. Army from 1841 to 1861.

4. Alexander William Doniphan (1808–1887) was a soldier and politician who fought in the Mexican-American War of 1846–1848 and went on to be a moderate Republican politician. Doniphan was involved in the early development of Kansas, Nebraska, and Missouri.

5. A classical reference to the myth of Minerva, the goddess of wisdom, who sprang fully formed from the head of her father, Jupiter (or Jove).

6. William McKendree Gwin (1805–1885) served as a Democratic senator for California from 1850 to 1855. In the original text Burke misspells his name as "Gwinn."

7. James Buchanan (1791–1868) was the fifteenth president of the United States, from 1857 to 1861.

8. *Deo volente* is Latin for "God willing."

9. Fort Hall, situated on the Snake River just north of the present-day site of Pocatello, Idaho, was an important stop on the Oregon Trail. It operated as a trading post from 1832 and was used as a military base from 1861 until its abandonment in 1866. In the original text Burke misspells Pocatello as "Pocatella."

10. Soda Springs, Idaho.

11. The river was named "Mary's River" by Peter Skene Ogden (1790–1854) of the Hudson's Bay Company, after the Indian wife of a trapper. How it acquired the "St." before her name is not known.

12. Hams Fork is at the present-day site of Granger, Wyoming.

13. Archduke Ferdinand Maximilian Joseph of Austria (1832–1867) was Emperor Maximilian I of Mexico from 1864 to 1867.

14. Green Mountain, Vermont.

15. Edward Creighton (1820–1874) was a prominent early Omaha businessman who was responsible for the founding of Creighton University.

16. Benjamin Holladay (1819–1887) was known as the "Stagecoach

King" until his routes were taken over by Wells Fargo in 1866. In the original text Burke misspells his surname as "Holliday."

17. Fought in August 1782, the battle of Blue Licks was one of the last to be fought in the Revolutionary War. Burke misses the final "s" in the original text. The site of the battle is in present-day Robertson County, Kentucky.

18. Joseph Smith (1805–1844) and Brigham Young (1801–1877) were two of the early leaders of the Church of Jesus Christ of Latter-Day Saints.

19. The residents of a Mormon settlement of Farwest, Caldwell County, Missouri, surrendered to Colonel Doniphan's forces on November 1, 1838.

20. John Warren Butterfield (1801–1869), whose Butterfield Overland Stage service carried mail and operated from 1857 to 1861, eventually being bought by Wells Fargo.

21. A reference to the best-known of the Leatherstocking Tales by James Fenimore Cooper (1789–1851), *The Last of the Mohicans*, which was first published in 1826.

22. A biblical reference to the portion mentioned in I Kings 9 and 10, in which King Solomon dispatches a fleet of ships to bring back treasures of gold and precious stones.

23. A classical reference to the River Pactolus in Turkey, which was famous for its golden sands. According to the myth of King Midas of the golden touch, the king was cured by washing his hands in the river. The term "Pactolian streams"—and more often "Pactolian floods"—was a common nineteenth-century reference to streams or floods of gold.

14. Held Up by Road Agents

1. Red Buttes was about nine miles south of Laramie, Wyoming.

2. Three Crossings Station was a Pony Express station south of the main overland trails on the Sweetwater River in Wyoming.

15. A Year of Adventures

1. Multiple creeks named Prairie Dog exist throughout the West. The one referred to here flows into the Republican River near the present-day town of Colby, Kansas.

2. Ite Omagazu or Rain in the Face (ca. 1836–1905) was a Hunkpapa Lakota leader popularly identified as the "Killer of Custer." His name

was immortalized in the poem "The Revenge of Rain in the Face" by Henry Wadsworth Longfellow (1807–1882).

3. Junction City, Kansas, is at the confluence of the Smoky Hill River and the Republican River.

4. Split Rock Station, Wyoming, was a Pony Express staging post located along present U.S. Highway 287 between Muddy Gap and Jeffrey City, Wyoming.

16. A Soldier of the Civil War

1. The Seventh Kansas Volunteer Cavalry, also known as Jennison's Jayhawkers, after their commander, Colonel Charles R. "Doc" Jennison (1834–1884).

2. Andrew Jackson Smith (1815–1897) was the commander of the corps of the U.S. Army in the West to which the Seventh Kansas Volunteer Cavalry belonged.

3. George Augustus Armes (1844–1919) was a controversial officer who fought through the Civil War and in the Indian Wars and left his own account of his colorful career.

4. William T. Rose (1831–1885) was an associate of William F. Cody involved in the founding of Rome, Kansas.

17. A Champion Buffalo-Hunter

1. Established as Fort Wise in 1860 on the site of a Santa Fe Trail trading post on the Arkansas River near present-day Las Animas, Colorado, Fort Lyon operated as a military establishment until its abandonment in 1868. It was renamed in 1862 in honor of Gen. Nathanial Lyon (1818–1861), who was the first Union general killed in the Civil War.

2. William Averill Comstock (1842–1868), sometimes known as "Medicine Bill," went on to be chief scout at Fort Wallace, Kansas, a position he held when he was killed by Lakota and Cheyenne Indians along the Solomon River about fifty miles from his post in August 1868.

3. In the original text Burke wrongly gives the caliber of the rifle as .42.

18. Scout, Guide, and Indian Fighter

1. The Hotametaneo'o, or Dog Men, was a Cheyenne Warrior Society. From the 1840s until the Battle of Summit Springs in 1869 the society

effectively functioned as a separate band within the Cheyenne nation.

2. Philadelphia doctor Morris Joseph Asch (1833–1902) was a leading U.S. Army surgeon during the Civil War. In the original text Burke wrongly refers to him as "Sergeant-General Arsch."

3. Boston actor John B. Studley (1831–1910) played leading roles in many Victorian melodramas in the late nineteenth and early twentieth centuries.

4. Nathan Salsbury (1846–1902) served through the Civil War in the Army of the Cumberland and, after discharge, became an actor and wrote several plays. In 1875 he organized Salsbury's Troubadours, a successful acting company, and in 1884 joined Buffalo Bill as co-owner of Buffalo Bill's Wild West.

19. Buffalo Bill's "Pards" of the Plains

1. Seth Kinman (1815–1888) was a noted frontiersman who in the 1850s explored and hunted in the Humboldt Bay area near present-day Eureka, California.

2. Thomas Cosgrove (d. 1876) was an Irish immigrant who served in the Confederate Army during the Civil War, settled in Wind River, Wyoming, about 1869, and married a Shoshone woman. Cosgrove supervised the Shoshone scouts attached to General Crook's command during the Great Sioux War of 1876 and fought at the Battle of the Rosebud.

3. Frank Joshua North (1840–1885) commanded the Pawnee scouts at the Battle of Summit Springs and was William F. Cody's partner in his Nebraska ranch on the Dismal River. He traveled with the original Buffalo Bill's Wild West as manager of the Indians, and died as a result of injuries sustained in a riding accident in Connecticut.

4. Frederick Gustavus Schwatka (1849–1892) was a noted explorer of northern Canada and Alaska.

5. John Frederick Finerty (1846–1908) was a correspondent for the *Chicago Times* during the Great Sioux War of 1876–1877.

6. English journalist Edward Fox (d. 1895) was a correspondent for the *New York Herald* who was nicknamed "Modoc" for his interview of Captain Jack during the Modoc War of 1872–1873.

7. James O'Kelly (1845–1916) was a correspondent for the *New York*

Herald during the Cuban uprising of 1870 and the Great Sioux War of 1876–1877 before returning to his native Ireland and becoming a Nationalist member of parliament from 1880.

8. Burke is referring here to the Ghost Dance troubles of 1890 and the resultant massacre at Wounded Knee, during which Samuel Harries Darrow of the *Washington Star* and *Harpers Weekly*, John B McDonough of the *New York World*, Gilbert E. Bailey of the *Chicago Inter Ocean*, William Fitch Kelley of the *Nebraska State Journal*, Charles H. Cressey of the *Omaha Bee*, Charles G. Seymour of the *Chicago Herald*, Charles W. Allen (1851–1942) of the *New York Herald*, and Robert J. Boylan (1862–1934) were all correspondents. In the original text Burke misspells the surnames of "Kelley" and "Cressey" as "Kelly" and "Cressy."

9. Frank Grouard (1850–1905), whose surname Burke misspells as "Gruard" in the original text, Baptiste "Little Bat" Garnier (d. 1900), Philip Wells (1850–1947), Louis Shangrau, Jean Baptiste "Big Bat" Pourier (1843–1928), and John Shangrau were men of mixed Indian and European heritage who served as scouts and interpreters for the U.S. Army around Pine Ridge Indian Agency. Philip Wells and both of the Shangraus acted as interpreters for Buffalo Bill's Wild West.

10. Tahu Wanica or No Neck, Miwakan Yuhala or George Sword, Ogle Sa or Red Shirt, and Sunkmanitu Ota or Plenty Wolf (also known as Yankton Charley), were Lakota men who appeared with Buffalo Bill's Wild West.

11. David Franklin "White Beaver" Powell (1847–1906) was a longtime associate of William F. Cody.

12. Big Papillion Creek is the main branch of Papillion Creek, which flows into the Platte River near the site of present-day Bellevue, Nebraska. The Emigrant Crossing was the point at which the Oregon Trail crossed the creek.

13. Until 1876 the Pawnee Indian Reservation was located near the site of present-day Genoa, Nebraska.

14. William P. Dole (1811–1889) was commissioner of Indian Affairs in 1864. The Mr. Rudy referred to here was Jacob Owen Rudy (1827–1916), husband of Dole's daughter, Persis Jane Dole Rudy (b. 1835).

15. Samuel Ryan Curtis (1805–1866), a West Point graduate who had

fought in the Mexican-American War and the Civil War, was commander of the Department of Kansas in 1864.

16. Burke is mistaken here. There is no indication that the great northern Oglala leader Mahpiya Luta or Red Cloud was involved in the disturbances around Julesburg, Colorado, in which Frank North and his Pawnee scouts were engaged.

17. The Battle of Platte Bridge Station–Red Buttes took place on July 26, 1865, near the site of present-day Casper, Wyoming, in which Lt. Caspar Collins (1845–1865) was killed.

18. Fort Sedgwick, originally called Camp Rankin, was located opposite the mouth of Lodgepole Creek about one mile from Julesburg, Colorado. It served as an army post from 1864 to 1871 and was named for Union general John Sedgwick (1813–1864), who was killed May 9 at the Battle of Spotsylvania Court House.

19. Tatanka Iyotake or Sitting Bull (1831–1890) was the great Hunkpapa Lakota spiritual leader of the second half of the nineteenth century who spent part of the 1884 season with Buffalo Bill's Wild West.

20. Fort Keogh was established in August 1876 as the Tongue River Cantonment near the site of present-day Miles City, Montana. It was subsequently renamed for Maj. Myles Walter Keogh (1840–1876), who had been killed at the Battle of Little Bighorn and operated as a military post until 1908.

21. The Standing Rock Agency, now the Standing Rock Indian Reservation, which straddles the border of North Dakota and South Dakota and encompasses present-day Sioux County, North Dakota, and Corson County, South Dakota, was established in 1869.

22. English-born Robert "Pony Bob" Haslam (1840–1912) was credited with having made the longest round-trip ride in the brief history of the Pony Express. He accompanied William F. Cody in his 1890 diplomatic mission to Sitting Bull.

23. The French term émeute, meaning "moved" or "startled," which is seldom used in English now. In the 1890s it was used in the sense of "riot" or "disturbance."

24. David Lewis Payne (1836–1884), a former army scout best remembered for his role as a lobbyist and activist for the opening of Indian Territory to settlement.

25. Carl Schurz (1829–1906) was a Germany-born Republican politician who held the office of U.S. Secretary of the Interior from 1877 to 1881.

26. Burke is mistaken about Salsbury's Civil War regimental affiliation. He served with the Ninth and Ninth Illinois Regiments, rather than the Fifteenth.

27. The name "Massachusetts" is generally regarded as deriving from one of two Algonquin expressions: either *mass-adchu-s-et*, with a meaning close to that given by Burke; or, from the initial element of the place name Moswetuset Hummock, in Quincy, Massachusetts, meaning "hill shaped like an arrowhead."

28. "Connecticut" is generally regarded as deriving from the Algonquin expression *quin-at-tuc-quet*, meaning "on the long river."

29. The etymology for "Alabama" that Burke gives was popularized by the politician and writer Alexander Beaufort Meek (1814–1865), who served as the state's attorney general, but it is without sound linguistic foundation. A more plausible etymology is its derivation from two Muskogean terms: *alba*, meaning "plants," and *amo*, meaning "to cut, trim or gather." This derivation indicates that the people who lived along the Alabama River either gathered plants or cleared the land for cultivation.

30. The Natchez people speak a Muskogean language, and it was a popular nineteenth-century misconception that "Mississippi" meant "Father of Waters" in the language. "Mississippi" in fact derives from the Algonquin expression *misi-ziibi*, meaning "Great River."

31. "Kansas" comes from the Siouan language of the Kansa people, who refer to themselves as *kikazhe*, which is variously translated as "People of the Waters" or "People of the South Wind." Arkansas is related to *akakaze*, a word from the Deghida language of the Quapaw people meaning "land of the Down-river People" or "land of the People of the South Wind."

32. "Tennessee" is from the name of the Overhill Cherokee village of Tanasi, which was located in Monroe County, Tennessee, but is now submerged as a result of the damming of the Tennessee River. The word Tanasi is of dubious etymology: it may be from a Cherokee expression meaning "place where the river bends" or from a Yuchee expression meaning "meeting place."

33. "Kentucky" is generally regarded as deriving from the Iroquoian expression *kane-tukee*, meaning "the meadow lands."

34. "Ohio" is generally regarded as deriving from the Iroquoian expression *ohi-yo*, meaning "the great river."

35. "Michigan" is generally regarded as deriving from the Algonquin expression *mishigamaa*, meaning "the big water or lake."

36. The name "Illinois" is of dubious etymology but the most plausible explanation is that it derives from *irenwe<middot>wa*, an Algonquin expression in the Miami-Illinois language signifying someone who speaks normally.

37. The name "Wisconsin" is of dubious etymology, with one plausible explanation being that it derives from *Meskon-sing*, an Algonquin expression meaning "it lies red" in reference to the red sandstone Dells of the Wisconsin River in the southern part of the state.

38. "Missouri" is from a Siouan expression, *ouemessourita*, applied to the Otoe-Missouri people and meaning "People with Dugout Canoes." The Missouri River is referred to as the "Muddy River" in a number of Plains Indian languages, such as the Lakota "mni-sosa," but this does not provide the etymology of the word itself.

39. "Kansas" is an Indian word for "smoky water."

40. "Iowa" derives from the Siouan Dakota word *ayuhwa*, for the Iowa people, which may be interpreted as Burke suggests.

41. "Minnesota" is from a Siouan expression *mni-sota* meaning "cloudy or sky-tinted water."

20. Border Poetry

1. William Edwards Annin (1856–1903) was associate editor of the *Omaha Bee* from 1879 to 1899.

2. Charles "Buffalo Chips" White (d. 1876) was a companion of William F. Cody and scout for the Fifth U.S. Cavalry during the Great Sioux War of 1876–1877. He was killed at the Battle of Slim Buttes, which took place near present-day Reva, South Dakota, on September 9–10, 1876. He is wrongly identified as "Jonathan White" on the historical marker at the battle site and is referred to by that name in Crawford's poem.

3. John Wallace "Captain Jack" Crawford (1847–1917), known as the poet scout, replaced William F. Cody as chief of scouts with the Fifth

Cavalry in late August 1976. The poem cited here first appeared in Jack Crawford's *The Poet Scout—A Book of Song and Story* (New York: Funk & Wagnalls, 1886), 130–31.

4. "Little Phil" was the nickname of Gen. Philip Henry Sheridan (1831–1888).

5. Crawford, *The Poet Scout*, 23–26.

6. In addition to being a prominent newspaper journalist and editor, businessman, and latterly showman, Hugh Alphonzo Wetmore (1851–1909) was also the husband of William F. Cody's sister, Helen Cody Wetmore.

21. From Prairie to Palace

1. Burke is referring to the so-called Wyoming Valley Massacre of July 3, 1778, in the Wyoming Valley of Pennsylvania, during which it was alleged that Iroquois allies of the Loyalist forces hunted down and butchered and tortured to death fleeing Patriot soldiers.

2. Burke overestimates Seventh Cavalry casualties at Little Bighorn in 1876 by about forty.

3. Queen Victoria (1819–1901), who reigned as Queen of England from 1837 to 1901.

4. Prince Albert Edward (1841–1910), the eldest son of Queen Victoria and future King Edward VII, who held the title of Prince of Wales from 1841 until he succeeded his mother to the throne in 1901.

5. Charles J. Murphy (1832–1921) fought in the Mexican-American War of 1846–1848 and the Civil War, winning the Medal of Honor at the first Battle of Bull Run–Manassas in July 1861, and went on to be a special envoy of the U.S. Department of Agriculture in Europe. He is credited with the introduction of California wines to the European market and won the nickname to which Burke refers for his role in introducing maize as a famine relief measure in Russia in 1881—an action for which he was also created a Knight of the Order of Saint Stanislaus by Tsar Alexander III (1845–1894).

6. According to her 1894 visiting card held at the British Library (Catalogue Pressmark Evan.6166), Annie I. Oppenheim "reads character at a glance, gives scientific and entertaining monologues on the art of character-reading from the face, illustrating every feature and explaining their

various characteristics. Attends at-homes, garden parties, etc., and gives examinations by appointment. Character delineated from photograph. Instruction given. For terms and vacant dates address—Professor Annie Oppenheim, 30, Redcliffe Square, S.W."

22. The Wild West at Sea

1. Lord Ronald Charles Sutherland-Leveson-Gower (1845–1916) was a prominent Liberal politician, writer, sculptor, and patron of the arts.

2. The exhibition took place at Earl's Court in West London.

3. Henry Irving was the stage name of John Henry Brodribb (1838–1905), the leading actor-manager on the London theater scene from 1871, when he became associated with the Lyceum Theatre. From 1895, when he was the first actor to be knighted for his theatrical work, he was known as Sir Henry Irving.

4. John Lawrence Toole (1830–1906) was a close associate of Henry Irving and another leading actor of the period.

5. Ellen Terry (1847–1928) was the leading Shakespearean actress of her generation. She was named a Dame Grand Cross of the Order of the British Empire in 1925, becoming only the second actress to be so honored.

6. Justin McCarthy (1830–1912) was an Irish Nationalist historian, novelist, and Liberal politician.

7. Edward John Phelps (1822–1900) was a lawyer, Democratic politician, and diplomat from Vermont who served as U.S. Minister to Great Britain from 1885 to 1889.

8. Thomas McDonald Waller (1840–1924), a lawyer and Democratic politician who served in the Civil War, was governor of the state of Connecticut from 1883 to 1885, and subsequently appointed U.S. consul general to London, an office that he held from 1885 to 1889.

9. Cornell University graduate Edmund Judson Moffat (1857–1929) became the U.S. Department of Agriculture's first overseas employee when he was appointed to the post of statistical agent in London in 1882, a role he fulfilled for ten years. Throughout this period he held the status of a deputy consul general of the State Department and was commonly referred to by that title.

10. Henry Du Pré Labouchère (1831–1912) was a prominent Liberal

politician, writer, publisher, and theater owner who served as member of Parliament for Windsor from 1865 to 1866, for Middlesex from 1866 to 1867, and for Northampton from 1880 to 1906.

11. Mary Antoinette Anderson (1859–1940), an American-born actress who was appearing in Shakespeare's *The Winter's Tale* at the Lyceum Theatre while Buffalo Bill's Wild West was in London in 1887.

12. Cora Urquhart Brown-Potter (1859–1936) was also a well-known American actress who was appearing on the London stage in 1887.

13. Charles Wyndham was the stage name of Charles Culverwell (1837–1919), the Liverpool-born doctor's son who himself qualified as a doctor and served as a volunteer surgeon with the Union Army during the Civil War before turning definitively to the stage. He became one of the leading actor-managers of the era and was knighted in 1902, taking the title Sir Charles Wyndham.

14. Sir Francis Philip Cunliffe-Owen (1828–1894) was a veteran exhibition organizer who in 1887 was serving as the director of the South Kensington Museum.

15. Henry Cyril Paget, Fifth Marquis of Anglesey (1875–1905), was a notorious figure on the London social and theatrical scenes in the 1880s and 1890s due to his lavish social life, on which he squandered his inheritance and by which he accumulated massive debts.

16. Charles William de la Poer Beresford, First Baron Beresford (1846–1919), known at the time as Lord Charles Beresford, was prominent both as a naval commander and a politician. In March 1906 he attended a performance of Buffalo Bill's Wild West in Genoa, Italy, together with two thousand of the sailors under his command.

17. Grand Duke Mikhail Mikhailovitch of Russia (1861–1929), grandson of Tsar Nicholas I, who spent most of the period between 1886 and 1888 in London before taking up permanent residence there in 1891.

18. Maria Louisa Long (1837–1920), known as Lady Monckton by virtue of her marriage to Sir John Braddick Monckton (1832–1902), was a well-known amateur actress.

19. Sir Francis Knollys, First Viscount Knollys (1837–1924), was private secretary to the Prince of Wales from 1870, becoming private secretary to the king when Prince Albert Edward succeeded his mother to the throne in 1901.

20. Alexander Ross Clarke (1828–1914), a leading figure in London society, was both an officer of the Royal Engineers and a member of the Royal Society. He served in Canada from 1851, and, upon returning to England, played a crucial role in developing the Ordinance Survey maps of Britain.

21. Leopold Agar Denys Montague (1861–1940) who, upon his retirement from the Sherwood Rangers cavalry regiment of the British Army in 1886, established a private museum and came to be well known as a collector and exhibitor of Egyptian, Greek, and Roman antiquities.

22. Lady Alice Josephine Bertie (1865–1950) was a noted beauty in London high society of the time. Burke wrongly gives her surname as "Beckie" in the original text.

23. The title "Lord Strathmore" might reasonably have been applied to any one of the seven sons of Claude Bowes-Lyon, Thirteenth Earl of Strathmore and Kinghorne (1824–1904), who were alive in 1887. Bowes-Lyon's fifth son, Patrick Bowes-Lyon (1863–1946), a leading tennis player who won the Wimbledon doubles title that year, would probably have been the best-known public figure at the time. His eldest son, Claude Bowes-Lyon (1855–1944), was the maternal grandfather of the present Queen Elizabeth II.

24. British nobleman and Conservative politician Robert George Windsor-Clive, First Earl of Plymouth (1857–1923), was known as "Lord Windsor" between 1869 and 1905.

25. New York–born Jeanette Jerome (1854–1921) became Lady Randolph Churchill in 1874 when she married Conservative politician Lord Randolph Henry Spencer-Churchill (1849–1895). She was the mother of British author and statesman Sir Winston Leonard Spencer-Churchill (1874–1965).

26. In 1866 New York–born Mary Louise Hungerford Mackay (1843–1928) married Ireland-born Comstock Lode millionaire John William Mackay (1831–1902). Shunned by much of New York society despite their great wealth, the couple spent a great deal of their time in Paris and London, and Mrs. John W. Mackay was well known for her lavish entertaining.

27. Cody's Scout's Rest Ranch is located in North Platte, Nebraska.

28. In 1887 Queen Victoria was celebrating the fiftieth anniversary of her ascent to the throne on June 20, 1837.

23. A Royal Welcome

1. William Ewart Gladstone (1809–1898) was a British politician who began his career as a Conservative before moving to the Liberal party. He served as prime minister on four occasions between 1868 and 1894 and as chancellor of the Exchequer on four occasions between 1853 and 1882.

2. The Reform Club is a London gentlemen's club on the south side of Pall Mall that was founded in 1836 as a social club for members of both Houses of Parliament. From the middle of the nineteenth century it became a bastion of liberal and progressive thought and was closely associated with the Liberal Party.

3. Prince George William Frederick Charles (1809–1904) held the title of Duke of Cambridge from 1850. He was the grandson of King George III and served as commander in chief of the British Army from 1856 to 1895.

4. The Mansion House is the official residence of the Lord Mayor of London, who in 1887 was Conservative politician Sir Reginald Hanson (1840–1905). His wife, Lady Constance Hanson née Hallett (1847–1905), was Lady Mayoress.

5. The Beaufort Club, located in Kings Road, Chelsea, is a gentlemen's dining club and polo club.

6. Conservative politician Henry Charles Fitzroy Somerset, Eighth Duke of Beaufort (1824–1899).

7. The Savage Club is a gentleman's club located in Whitehall Place, London.

8. Wilson Barrett (1846–1904) was an English actor, theater manager, and playwright who enjoyed success on both sides of the Atlantic.

9. The United Arts Club was an exhibition society located at Lancaster House in St. James Street, Savoy, London.

10. Prince Francis Paul Charles Louis Alexander (1837–1900) was a member of the British royal family who held the title of Duke of Teck from 1871 until his death.

11. The St. George's Club was a gentlemen's club and chess club located in Cavendish Square, Covent Garden, London.

12. Canada-born British nobleman Victor Alexander Bruce, Ninth Earl of Elgin, 13th Earl of Kincardine (1849 1917).

13. Liberal Conservative politician and colonial administrator William

Waldegrave Palmer, Second Earl of Selborne (1859–1942), was known as the Viscount Wolmer between 1882 and 1895. Burke wrongly gives his title as "Woolmer" in the original text.

14. Oliver Henry Wallop, Eighth Earl of Portsmouth (1861–1943), was known as Viscount Lymington until he assumed the Earldom from his brother in 1925.

15. Sir Christopher Sykes (1831–1898) was a Conservative politician and close friend of the Prince of Wales.

16. Herbert John Gladstone, First Viscount Gladstone (1854–1930), was a Liberal politician and the youngest son of William Ewart Gladstone.

17. A number of Lady McGregors or MacGregors resided in London at the time. Burke is most likely referring to the widow of Sir Charles Macgregor, Third Baronet of Savile Row (1819–1879), a well-known figure on the London theater scene and a keen supporter of the Lyceum Theatre in particular.

18. Lady Emma Bailey Rowcliffe Tenterden (d. 1928) was the widow of British nobleman and diplomat Charles Stuart Aubrey Abbott, Third Baron Tenterden (1834–1882).

19. American actress Elizabeth Jackson (d. 1899), whose stage name was Lizzie Weston, was the widow of the famous British actor Charles James Mathews (1803–1878). She was also known as Mrs. A. H. Davenport due to the surname of her first husband, whom she divorced in 1856.

20. British novelist and playwright Edmund Hodgson Yates (1831–1894).

21. Great Marlow in Buckinghamshire was the home of leading writer Jerome Klapka Jerome (1859–1927) at the time.

22. The annual gala parade of the London Coaching Club, which took place in July of each year.

23. The Honourable Artillery Company of London was incorporated by Royal Charter in 1537 by King Henry VIII. In addition to its continued existence as a unit of the British Territorial Army Reserve, it fulfills an important ceremonial function, with both serving members and veterans of the company regularly providing guards of honor for members of the British royal family and visiting heads of state.

24. The Lakota Agency at Pine Ridge, South Dakota, now Pine Ridge Indian Reservation.

25. The Princess of Wales was Princess Alexandra Caroline Marie Charlotte Louise Julia of Denmark (1844–1925); the children referred to by Burke were the Princess Royal Victoria Alexandra Dagmar (1867–1931), Princess Victoria Alexandra Olga Mary (1868–1935), and Princess Maud Charlotte Mary Victoria (1869–1938), the latter of whom would go on to be Queen of Norway from 1905 to 1938.

26. Princess Louise Caroline Alberta (1848–1939) and her husband John George Edward Henry Douglas Sutherland Campbell, Ninth Duke of Argyll and Marquis of Lorne (1845–1914).

27. His Serene Highness Prince Adolphus Charles Alexander Albert Edward George Philip Louis Ladislaus of Teck (1868–1927) and his son, Alexander Augustus Frederick William Alfred George Cambridge, First Earl of Athlone (1874–1957), known at the time as Prince Alexander of Teck.

28. María Isabel Francisca de Asís Antonia Luisa Fernanda Cristina Amelia Felipa Adelaide Josefa Elena Enriqueta Carolina Justina (1848–1919), known as Princess Marie-Isabelle d'Orléans, Comtesse de Paris, was the wife of Louis-Philippe d'Orléans (1838–1894), a claimant to the French throne under the putative title of Philippe VII of the House of Orléans.

29. Prince Christian Frederik Vilhelm Carl (1843–1912) subsequently reigned as King Frederick VII of Denmark from 1905 to 1912.

30. Cecilia Annetta Baring (1834–1911) of the famous banking family, became Lady Suffield in 1854 when she married Charles Harbord, Fifth Baron Suffield (1830–1914).

31. Charlotte Marion Baird (d. 1937) was known first as Lady Cole from 1869 by virtue of her marriage to Lowry Edgerton Cole (1845–1924) and subsequently as Lady Enniskillen when her husband became the Fourth Earl of Enniskillen in 1886.

32. Lord Edward William Henry Somerset (1866–1890).

33. John Young Nelson (b. 1826) was a former scout who served as driver for the Deadwood coach with Buffalo Bill's Wild West. His Oglala Lakota wife, Upan Ziwim or Yellow Elk Woman, and their five children traveled to London with him. Their youngest daughter, Rose, who would later take the stage name Prince Blue Waters, was the focus of the attention to which Burke refers.

34. Fenimore Cooper's novels *The Pioneers* (1823), *The Last of the Mohicans*

(1826), *The Prairie* (1827), *The Pathfinder* (1840), and *The Deerslayer* (1841) are known collectively as his *Leather Stockings' Tales* but there is no novel called *Leather Stocking*. "Leather Stockings" is a nickname for the main character, Nathanial "Natty" Bumppo, who is also known as "Hawkeye."

35. Sir Walter Scott (1771–1832) was a hugely influential Scottish Romantic novelist.

36. Prentiss Ingraham (1843–1904) was a colonel in the Confederate Army during the Civil War and a prolific writer of fiction who penned numerous stories about Buffalo Bill.

37. Radical politician, educationalist, and reformer John Bright (1811–1889) was highly critical of British foreign policy and committed himself to ensuring a better relationship between Britain and the United States.

38. Granville George Leveson Gower, Second Earl Granville (1815–1891), was leader of the Liberal Party in the House of Lords in 1887.

39. Ireland-born Field Marshal Garnet Joseph Wolseley, First Viscount Wolseley (1833–1913), was one of the most distinguished British military figures of the nineteenth century. In 1887 he was adjutant-general of the Army.

24. A Visit from Queen Victoria

1. Prince Henry Maurice (1858–1896) and Princess Beatrice Mary Victoria Feodore (1857–1944) were the Prince and Princess of Battenberg. Burke wrongly gives their title as "Battenburg" in the original.

2. Anne Home-Drummond Murray (1814–1897) was a Scottish courtier and close friend of Queen Victoria, who assumed the title Dowager Duchess of Atholl in 1864 upon the death of her husband, George Augustus Frederick John Murray, Sixth Duke of Atholl (1814–1864). Burke wrongly gives her title as "Athole" in the original text.

3. The Honorable Ethel Henrietta Maria Cadogan (1853–1930) was a lady-in-waiting to Queen Victoria.

4. Sir Henry Frederick Ponsonby (1825–1895) was Queen Victoria's private secretary; his wife was the Honorable Mary Elizabeth Bulteel (1832–1916).

5. Sir Henry Lynedoch Gardiner (1820–1897) was Equerry to Queen Victoria.

6. Sir Richard Henry Ewart (1864–1928) was Equerry in Waiting to Queen Victoria.

7. Controversial Republican politician James Gillespie Blaine (1830–1893) served as the senator for Maine from 1876 to 1881 and as U.S. secretary of state from 1889 to 1892.

8. Hungarian American Joseph Pulitzer (1847–1911) was a prominent newspaper publisher and member of the Democratic Party.

9. Chauncey Mitchell Depew (1834–1928) was an attorney, railway entrepreneur, and liberal Republican-Democrat politician who served as a U.S. senator for New York from 1899 to 1911.

10. Lawrence Jerome (1820–1888) was a newspaper publisher and local New York politician who, after he had made a substantial fortune on the stock market, became a well-known socialite in New York, London, and Paris.

11. Murat Halstead (1829–1908) was an essayist, journalist, and newspaper editor.

12. Joseph Roswell Hawley (1826–1905) was a newspaper editor and Republican politician who served with the U.S. Volunteers through the Civil War and attained the brevet rank of major general.

13. Simon Cameron (1799–1889) was a Democratic politician who served as both secretary of war and minister to Russia during Abraham Lincoln's administration. He was sometimes referred to as "General Simon Cameron."

14. King Christian IX (1818–1906) of the House of Schleswig-Holstein-Sonderburg-Beck was King of Denmark from 1863 to 1906.

15. Frederick Augustus Albert Anton Ferdinand Joseph Karl Maria Baptist Nepomuk Wilhelm Xaver Georg Fidelis (1828–1902) reigned as King Albert of Saxony from 1873 to 1902.

16. Léopold Louis Philippe Marie Victor (also Leopold Lodewijk Filips Maria Victor) (1835–1909) of the House of Saxe-Coburg Goethe reigned as King Leopold II of Belgium from 1865 to 1909. His wife, Queen Marie Henriette, was the former Princess Marie Henriette Anne (1836–1902) of Austria, a member of the House of Habsburg Lorraine.

17. King George I of Greece, who reigned from 1863 to 1913, was the Denmark-born Prince Christian Wilhelm Ferdinand Adolf Georg of

Schleswig-Holstein-Sonderburg-Glücksburg (1845–1913). He was the son of King Christian IX of Denmark.

18. Archduke Rudolf Franz Karl Joseph (1858–1889), of the House of Habsburg Lorraine, was known as Crown Prince Rudolph of Austria. He shot himself in what was believed to be a murder-suicide pact with his seventeen-year-old mistress, Baroness Marie Vetsera.

19. Prince Friedrich Johann Bernhard Hermann Heinrich Moritz (1861–1914) was Prince of Saxe-Meiningen, Duke of Saxony. His wife was the Countess Adelaide of Lippe-Biesterfeld (1870–1948).

20. Crown Prince Frederick William Victor Albert of Prussia (1859–1941) was Queen Victoria's grandson who later became Kaiser Wilhelm II of Germany the following year. His wife was Princess Victoria Friederike Luise Feodora Jenny von Schleswig-Holstein-Sonderburg-Augustenburg (1858–1921).

21. Prince Oscar Gustaf Adolf (1858–1950) was the Crown Prince of Sweden and Norway who went on to reign as King Gustav V from 1907 to 1950. Gustav never assumed the Norwegian throne, as the union of the two crowns was dissolved in 1905.

22. Princess Friederike Amalia Wilhelmine Viktoria (1866–1929), who was known as Princess Victoria of Prussia, was the second daughter of the reigning Kaiser Frederick III of Germany (1831–1888) and the granddaughter of Queen Victoria, her mother having been the queen's eldest daughter, the Princess Victoria.

23. The title Duke of Sparta is given to the eldest son of the King of Greece and in this case denominates Prince Constantine (1868–1923), who would reign as King Constantine I of Greece from 1913 to 1917 and 1922 to 1923.

24. Grand Duke Michael Nikolaevich (1832–1909) of the House of Romanov was the fourth son and seventh child of Tsar Nicholas I of Russia.

25. Prince George of Greece and Denmark (1869–1957) was the second son of King George I of Greece.

26. Prince Louis (or Ludwig) of Baden (1865–1888) was the younger son of the Grand Duke Fredreich I of Baden (1826–1907).

27. Sir Dighton MacNaughton Probyn (1833–1924) served as keeper of the privvy purse and secretary to the Prince of Wales. He was a

decorated war hero who had won the Victoria Cross, the British Army's highest award for gallantry, during the Indian Mutiny of 1857.

28. The battle of Cressy took place near Crécy in Northern France on August 26, 1346. King John of Bohemia (1296–1346) was killed in the battle and Prince Edward of Wales and Aquitaine and Duke of Cornwell (1330–1376), who was known as the Black Prince, was one of the commanders of the English forces at the battle.

29. Prince Frederick William George Ernest (1826–1902) of the House of Hohenzollern was known as Prince George of Prussia. Burke wrongly gives his title as Prince George of Russia in the original text.

25. The Home Trail

1. According to Aristotle, Thespis of Icaria was the first person ever to appear on stage as an actor. His name gave rise to the term "thespian," meaning actor.

2. Sir John Richard Somers Vine (1847–1929) was a noted political figure and writer.

3. Edward Joseph Hale (1815–1936) was U.S. consul in Manchester from 1885 to 1889.

26. Swinging Around Europe

1. Thomas Alva Edison (1847–1931) was a leading American businessman, inventor, and scientist.

2. *Capitale des deux mondes* is French for "capital of both worlds."

3. Marie François Sadi Carnot (1837–1894) served as fifth president of the French Republic from 1887 until his assassination in 1894. His wife was Marie Pauline Cécile Dupont-White (1841–1898).

4. Republican politician Whitelaw Reid (1837–1912) served as U.S. ambassador to France from 1889 to 1892.

5. Minnie Garrison (d. 1934) was the U.S.-born wife of Count Gaston Chandon de Briailles (1842–1914).

6. *Haut ton* is French for "high tone," a term used to denote the upper echelons of society.

7. Queen Isabella II (1830–1904) of the House of Bourbon had abdicated as queen of Spain in 1870 and thereafter spent most of her life living in exile in France.

8. *Bijouterie* is French for jewelry.

9. Herculaneum and Pompeii were two of the four Roman settlements destroyed by the eruption of Vesuvius in 79 AD.

10. Vincenzo Gioacchino Raffaele Luigi Pecci (1810–1903) headed the Roman Catholic Church as Pope Leo XIII from 1878 to 1903.

11. Romulus, together with his brother, Remus, was one of the mythical twins who founded the city of Rome. The term Caesar, when used alone, is generally a reference to Gaius Julius Caesar; Nero was Nero Claudius Caesar Augustus Germanicus, who was Roman emperor from 54 AD to 68 AD.

12. *Morituri te salutant* is a Latin quotation from Suetonius, roughly translated as "those about to die salute you." In Burke's day it was popularly believed that gladiators said this before they entered the arena but there is no historical evidence for such a belief.

13. Onorato Caetani (1842–1917) was an Italian nobleman and politician whose full title was Prince of Teano and Duke of Sermoneta.

14. British nobleman and politician Frederick Temple Hamilton Temple Blackwood (1826–1902) was the first marquis of Dufferin, the British ambassador in Rome at the time of the Wild West's visit.

15. Francesco Crispi (1818–1901) served as Italian prime minister from 1887 to 1891 and 1893 to 1896.

16. Prince Leopoldo Torlonia (1853–1918) was a nobleman and politician who held the titles Duke of Poli and Duke of Guadagnolo and who had served as mayor of Rome in 1887.

17. Amalia Flarer Depretis (1847–1922) was the France-born widow of the Italian radical politician and former prime minister Agostino Depretis (1813–1887).

18. The widow of Prince Calogero Gabriele Colonna (1841–1878) was born Baroness Emmelina Sonnino (1851–1944) and was the sister of Sidney Costantino Sonnino (1842–1922), who served as Italian premier in 1906. In the original text Burke misspells the surname as "Collona."

19. Mary Elizabeth Hickson Field (1846–1907), who came from a prominent New York family, was the wife of the Italian nobleman and patron of the arts Salvatore Brancaccio (1842–1924), Prince of Ruffano and Triggiano. Burke misspells the name as "Brancaccia" in the original text.

20. It has not been possible to identify the parties that Burke refers to by the names Gravina Antonelli, Baroness Reugis, and Grave Giannotti. There may be transcription or editing errors in the names.

21. The main square in Venice is the Piazza San Marco, or St. Mark's Square, which is named for the city's patron saint. The Molo di San Marco, which the writer translates as St. Mark's pier, is the main landing point on the Venice lido for visitors to the square but is on the adjoining Piazzetta di San Marco.

22. Vittorio Emanuele Maria Alberto Eugenio Ferdinando Tommaso of Savoy (1820–1878) reigned as King Victor Emanuel II of Italy from 1861 to 1878.

23. Gaius Aurelius Valerius Diocletianus Augustus (244–311) reigned as the Roman emporer Diocletian from 284 to 305.

24. Theodoric the Great (454–526) is known in the Gothic saga tradition as Dietrich of Bern. He was ruler from 493 to 526 and his capital was at Verona.

25. Napoleon Bonaparte (1769–1821) was Emperor Napoleon I from 1804 to 1815.

26. Michelangelo di Lodovico Buonarroti Simoni (14–75–1564) and Raffaello Sanzio da Urbino (1483–1520) were two of the leading artists of the Italian Renaissance.

27. The Oglala Lakota Inyan Mato, or Rocky Bear, was one of the leading Indian performers with Buffalo Bill's Wild West.

28. The right of leading Roman noble families to the titles of prince and duke were recognized by the Congregazione Araldica Capitolina in 1854; those listed by Burke are all members of such families, as follows: Prince Luigi Marcantonio Francesco Rodolfo Scipione Borghese (1871–1927) and his wife, Princess Anna Maria de Ferrari (1874–1924); Marquis Francesco Serlupi (1839–1929); Princess Elena di Bandini Newburgh (1853–1950); Caterina Lante Montefeltro della Rovere di Garzioli (1828–1897); Prince Filippo-Massimiliano Massimo (1843–1915) and his wife, Princess Elisabetta Aldobrandini di Massimo (1847–1937); and Prince Alessandro dei Ruspoli (1844–1916) and his England-born wife, Princess Eva Capel Broadwood dei Ruspoli (1858–1948).

29. Formally entitled the Sovereign Military Hospitaller Order of

Saint John of Jerusalem of Rhodes and of Malta, the Knights of Malta are a lay Roman Catholic Religious Order and the oldest Order of Chivalry in existence.

30. *Praetor* was an ancient Roman honorary title given to an army commander or an elected magistrate.

31. The Appian Way was the ancient road from Rome to the port of Brindisi.

32. Marcus Tullius Cicero (106BC–43BC) was a Roman orator, philosopher, and statesman.

33. Publius Cornelius Scipio Africanus (235 BC–183 BC) was a Roman general best known for his defeat of the Carthaginian Hannibal (247 BC–183 BC) in the Second Punic War of 218 BC to 202 BC.

27. The Last Indian War

1. Leonard Wright Colby (1846–1924), of the National Guard of the State of Nebraska, tended to the Indian casualties at Wounded Knee and adopted one of the surviving orphaned Lakota children, who later came to be known as the "Lost Bird of Wounded Knee."

2. Si Tanka, or Big Foot, was the leader of the Lakota people whose village was attacked at Wounded Knee. Tatanka Ptecela, or Short Bull, and Mato Wanahtaka, or Kicking Bear, were Lakota leaders of the Ghost Dance.

3. There is no Lakota group generally known as "Wassaohas." There is a band of Lakotas known as Wazhazhe, which would appear to be closest to Burke's transliteration. From the context, however, he appears to be referring to the the Miniconjou Lakotas, who were with Big Foot.

4. Tasunke Kokipapi, or (Young) Man-Afraid-of-his-Horses, was an Oglala Lakota leader on Pine Ridge Reservation at the time of Wounded Knee.

5. John Rutter (or Ruller) Brooke (1838–1926) and Francis Wheaton (1833–1903) were both career soldiers and Civil War veterans. General Brooke was commander of the Department of the Platte in December 1890 and General Wheaton was in command of the Second U.S. Infantry at the time.

28. Back to Europe

1. Tatanka Wanjila, or Lone Bull, Kalala, or Scatter, and Watoki-cun, or Revenge, were among the Lakota prisoners of war who were released to William F. Cody's custody and who traveled to Europe with The Wild West.

2. The battle of Thermopylae of 480 BC, at which a small Spartan army repelled the much larger Persian army and prevented the invasion of Greece.

3. *Mal de mer* is French for "seasickness."

4. *The Descent from the Cross* is the center panel of a triptych in the Cathedral of Our Lady in Antwerp, Belgium, that was painted by the Flemish Baroque painter Peter Paul Rubens (1577–1640) between 1612 and 1614.

5. *Peau rouge* is French for "red skin."

6. Charlemagne (ca. 742–814) or, in Italian, Carlo Magno, was King of the Franks from 768 and the first Holy Roman Emperor from 800, holding both titles until his death.

7. Otto III (980–1002) was Holy Roman Emperor from 983. He is reputed to have opened the tomb of Charlemagne at Aachen in the year 1000 and found the body as described by Burke.

8. *La belle France* is French for "beautiful France."

9. The battle of Waterloo on June 18, 1815, marked the end of the Napoleonic Wars.

An Episode Since the Return from Europe

1. Frank Dwight Baldwin (1842–1923) was a career soldier who served through the Civil War, Indian Wars, and Spanish-American War, and who was twice awarded the Medal of Honor.

2. Sir William Henry Mackinnon (1852–1929) was an officer of the British Grenadier Guards who served through the Second Boer War and the First World War, attaining the rank of general.

3. Sir Henry Paulet St. John Mildmay (1853–1916) was an English baron who held the rank of major in the Grenadier Guards and played county cricket for Hampshire.

4. Col. Allison Nailor (1836–1908).

5. Elder Junius Free Wells (1854–1930) was the first leader of the

Young Men's Mutual Improvement Association of the Church of Jesus Christ of Latter-Day Saints.

6. Horton S. Boal (1866–1902) was William F. Cody's son-in-law.

7. John Hance (1840–1919) is thought to have been the first non-Indian resident of the Grand Canyon.

BIBLIOGRAPHY

Aleshire, Peter. *The Fox and the Whirlwind: General George Crook and Geronimo*. New York: John Wiley & Sons/Castle, 2000.

Allen, Charles W. *From Fort Laramie to Wounded Knee in the West that Was*. Lincoln: University of Nebraska Press, 1997.

Alter, J. Cecil. *Jim Bridger*. Norman: University of Oklahoma Press, 1979.

Armes, George Augustus. *Ups and Downs of an Army Officer*. Washington DC: n.p. 1900.

Aron, Stephen. *How the West was Lost: The Transformation of Kentucky from Daniel Boone to Henry Clay*. Baltimore: Johns Hopkins University Press, 1996.

Athearn, Robert G. *William Tecumseh Sherman and the Settlement of the West*. Norman: University of Oklahoma Press, 1956.

Bailey, John W. *Pacifying the Plains: General Alfred Terry and the Decline of the Sioux, 1866–1890*. Westport CT: Greenwood, 1979.

Barnett, Louise. *Touched by Fire: The Life, Death, and Mythic Afterlife of George Armstrong Custer*. Lincoln: University of Nebraska Press, 2006.

Berger, Jason. "Buffalo Bill's Wild West and John M. Burke: Exploring the Origins of Celebrity Brand Management." *Journal of Promotion Management* 7, nos. 1 & 2 (2002): 225–52.

Berthrong, Donald J. *The Southern Cheyennes*. Norman: University of Oklahoma Press, 1963.

Bierman, John. *Dark Safari: The Life behind the Legend of Henry Morton Stanley*. New York: Alfred A. Knopf, 1990.

Blackstone, Sarah J. *Buckskins, Bullets and Business: A History of Buffalo Bill's Wild West*. In *Contributions to the Study of Popular Culture* 14. New York: Greenwood, 1986.

———. *The Business of Being Buffalo Bill: Selected Letters of William F. Cody 1879–1917*. New York: Greenwood, 1988.

Bonds, Russell S. *War Like the Thunderbolt: The Battle and Burning of Atlanta*. Yardley: Westholme, 2009.

Bonsal, Stephen. *Edward Fitzgerald Beale: A Pioneer in the Path of Empire*. New York: G. P. Putnam's Sons, 1912.

Bourke, John G. *On the Border with Crook*. New York: Charles Scribner's Sons, 1892.

Bowman, Eldon G., and J. B. Smith. *Beale's Road through Arizona*. Flagstaff: Flagstaff Corral of Westerners International, 1979.

Bridger, Bobby. *Buffalo Bill and Sitting Bull: Inventing the Wild West*. Austin: University of Texas Press, 2002.

Brisbin, James S. *The Beef Bonanza or How to Get Rich on the Plains*, Philadelphia: Lippincott, 1881.

———. *Brisbin's Stories of the Plains or Twelve Years among the Wild Indians*. Whitefish: Kessinger, 2010.

Broome, Jeff. *Dog Soldier Justice: The Ordeal of Susanna Alderdice in the Kansas Indian War*. Lincoln NE: Lancaster County Historical Society, 2003.

Brown, Meredith M. *Frontiersman: Daniel Boone and the Making of America*. Baton Rouge: Louisiana State University Press, 2008.

Burke, John M. *From Prairie to Palace: The Lost Biography of Buffalo Bill*. Edited by Tim Connor and with an introduction by Jason Berger. Spokane: Marquette, 2005.

Carter, Harvey L. *"Dear Old Kit": The Historical Christopher Carson*. Norman: University of Oklahoma Press, 1968.

Carter, Robert A. *Buffalo Bill Cody: The Man Behind the Legend*. Edison NJ: Castle, 2005.

Castel, Albert. *The Civil War in Kansas: Reaping the Whirlwind*. Lawrence: University Press of Kansas, 1997.

Chaffin, Tom. *Pathfinder: John Charles Frémont and the Course of American Empire*. New York: Hill and Wang, 2002.

Chalfant, William Y. *Hancock's War: Conflict on the Southern Plains*. Norman: Arthur H. Clark, 2010.

Clarke, Dwight L. *William Tecumseh Sherman: Gold Rush Banker*. San Francisco: California Historical Society, 1969.

Clayton, Lawrence A., Vernon J. Knight, and Edward C. Moore, eds. *The De Soto Chronicles: The Expedition of Hernando de Soto to North America in 1539–1543*. Tuscaloosa: University of Alabama Press, 1996.

Cody, William F. *The Life of Hon. William F. Cody, Known as Buffalo Bill: The Famous Hunter, Scout and Guide. An Autobiography*. With a foreword by Don Russell. Lincoln: University of Nebraska Press, 1978.

Coleman, William S. E. *Voices of Wounded Knee*. Lincoln: University of Nebraska Press, 1991.

Cooper, Edward S. *William Babcock Hazen: The Best Hated Man*. Madison: Fairleigh Dickinson University Press, 2005.

Corbett, Christopher. *Orphans Preferred: The Twisted Truth and Lasting Legend of the Pony Express*. New York: Broadway, 2003.

Crawford, Jack. *The Poet Scout: A Book of Song and Story*. New York: Funk & Wagnalls, 1886.

Crockett, David. *A Narrative of the Life of David Crockett of the State of Tennessee*. Edited by Paul A. Hutton. Lincoln: University of Nebraska Press, 1987.

Crockett, Albert S. *When James Gordon Bennett was Caliph of Bagdad*. New York: Funk & Wagnalls, 1926.

Cunningham, Tom F. *Your Fathers the Ghosts: Buffalo Bill's Wild West in Scotland*. Edinburgh: Black & White, 2007.

Curtis, E. G. "John Milton Thayer." *Nebraska History* 29 (March–June 1948): 134–50.

Custer, Elizabeth B. *Boots and Saddles or, Life in Dakota with General Custer*. New York: Harper & Brothers, 1885.

———. *Following the Guidon*. New York: Harper & Brothers, 1890.

———. *Tenting on the Plains; Or, General Custer in Kansas and Texas*. New York: C. L. Webster, 1887.

Custer, George A. *My Life on the Plains*. New York: Sheldon, 1874.

Daniel, Larry J. *Shiloh: The Battle that Changed the Civil War*. New York: Simon & Schuster, 1997.

Darling, Roger. *A Sad and Terrible Blunder: Generals Terry and Custer at the Little Big Horn—New Discoveries*. Vienna VA: Potomac-Western, 1990.

Davies, Henry E. *Ten Days on the Plains*. Edited by P. A. Hutton. Dallas: Southern Methodist University Press, 1985.

De Barthe, Joseph. *The Life and Adventures of Frank Grouard, Chief of Scouts U.S. Army*. St Joseph MO: Combe, 1894.

DeMontravel, Peter R. *A Hero to His Fighting Men: Nelson A. Miles, 1839–1925*. Kent OH: Kent State University Press, 1998.

Denison, Charles W., and George B. Herbert. *Hancock "The Superb": The Early Life and Public Career of Winfield S. Hancock, Major-General U.S.A.* Philadelphia: National, 1880.

Dilke, Charles W. *Greater Britain: A Record of Travel in English-Speaking Countries during 1866 and 1867*. Cambridge: Cambridge University Press, 2009 (1st Edition).

———. *Problems of Greater Britain*. London: MacMillan, 1890.

Dippie, Brian W. *Remington & Russell*. Austin: University of Texas Press, 1994.

Dixon, David. *Hero of Beecher Island: The Life and Military Career of George A. Forsyth*. Lincoln: University of Nebraska Press, 1994.

Dodge, Richard I. *The Black Hills: A Minute Description of the Routes, Scenery, Soil, Climate, Timber, Gold, Geology, Zoölogy, etc., with an Accurate Map, Four Sectional Drawings, and Ten Plates from Photographs, Taken on the Spot*. Minneapolis: Ross & Haines, 1965.

———. *Hunting Grounds of the Great West*. London: Chatto & Windus, 1877.

———. *Our Wild Indians*. Hartford: A. D. Worthington, 1883.

Donovan, James M. *A Terrible Glory: Custer and the Little Bighorn—The Last Great Battle of the American West*. New York: Little, Brown, 2008.

Drum, Richard C. "Reminiscences of the Indian Fight at Ash Hollow, 1855." In *Collections of the Nebraska State Historical Society* 16, 143–51. Lincoln: Nebraska State Historical Society, 1911.

Dugard, Martin. *Into Africa: The Epic Adventures of Stanley and Livingstone*. New York: Broadway, 2003.

Duncan, David E. *Hernando de Soto: A Savage Quest in the Americas*. Norman: University of Oklahoma Press, 1997.

Dunlay, Thomas W. *Kit Carson and the Indians*. Lincoln: University of Nebraska Press, 2000.

Eicher, John H., and David J. Eicher. *Civil War High Commands*. Palo Alto: Stanford University Press, 2001.

Elliot, Michael A. *Custerology: The Enduring Legacy of the Indian Wars and*

George Armstrong Custer. Chicago: University of Chicago Press, 2008.

Ellis, Richard N. *General Pope and U.S. Indian Policy.* Albuquerque: University of New Mexico Press, 1970.

Etulian, Richard W. *Does the Frontier Experience Make America Exceptional?* Boston: Bedford–St. Martin's, 1999.

Faragher, John M. *Daniel Boone: The Life and Legend of an American Pioneer.* New York: Holt, 1992.

Fellows, Dexter W., and A. A. Freeman. *This Way to the Big Show—The Life of Dexter Fellows.* New York: Viking, 1936.

Flood, Renee S. *Lost Bird of Wounded Knee—Spirit of the Lakota.* New York: Da Capo, 1998.

Forsyth, George A. *The Story of a Soldier.* New York: D. Appleton, 1900.

———. *Thrilling Days of Army Life.* New York: Harper & Brothers, 1900.

Galland, Antoine. *Les mille et une nuits.* Paris: Garnier Flammarrion, 1704, rpt. 1965.

Gallop, Alan. *Buffalo Bill's British Wild West.* Phoenix Mill, UK: Sutton, 2001.

Gibbon, John. *Adventures on the Western Frontier.* Edited by Alan D. Gaff and Maureen Gaff. Bloomington: Indiana University Press, 1994.

———. *Gibbon on the Sioux Campaign of 1876.* Bellevue NE: The Old Army Press, 1970.

———. *Personal Recollections of the Civil War.* New York: G. P. Putnam's Sons, 1928.

Goodrich, Frederick E., and Frederick O. Prince. *The Life and Public Services of Winfield Scott Hancock, Major-General, U.S.A.* Boston: Lee & Shepard, 1880.

Gordon-McCutchan, R. C., ed. *Kit Carson: Indian Fighter or Indian Killer?* Boulder: University Press of Colorado, 1996.

Green, Jerome A. *Slim Buttes, 1876: An Episode of the Great Sioux War.* Norman: University of Oklahoma Press, 1990.

———. *Yellowstone Command: Colonel Nelson A. Miles and the Great Sioux War of 1876–1877.* Norman: University of Oklahoma Press, 2006.

Griffin, Charles E. *Four Years in Europe With Buffalo Bill.* Lincoln: University of Nebraska Press, 2010.

Grimsley, Mark. *The Hard Hand of War: Union Military Policy toward Southern Civilians, 1861–1865.* Cambridge: Cambridge University Press, 1997.

Grinnell, George B. *The Fighting Cheyennes*. Norman: University of Oklahoma Press, 1955.

Gwynn, Stephen, and Gertrude Tuckwell. *The Life of the Rt. Hon. Sir Charles W. Dilke*. London: John Murray, 1917.

Hancock, Almira R. *Reminiscences of Winfield Scott Hancock*. New York: Charles L. Webster, 1887.

Hazen, William B. *A Narrative of Military Service*. Huntington: Blue Acorn, 1993.

———. *Our Barren Lands: The Interior of the United States West of the 100th Meridian and East of the Sierra Nevadas*. Cincinnati: R. Clarke, 1875.

———. *The School and the Army in Germany and France: With a Diary of Siege Life at Versailles*. New York: Harper & Bros., 1872.

Healy, David. *James G. Blaine and Latin America*. Columbia: University of Missouri Press, 2001.

Hedren, Paul L., and Don Russell. *First Scalp for Custer: The Skirmish at Warbonnet Creek Nebraska, July 17, 1876*. Lincoln: University of Nebraska Press, 1976.

Helferich, Gerald. *Humboldt's Cosmos: Alexander von Humboldt and the Latin American Journey that Changed the Way We See the World*. New York: Gotham, 2004.

Hirshson, Stanley P. *The White Tecumseh: A Biography of General William T. Sherman*. Hoboken: John Wiley & Sons, 1997.

Hoig, Stan. *David L. Payne, the Oklahoma Boomer*. Oklahoma City: Western Heritage, 1980.

Hudson, Charles M., *Knights of Spain, Warriors of the Sun: Hernando De Soto and the South's Ancient Chiefdoms*. Athens: University of Georgia Press, 1997.

Hutton, Paul A. *Phil Sheridan and His Army*. Lincoln: University of Nebraska Press, 1985.

Jaffe, Mark. *The Gilded Dinosaur: The Fossil War Between E. D. Cope and O. C. Marsh and the Rise of American Science*. New York: Crown, 2000.

Jamieson, Perry D. *Winfield Scott Hancock: Gettysburg Hero*. Civil War Campaigns and Commanders Series. Abilene KS: McWhiney Foundation, 2003.

Jeal, Tim. *Stanley—The Impossible Life of Africa's Greatest Explorer*. London: Faber & Faber, 2007.

Jenkins, Roy. *Sir Charles Dilke: A Victorian Tragedy.* London: Papermac, 1996.

Jonnes, Jill. *Eiffel's Tower and the World's Fair Where Buffalo Bill Beguiled Paris, the Artists Quarreled, and Thomas Edison Became a Count.* New York: Viking–Penguin, 2009.

Jordan, David M. *Winfield Scott Hancock: A Soldier's Life.* Bloomfield: Indiana University Press, 1988.

Kasson, Joy S. *Buffalo Bill's Wild West: Celebrity, Memory, and Popular History.* New York: Hill & Wang, 2000.

Kelley, William F. *Pine Ridge 1890: An Eye Witness Account of the Events Surrounding the Fighting at Wounded Knee.* Edited by A. Kelley and P. Bovis. San Francisco: Bovis, 1971.

Kennett, Lee B. *Sherman: A Soldier's Life.* London: HarperCollins, 2001.

Kime, Wayne R. *Colonel Richard Irving Dodge: The Life and Times of a Career Army Officer.* Norman: University of Oklahoma Press, 2006.

———, ed. *The Black Hills Journals of Colonel Richard Irving Dodge.* Norman: University of Oklahoma Press, 1996.

———. *The Indian Territory Journals of Colonel Richard Irving Dodge.* Norman: University of Oklahoma Press, 2000.

———. *The Powder River Expedition Journals of Colonel Richard Irving Dodge.* Norman: University of Oklahoma Press, 1997.

———. *The Sherman Tour Journals of Colonel Richard Irving Dodge.* Norman: University of Oklahoma Press, 2002.

King, Charles. *Campaigning with Crook and Stories of Army Life.* New York: Harper & Brothers, 1890.

King, James T. *War Eagle: A Life of General Eugene A. Carr.* Lincoln: University of Nebraska Press, 1964.

Knight, Oliver. *Following the Indian Wars: The Story of the Newspaper Correspondents among the Indian Campaigners.* Norman: University of Oklahoma Press, 1960.

LaPointe, Ernie. *Sitting Bull—His Life and Legacy.* Layton UT: Gibbs Smith, 2009.

Lavery, Dennis S., and Mark H. Jordan. *Iron Brigade General: John Gibbon, Rebel in Blue.* Westport: Greenwood, 2003.

Lesley, Lewis B. *Uncle Sam's Camels: The Journal of May Humphreys Stacey Supplemented by the Report of Edward Fitzgerald Beale (1857–1858).* Cambridge: Harvard University Press, 1929.

Liebowitz, Daniel, and Charles Pearson. *The Last Expedition: Stanley's Mad Journey through the Congo*. New York: W. W. Norton, 2005.

Lofaro, Michael A. *Daniel Boone: An American Life*. Lexington: University Press of Kentucky, 2003.

——, ed. *Davy Crockett: The Man, The Legend, The Legacy, 1786–1986*. Knoxville: University of Tennessee Press, 1985.

Maddra, Sam A. *Hostiles?: The Lakota Ghost Dance and Buffalo Bill's Wild West*. Norman: University of Oklahoma Press, 2006.

Magnum, Neil C. *Battle of the Rosebud: Prelude to the Little Big Horn*. El Segundo: Upton & Sons, 1988.

Manzione, Joseph. *"I Am Looking to the North for My Life": Sitting Bull, 1876–1881*. Salt Lake City: University of Utah Press, 1991.

Marill Escudé, Josep. *Aquell hivern . . . L'espectacle de Buffalo Bill a Barcelona*. Palma de Mallorca: Hesperus, 1998.

Marszalek, John F. *Sherman: A Soldier's Passion for Order*. Carbondale: Southern Illinois University Press, 2007.

Martin, George W. "Indian Fight in Ford County in 1859." *Collections of the State Historical Society of Kansas* 12 (1912).

Meigs, William M. *The Life of Thomas Hart Benton*. Philadelphia: J. B. Lippincott, 1904.

Miles, Nelson A. *Personal Recollections and Observations of General Nelson A. Miles*. Chicago: Werner, 1896.

Miller, Darlis A. *Captain Jack Crawford—Buckskin Poet, Scout, and Showman*. Albuquerque: University of New Mexico Press, 1993.

Mooney, James. *The Ghost Dance Religion and the Sioux Outbreak of 1890*. Edited by R. J. DeMaillie. Lincoln: University of Nebraska Press, 1991.

Moore, John H. *The Cheyenne*. Oxford: Blackwell, 1996.

Morris, James M. *Pulitzer: A Life in Politics, Print and Power*. London: Harper Collins, 2010.

Morris, Roy, Jr. *Sheridan: The Life and Wars of General Phil Sheridan*. New York: Crown, 1992,

Moses, L. G. *Wild West Shows and the Images of American Indians, 1883–1933*. Albuquerque: University of New Mexico Press, 1996.

Nevins, Allan. *Fremont: Pathmaker of the West*. Lincoln: University of Nebraska Press, 1992.

Norris, L. David, James C. Milligan, and Odie B. Faulk. *William H. Emory: Soldier–Scientist*. Tucson: University of Arizona Press, 1998.

O'Connor, Richard. *The Scandalous Mr. Bennett*. New York: Doubleday, 1962.

———. *Sheridan—The Inevitable*. New York: Bobbs-Merrill, 1953.

O'Reilly, Harrington. *Fifty Years on the Trail: A True Story of Western Life, The Adventures of John Young Nelson as Described to Harrington O'Reilly*. Norman: University of Oklahoma Press, 1969.

Ostler, Jeffrey. *The Plains Sioux and U.S. Colonialism from Lewis and Clark to Wounded Knee*. Cambridge: Cambridge University Press, 2004.

Page, Walter H., and Arthur W. Page. *"General William J. Palmer—A Builder of the West."* In *The World's Work . . . : A History of Our Time* 15, 9899–9903. New York: Doubleday, Page, 1908.

Parker, Lew. *Odd People I Have Met*. n.p., n.d.

Pierce, Michael D. *The Most Promising Young Officer: A Life of Ranald Slidell Mackenzie*. Norman: University of Oklahoma Press. 1993.

Pope, J. *The Military Memoirs of General John Pope*. Edited by P. Cozzens, and R. I. Girardi. Chapel Hill: University of North Carolina Press, 1998.

Powell, Peter J. *Sweet Medicine: The Continuing Role of the Sacred Arrows, the Sun Dance, and the Sacred Buffalo Hat in Northern Cheyenne History*. Norman: University of Oklahoma Press, 1969.

Price, Geroge F. *Across the Continent with the Fifth Cavalry*. New York: D. Van Nostrand, 1883.

Reavis, L. U., and Cassius M. Clay. *The Life and Military Services of General Harney*. St Louis: Bryan, Brand, 1878.

Reddin, Paul. *Wild West Shows*. Urbana: University of Illinois Press, 1999.

Rennert, Jack. *100 Posters of Buffalo Bill's Wild West*. New York: Darien House, 1976.

Ricker Eli S. *Voices of the American West, Volume 1: The Indian Interviews*. Lincoln: University of Nebraska Press, 2005.

Rister, Carl C. *Land Hunger: David L. Payne and the Oklahoma Boomers*. Norman: University of Oklahoma Press, 1942.

Roberts, David A. *Newer World: Kit Carson, John C. Fremont, and the Claiming of the American West*. New York: Touchstone, 2001.

Roberts, R. H., ed. *Seth Kinman's Manuscript and Scrapbook*. Ferndale CA: Ferndale Museum, 2010.

Robinson, Charles M., III. *Bad Hand: A Biography of General Ranald S. MacK-enzie*. Buffalo Gap TX: State House, 1993.

———. *General Crook and the Western Frontier*. Norman: University of Okla-homa Press, 2001.

———. *The Indian Trial: The Complete Story of the Warren Wagon Train Mas-sacre and the Fall of the Kiowa Nation*. Chicag: A. H. Clark, 1997.

———. *Satanta: Life and Death of a War Chief*. Buffalo Gap TX: State House, 1997.

Rolde, Neil. *Continental Liar from the State of Maine: James G. Blaine*. Gar-diner: Tilbury House, 2006.

Rolle, Andrew F. *John Charles Fremont: Character as Destiny*. Norman: Uni-versity of Oklahoma Press, 1991.

Roosevelt, Theodore. *The Life of Thomas Hart Benton—American Statesman*. Cambridge: Riverside, 1886.

Rosa, Joseph G. *Wild Bill Hickok Gunfighter: An Account of Hickok's Gunfights*. Norman: University of Oklahoma Press, 2006.

———. *Wild Bill Hickok: The Man and His Myth*. Topeka: University Press of Kansas, 1996.

Royster, Charles. *The Destructive War: William Tecumseh Sherman, Stone-wall Jackson, and the Americans*. New York: Alfred A. Knopf, 1991.

Rupke, Nicolaas A. *Alexander von Humboldt: A Metabiography*. Chicago: University of Chicago Press, 2008.

Russell, Don. *The Lives and Legends of Buffalo Bill*, Norman: University of Oklahoma Press, 1960.

Rusell, Don, with Paul L. Hedren. *Campaigning with King: Charles King, Chronicler of the Old Army*. Lincoln: University of Nebraska Press, 1990.

Rydell, Robert W., and Rob Kroes. *Buffalo Bill in Bologna: The American-ization of the World, 1869–1922*. Chicago: University of Chicago Press, 2005.

Sabin, Edwin L. *Kit Carson Days*. 2 vols. Lincoln: University of Nebras-ka Press, 1995.

Sachs, Aaron. *The Humboldt Current: A European Explorer and His American Disciples*. Oxford: Oxford University Press, 2008.

Sagala, Sandra K. *Buffalo Bill on Stage*. Albuquerque: University of New Mexico Press, 2008.

Samuels, Peggy, and Samuels, Harold. *Frederic Remington: A Biography.* New York: Doubleday, 1982.

Schmitt, Martin F., ed. *General George Crook: His Autobiography.* Norman: University of Oklahoma Press, 1986.

Schwatka, Frederick. *Along Alaska's Great River.* New York: Cassell, 1885.

———. *Children of the Cold.* New York: Cassell, 1886.

———. *In the Land of Cave and Cliff Dwellers.* New York: Cassell, 1893.

———. *Nimrod in the North.* New York: Cassell, 1885.

———. *A Summer in Alaska.* St Louis: J. W. Henry, 1894.

Seitz, Don C. *The James Gordon Bennetts: Father and Son, Proprietors of the New York Herald.* Indianapolis: Bobbs-Merrill, 1928.

Shackford, James A. *David Crockett: The Man and the Legend.* Chapel Hill: University of North Carolina Press, 1994.

Shea, William L., and Earl J. Hess. *Pea Ridge: Civil War Campaign in the West.* Chapel Hill: University of North Carolina Press, 1992.

Sheridan, Philip H. *Personal Memoirs of P. H. Sheridan, General United States Army.* 2 vols. New York: Charles L. Webster, 1888.

Sides, Hampton. *Blood and Thunder: The Epic Story of Kit Carson and the Conquest of the American West.* New York: Doubleday, 2006.

Simmons, Marc. *Kit Carson and His Three Wives.* Albuquerque: University of New Mexico Press, 2003.

Smith, Rex A. *The Moon of Popping Trees: The Tragedy at Wounded Knee and the End of the Indian Wars.* Lincoln: University of Nebraska Press, 1975.

Sorg, Eric V. *Doctor, Lawyer, Indian Chief: The Life of White Beaver Powell, Buffalo Bill's Blood Brother.* Austin: Eakin, 2002.

Stanwood, Edward. *James Gillespie Blaine.* Boston: Houghton, Mifflin, 1905.

Terry, Alfred H. *The Field Diary of General Alfred H. Terry: The Yellowstone Expedition, 1876.* Bellevue: Old Army Press, 1978.

———. *The Terry Letters: The Letters of General Alfred Howe Terry to His Sisters during the Indian War of 1876.* La Mirada: J. Willert, 1980.

Terwin, Wendy. *All on Stage: Sir Charles Wyndham and the Alberys.* London: Harrap, 1980.

Thompson, Gerald. *Edward F. Beale and the American West.* Albuquerque: University of New Mexico Press, 1983.

Tucker, Glenn. *Hancock the Superb.* Indianapolis: Bobbs-Merrill, 1960.

Turner, Frederick J. "The Significance of the Frontier in American History." In *Report of the American Historical Association for 1893*, 199–227. Chicago: American Historical Association, 1893.

Turner, Thadd M. *Wild Bill Hickok: Deadwood City—End of Trail*. Boca Raton: Universal, 2001.

Utley, Robert M. *The Lance and the Shield: The Life and Times of Sitting Bull*. New York: Henry Holt, 1993.

Van de Logt, Mark. *War Party in Blue: Pawnee Scouts in the U.S. Army*. Norman: University of Oklahoma Press, 2010.

Vestal, Stanley. *Jim Bridger Mountain Man*. Lincoln: University of Nebraska Press, 1970.

———. *Sitting Bull: Champion of the Sioux, a Biography*. New York: Houghton Mifflin, 1932.

Walker, General Francis A. *General Hancock*. New York: D. Appleton, 1894.

Wallace, Ernest. *Ranald S. MacKenzie and the Texas Frontier*. College Station: Texas A&M University Press, 1993.

Wallis, Michael. *David Crockett—The Lion of the West*. New York: W. W. Norton, 2011.

Warren, Louis S. *Buffalo Bill's America: William Cody and the Wild West Show*. New York: Alfred A. Knopf, 2005.

Werner, Fred H. *The Slim Buttes Battle*. San Luis Obispo: Werner, 1981.

Wetmore, Helen Cody. *Last of the Great Scouts*. Chicago: Duluth, 1899.

White, Richard. "Frederick Jackson Turner and Buffalo Bill." In Richard White and Patricia N. Limerick, eds, *The Frontier in American Culture*, 7–55. Berkley: University of California Press, 1994.

———. "When Frederick Jackson Turner and Buffalo Bill Cody Both Played Chicago in 1893.", In Richard W. Etulian, ed., *Does The Frontier Experience Make America Exceptional?* 45–57. Boston: Bedford–St. Martin's, 1999.

White, Richard, and Patricia N. Limerick, eds. *The Frontier in American Culture*. Berkley: University of California Press, 1994.

Whittaker, Frederick. *A Complete Life of General George A. Custer*. 2 vols. Lincoln: University of Nebraska Press, 1993.

Wittenberg, Eric J. *Little Phil: A Reassessment of the Civil War Leadership of Gen. Philip H. Sheridan*. Washington DC: Potomac, 2002.

Woodworth, Steven E. *Nothing but Victory: The Army of the Tennessee, 1861–1865*. New York: Alfred A. Knopf, 2005.

———. *Sherman: Lessons in Leadership*. London: Palgrave Macmillan, 2010.

Wooster, Robert. *Nelson A. Miles and the Twilight of the Frontier Army*. Lincoln: University of Nebraska Press, 1996.

Wyndham-Quin, W. T. *Hunting in the Yellowstone or On the Trail of the Wapiti with Texas Jack in the Land of Geysers*. London: MacMillan, 1925.

Yenne, Bill. *Sitting Bull*. Yardley: Westholme, 2008.

Yost, Nellie Irene Snyder. *Buffalo Bill: His Family, Friends, Fame, Fortune and Failures*. Chicago: Sage–Swallow, 1979.

INDEX

Big Foot (Si Tanka), 272, 274,
340nn2–3
Big Horn and Yellowstone expedition
(1876), 20, 23
Big Sandy Lake, 106, 316ch10n2
Black Hawk co, 112, 318n8
Black Prince, 239, 337n28
Blaine, Hon. James Gillespie, 236,
335n7
Blue Licks (battlefield), 123, 320n16
Blue Water Creek ne, 106, 317n5
Blunt, Gen. James Gilpatrick, 30,
311n50
Boal, Horton S., 291, 342n6
Bologna, Italy, 264
Bonheur, Rosa, ix, 47, 252, 253–54,
313n8
Boone, Daniel, 35, 119, 166, 207, 312n2
Bradford, Edward, 291
Bridger, James "Jim," 8, 18, 23, 24, 166,
299n5, 317n9
Brigham (horse), 51, 53
Brisbin, Gen. James Sanks, 18, 302n8
Brooke, Gen. John R., 276, 340n5
Brown-Potter, Cora Urquhart, 215,
329n12
Bruce, Lord Victor Alexander, 221,
331n12
Brulé Indians. See Sioux Indians
Buckskin Joe (horse), 23, 51–53, 160,
309n41
"Buffalo Chips." See White, Charles
"Buffalo Chips"
Burke, John M. "Arizona John," xii–
xvii, xix–xx, xxiii, 2, 3, 90, 287, 290,
291, 297n6, 298n16, 298n25, 299n1,
299n26
Butterfield, John Warren, 124, 320n20
Butterfield Overland Despatch. See
Butterfield Overland Stage Com-
pany

Butterfield Overland Mail. See Butterfield Overland Stage Company
Butterfield Overland Stage Company,
310n45, 320n20

"California Joe." See Milner, Moses
"California Joe"
Cameron, Simon, 236–37, 335n13
Canby, Gen. Edward Richard Sprigg,
30, 311n50
"Captain Jack." See Crawford, John
Wallace "Captain Jack"
Carr, Gen. Eugene Asa, viii, 18, 31, 90,
90, 91, 157, 276, 303n13
Carson, Christopher "Kit," 8, 10, 18,
31, 35, 152, 166, 180, 207, 299n6
Cheyenne Indians, 230, 306–7n24,
321ch18n1; and Custer, 31, 181,
307n25, 307n26; and death of Wil-
liam Averill Comstock, 321ch17n2;
and Maj. Frank North, 175–77; as
opponents of William F. Cody, 28–9,
85, 106; in poetry, 189, 198; as show
Indians, 209
Cheyenne Pass wy, 111, 317n1
Cheyenne Warrior Society. See Dog
Soldiers
Chicago World's Fair. See World's
Columbian Exposition
chief of scouts, 17, 22, 27, 29, 83,
91–92, 95, 96, 157, 162, 326n3
Churchill, Lady Randolph (née Jea-
nette Jerome), 215, 221, 330n25
Churchill, Lord Randolph. See
Spencer-Churchill, Lord Randolph
Henry
Churchill, Sir Winston. See Spencer-
Churchill, Sir Winston Leonard
"Cimarron Scout." See Payne, Capt.
David Lewis "Oklahoma Payne"
City of Nebraska (steamship). See State
of Nebraska (steamship)

Civil War (United States), 145–48
Clarke, Col. Alexander Ross, 215, 223,
    330n20
Coaching Club Parade (London), 222,
    332n22
Cody, Arta, 53, 275, 314n11
Cody, Elijah, 100, 316ch9n2
Cody, Isaac (father), 10, 99–103,
    300n2, 316ch9n2, 316n6
Cody, Louisa Frederici, 146
Cody, Mary (mother), 12, 99, 102–3,
    105, 112, 137, 145
Cody, Orra, 275
Colby, Gen. Leonard Wright, 270–71,
    272, 340n1
Colon, Cristobal. See Columbus,
    Christopher
Colorado, 37, 228–29, 293
Colorado River, 291, 299n3
Colosseum of Rome, ix, 12, 227, 256,
    256–57, 259, 263–64
Columbian Exhibition. See World's
    Columbian Exposition
Columbus, Christopher, xviii, 35, 115,
    201, 207, 255, 301n7
Comanche Indians, 17, 75, 306n24
Comstock, William Averill "Medicine
    Bill," 153–56, 166, 321ch17n2
Connecticut, 186, 325n28
Cooper, James Fenimore, 226, 320n21,
    333n34
Cortés de Monroy y Pizarro, Hernán,
    46, 47, 115, 313n4
Cortez, Hernán. See Cortés de Mon-
    roy y Pizarro, Hernán
Cosgrove, Thomas, 166, 322ch19n2
Cossacks, 41, 43, 313n3
cowboy band, 210, 211, 213, 219
Cox, Maj. Charles G., 79, 315n10
Crawford, John Wallace "Captain
    Jack," 191–97, 326n3, 327ch20n5

Crittenden, Gen. Eugene W., 30,
    311n50
Crockett, David, 35, 207, 312n3
Crook, Gen. George R., viii, 18, 27, 89,
    89, 91, 162, 179, 189, 191, 304n15
Curtis, Gen. Samuel Ryan, 175, 323n15
Custer, Gen. George Armstrong, ix,
    18, 23; and California Joe, 91, 147,
    309n43; and Cheyenne Indians, 31,
    181, 307n25, 307n26; and Cody, 153;
    and Comstock, 162, 178, 203; and
    Fifth Cavalry, 181, 181; and Little Big-
    horn, 178–79, 307n25; in poetry, 190,
    198, 320n2; and Sitting Bull, 180

Dakota Territory, 37, 189, 269, 282
Deadwood coach, 230, 238, 251, 333n33
Deadwood SD, 170, 307n27
"Denver Jim." See Keller, James Mad-
    dison "Denver Jim"
Depew, Chauncey Mitchell, 236, 335n9
Dilke, Sir Charles Wentworth, 11,
    300n5
Dismal River, 176, 322ch19n2
Dodge, Gen. Richard Irving, 17, 21, 29,
    30, 301n1
Dog Men. See Dog Soldiers
Dog Soldier Indians. See Dog Soldiers
Dog Soldiers, 22, 83, 157, 321ch18n1
Doniphan, Alexander William, 115,
    123, 319n4
Dowd, William B., 291
Drum, Gen. Richard Coulter, 92, 315n1
Dudley, Gen. Nathan Augustus Mon-
    roe, viii, 30, 96, 96
Duke Alexis. See Grand Duke Alexis
    Alexandrovich Romanov of Russia
Duke of Beaufort (Henry Charles
    Fitzroy Somerset), 221, 331n6
Duke of Cambridge (Prince George
    William Frederick Charles), 221,
    223, 331n3

Duke of Sonora. *See* Gwin, Sen. William McKendree (Duke of Sonora)
Duke of Teck (Prince Francis Paul Charles Louis Alexander), 221, 223, 331n10
Duncan, Gen. Thomas, 18, 306n22

Earl of Dunraven. *See* Wyndham-Quin, Windham Thomas (Earl of Dunraven)
Earl's Court (London), ix, 219, *284*, 328n2
Emory, Gen. William Hemsley, viii, 18, 23, 92, *92*, 302n9, 310n43
England, xii, 70, 185, 203–5, 211–41, 246, 250, 281, 284, 289–91
Everhart, Hon. George P., 291
Exposition Universelle of 1889 (Paris Exposition), 250–51, 308n30, 313n8

Fellows, Dexter, xv–xvi, xvii, 298nn10–13, 298n17
Fifth Cavalry, U.S., 21–27, 83, 95, 157, 309n38
First Cavalry, U.S., 96
Florence, Italy, 264
Flowers, Lt. Lem, 142
Forsyth, Gen. James William, viii, 18, 93, *93*, 166, 276
Forsyth, George Alexander "Sandy," 18, 30, 157, 160, 302ch2n6, 311n50
Fort Bridger WY, 108, 317n9
Fort Dodge KS, 25–26, 78–80, 310n47
Fort Hall ID, 117, 319n9
Fort Hays KS (formerly Fort Fletcher), 25–27, 77–79, 81, 147–48, 181, 310n46
Fort Kearny NE (formerly Fort Childs), 106, 117, 121, 176, 229, 316ch10n1, 317n4
Fort Keogh MT, 179, 324n20
Fort Laramie WY (formerly Fort William), 111, 117, 190

Fort Larned KS, 25–26, 75–81, 147, 310n45
Fort Leavenworth KS, 10, 100, 106, 108, 110, 111, 113, 118, 141, 145, 180
Fort Lyon CO (formerly Fort Wise), 152, 321ch17n1
Fort McPherson NE, 20, 22, 52, 159, 178, 309n37
Fort Riley KS, 229, 231
Fort Sedgwick CO, 176, 324n18
Fort Zarah KS, 75, 314ch7n2
Fourth Cavalry, U.S., 95
France, xvi, 203, 205, 250, 254, 266, 283, 291
Fremont, John Charles, 8, 10, 31, 115, 117, 166, 207, 299n2, 299n4, 299n6
Fry, Gen. James Barnet, viii, 30, 87, *87*, 87, 311n50

the Gaucho, 41, 44
Germany, 203, 205, 238, 259, 265, 283; cities in visited by Buffalo Bill's Wild West, 283
Gibbon, Gen. John Oliver, 18, 179, 303n10
Gladstone, William Ewart (prime minister), 219–20, 331n1, 332n16
Gladstone, Rt. Hon. Herbert John, 221, 332n16
Gore, Sir St. George, 18, 307n28
Gower, Lord (Ronald Charles Sutherland-Leveson-Gower), 212, 215, 219, 234, 328n1
Grand Cañon of the Colorado, 291, 293
Grand Duke Alexis Alexandrovich Romanov of Russia, 17–18, 22, 160, 302n4, 305n18, 308n33, 311n50
Grand Duke Michael (Mikhail) Mikhailovitch of Russia, 215, 238, 329n17

Paget, Lord Henry Cyril, 215, 329n15
Palmer, Gen. William Jackson, 18,
    306n23
Paris, France, 47, 250–51, 253
Paris Exposition. *See* Exposition Uni-
    verselle of 1889 (Paris Exposition)
Parker, Capt. Charles, 75, 77–78,
    314ch7n1
Parker, Lew, xvi, 298nn14–15
Pawnee Fork, 76, 79, 310n45, 310n48,
    315n9
Pawnee Indians, 175–76, 230, 323n13;
    on reservation, 175–76; as scouts,
    175, 322ch19n3, 324n16; as show
    members, 209
Pawnee language, 175
Pawnee Rock, 75, 314n3, 315n6
Payne, Capt. David Lewis "Oklahoma
    Payne," 180–81, 183, 324n24
Penrose, Gen. William Henry, 18, 30,
    157, 306n24, 311n50
Persian Monarch (steamship), 246–47,
    250
Phelps, Edward John, 215, 328n7
Pine Ridge Indian Agency SD, 180,
    222, 271–74, 284, 323n9, 332n24,
    340n4
Pizarro González, Francisco, 115, 318n1
Platte River, 106, 113, 117, 131,
    316ch10n1, 317n4, 323n12. *See also*
    North Platte River; South Platte
    River
Plenty Horses (Tasunka Ota), vii, *82*
Plenty Wolf (Sunkmanitu Ota, "Yank-
    ton Charley"), 168, 279, 323n10
Poet Scout. *See* Crawford, John Wal-
    lace "Captain Jack"
Ponsonby, Lady Mary Elizabeth
    Bulteel, 234, 334n4
Ponsonby, Sir Henry, 234, 235, 324n4

Pony Express, viii, 5, 11, 115–24, 119,
    123–24, 141, 316n5, 318n10; riders,
    viii, 12, 25, 103, 113–14, *117*, 131–32,
    315n7, 324n22; trail, 125, 317n3, 317n9,
    318n10, 320ch14n2, 321ch15n4
Pope, Gen. John, 18, 304n16
Pope Leo XIII, ix, 205, 255, 262–63,
    262, 338n10
Pourier, Jean Baptiste "Big Bat," 168,
    323n9
Powder-Face (horse), 51
Powell, David Franklin "White Bea-
    ver," viii, 171–74, *172*, 179, 323n11
Prairie Dog Creek, 22, 137, 320n1
Price, Capt. George Frederick, 21, 22,
    309n38
Prince Alexander of Teck (Alexander
    Augustus Frederick William Alfred
    George Cambridge), 333n27
Prince Louis (Ludwig) of Bade, 238,
    336n26
Prince of Wales, 205, 215, 221, 222–23,
    228–31, 238–40, 327ch21n4
Princess of Wales, 223, 228–29, 230–31,
    238–39
Probyn, Gen. Sir Dighton, 239, 336n27
Pulitzer, Joseph, 236, 335n8

Queen Victoria, 6, 217, 233–41,
    327nn3–4, 330n28

Rain-In-The-Face (Ite Omagazu), 139,
    320ch15n2
Red Buttes WY, 131, 320ch14n1
Red Cloud (Mahpiya Luta), 176, 198,
    324n16
Red Shirt (Ogle Sa), 168, 210–11, 219,
    224, 226, 228, 235, 323n10
Reform Club (London), 221, 331n2
Remington, Frederic Sackrider, 18,
    308n32

Republican River, 22, 52, 83, 85, 137, 320ch15n1, 321ch15n3
Republican River expedition, 22
Revenge (Watokicun), 279, 282, 341ch28n1
Reynolds, Gen. John Fulton, 30, 311n50
River Thames, 228, 290
Rocky Bear (Inyan Mato), 261–62, 276, 339n27
Rocky Mountains, 9, 12, 87, 107, 166, 230
Rome, Italy, ix, 12, 227, 253–64, *254*, 338n11, 338n14, 338n16, 340n31
Rome KS, 148, 321ch16n4
Rose, William T., 147–48, 321ch16n4
Rosebud MT, battle of, 189, 304n15, 311n50, 312n50, 322ch19n2
Royall, Gen. William Bedford, viii, 18, 95, *95*, 157, 305n20
Rucker, Gen. Edmund Winchester, 30, 159, 311n50
Rudy, Jacob Owen, 175, 323n14
Russell, Majors & Waddell, 103, 107–8, 113, 115, 118. *See also* Russell & Majors
Russell, William Hepburn, 116, 119, 316n5, 319n14. *See also* Russell & Majors; Russell, Majors & Waddell
Russell & Majors, 101, 105, 170, 316n5. *See also* Russell, Majors, & Waddell

Salsbury, Nathan "Nate," ix, xvii, 163, *182*, 183–86, 209, 211, 214, 219, 223, 235, 261, 269, 286, 287, 290, 322nch18n4, 325n26. *See also* Salsbury's Troubadours
Salsbury's Troubadours, 184–85, 322ch18n4
Salt Creek Valley, 100, 137, 147, 316n4
Satanta (White Bear), 75, 77, 314n4
Savage Club, 221, 331n7

Scatter (Kalala), 279, 282, 341ch28n1
Schurz, Carl, 183, 325n25
Scotland, 185
Scott, Gen. Winfield, 115, 319n3
Scott, Sir Walter, 226 334n35
Scott County IA, 99
Scout's Rest Ranch (Nebraska), 52, 202, 216, 253, 291, 330n27
Sedgwick County KS, 181
Seigmiller, Daniel, 291
Seventh Cavalry, U.S., 93, 166, 190, 315n10, 327n2
Seventh Kansas Volunteer Cavalry (Jennison's Jayhawkers, Seventh Kansas Jayhawkers), 145, 321ch16nn1–2
Shakespeare, William, 49–50, 313n9
Shangrau, John, 168, 323n9
Shangrau, Louis, 168, 323n9
Sheridan, Gen. Philip Henry "Little Phil," viii, 17, 19, 21–23, 75, 77–82, *86*, 86–87, 91, 157, 159–60, 162, 192, 301n3, 327ch20n4
Sherman, Gen. William Tecumseh, vii, 17, 85, *85*, 226, 228–31, 261, 301nn1–2
Short Bull (Tatanka Ptecela), 273, 279, 282, 342n2
Simpson (Lewis), 107–10
Sioux Indians, 22–23, 175, 230 302n5; Brulé, 273, 274, 276; and Battle of Blue Water Creek, 106, 317n5; and death of William Averill Comstock, 321ch17n2; Hunkpapa, 320ch15n2, 324n19; and John Young Nelson, 333n33; Miniconjou, 340n3; Oglala, vii, *54*, 67, 82, 209, 273–76, 282, 324n16, 333n33, 339n27, 340n4; as opponents of Cody, 89, 95, 96, 139, 142; in poetry, 189–92, as show members, 209, 247, 256, 261, 323n10, 324n19,

In the Papers of William F. "Buffalo Bill" Cody series

Four Years in Europe with Buffalo Bill
Charles Eldridge Griffin
Edited and with an introduction by Chris Dixon

The Life of Hon. William F. Cody, Known as Buffalo Bill
William F. Cody
Edited and with an introduction by Frank Christianson

Buffalo Bill from Prairie to Palace
John M. Burke
Edited and with an introduction by Chris Dixon

The Wild West in England
William F. Cody
Edited and with an introduction by Frank Christianson

To order or obtain more information on these
or other University of Nebraska Press titles,
visit www.nebraskapress.unl.edu.